ETRURIA HALL, WEDGWOOD'S HOME.

A dish from the service made for Catherine II., Empress of Russia, for the Palace of La Grenouillête. Lent by Josiah Wedgwood & Sons.

Frontispiece]

Collecting Old English Pottery

J. F. Blacker

COLES

© COPYRIGHT 1980 AND PUBLISHED BY
COLES PUBLISHING COMPANY LIMITED
TORONTO — CANADA
PRINTED IN CANADA

Originally published in United Kingdom - which accounts for British references.

PREFACE

THE desire expressed by many collectors that my various articles on collecting "Old Pottery" should be embodied in a book is responsible for the appearance of this volume, which will be followed by a new edition of the "A B C of Collecting Old China," by the same publishers. The "China Book" had a marvellous success, no less than ten thousand being sold in about ten months. This encourages the hope that this Pottery Book will meet with many friends to whom the pleasure and profit of collecting are relaxation, recreation, pure enjoyment, and more. As Cowper says:—

> "Variety's the very spice of life
> That gives it all its flavour."

Variety and change of occupation can be secured by collecting, and no object is more worthy of the attention of collectors than Old Pottery.

For those who possess pottery, and for those, too, who wish to learn about it, much information and many illustrations have been gathered together. The sketches may not be fine; they will nevertheless be instructive, and they are freely distributed in the text. The thirty-two pages of half-tone blocks include the later cottage pottery, which needs no description. Throughout, notes are given on values, and an Appendix furnishes reliable information as to Auction Prices. All fine Old Pottery is rising in value, though as yet the cost is not prohibitive to the man of moderate means. Collectors who have, in the past, bought well, can realise handsomely to-day.

In order to form an accurate judgment, reading, seeing and handling are necessary, but handling is of the first importance. It is the best education, though the value of the Museum must not be ignored. There is a something, I do not know what, in the feel, the weight, the glaze, and the whole appearance of Old Pottery which no book can teach: it is pure experience, trained by practice until it develops into an instinctive faculty. Examination by handling is a necessity, but the best results can only be gained from it when accurate comparisons are made and, during the early stages at least, under careful guidance.

The buyer who wishes to avoid risks puts his trust in a responsible dealer, who will nearly always take back any article which does not give perfect satisfaction. No great bargains can be expected in adopting this system, which is safe and sure, although current prices must be paid. A ripe judgment may, in time, reward the man who is content to go slowly. Still, whilst human nature remains, others, "who grasp the skirts of happy chance," prefer the attraction—the prizes, the risks—which results from hunting on their own account. Experience gives them power.

The Earl of Shaftesbury (1671-1713) describes the position of the ideal collector: "I like, I fancy, I admire! How? By accident, or as I please? No. But I learn to fancy, to admire, to please as the subjects themselves are deserving and can bear me out. And if I expect the knowledge should come to me by accident or in play, I shall be grossly deluded, and prove myself, at best, a mock virtuoso or mere pedant of the kind."

Fortunately, the many varieties of Old Pottery give free

PREFACE

scope for individual taste. One collector finds his happiness in Roman or Mediæval Pottery, another has a fancy for Salt Glaze, a third prefers Old Wedgwood; this one likes Toby Jugs, that one chooses Staffordshire Figures. Yet all have a common bond of sympathy in desiring to form a collection illustrative of the potter's art. There may be money in it, but apart and aside from monetary considerations, there is much real and lasting pleasure in the pursuit of Old Pottery, much happiness in its possession, and much distraction from the teasing worries of life's daily routine.

Good feeling and kindly assistance have been forthcoming from distinguished collectors, noted manufacturers and well-known dealers, for which my acknowledgment of gratitude is due. Such kindness, received from so many, appears to emphasise the necessity for the book—indeed, it enhances its value, especially where information from authentic sources appears for the first time. My special thanks for the use of illustrations are tendered to Miss Edith Feilden, who, in addition to those having her name attached, lent that on page 223, to Mr. A. M. Broadley, Colonel Bemrose, Captain H. D. Terry, Messrs. E. Norman, S. H. Eglington, S. Fair, and others.

MacArthur wrote, "Two names stand pre-eminent in the historical development of the potter's art—Bernard Palissy, of France, and Josiah Wedgwood of England." It is to the descendants of our great English potter, to Messrs. Cecil and Frank Wedgwood, that I owe many illustrations and much information, especially about the "Finds" and the "Date Marks." I am fully sensible of my obligations to them, and to W. Adams & Co., W. T. Copeland & Sons, Doulton & Co., and Mr. Henry Booth.

My appreciation is warmly tendered to that expert in old Wedgwood, Mr. F. Rathbone, who has helped me with illustrations; to Mr. Cyril Andrade; to Mr. S. G. Fenton, whose two seated figures on page 235 await identification; but above all, to Mr. George Stoner, of King Street, St. James's Square, not only for illustrations of fine pottery, but also for reading the letterpress in proof. His practical knowledge, helpful suggestions and unfailing kindness have been invaluable. "My first thought," he wrote, after reading the proofs, "is to tender my congratulations. I am perfectly sure it is a work that will find appreciative readers."

J. F. BLACKER.

CONTENTS

	PAGE
PREFACE	5
LIST OF HALF-TONE ILLUSTRATIONS	11

CHAPTER

I.	INTRODUCTION	13
II.	ETRUSCAN OR GREEK VASES AND TAZZAS	17
III.	ROMAN RED LUSTROUS WARE	23
IV.	EARLY ENGLISH AND MEDIÆVAL POTTERY	35
V.	OLD TILES	46
VI.	GREYBEARDS OR BELLARMINES	51
VII.	PUZZLE JUGS	55
VIII.	LAMBETH DELFT WARE.	59
IX.	BRISTOL DELFT WARE	69
X.	LIVERPOOL DELFT WARE	76
XI.	SLIP WARE	89
XII.	WHIELDON WARE	107
XIII.	FULHAM WARE	112
XIV.	PLACE'S WARE	120
XV.	ELERS WARE	123
XVI.	ASTBURY WARE	127

CONTENTS

CHAPTER		PAGE
XVII.	SALT GLAZE WARE	129
XVIII.	WEDGWOOD	144
XIX.	WEDGWOOD (*continued*)	158
XX.	OLD WEDGWOOD MARKS	177
XXI.	THE STORY OF THE WEDGWOOD "FINDS"	180
XXII.	WEDGWOOD AND HIS RIVALS	186
XXIII.	LUSTRE WARE	206
XXIV.	LEEDS WARE	218
XXV.	SWANSEA POTTERY	226
XXVI.	JACKFIELD POTTERY	230
XXVII.	VOYEZ AND HIS WORK	233
XXVIII.	YARMOUTH POTTERY	237
XXIX.	NOTTINGHAM POTTERY—STONEWARE	241
XXX.	QUAINT JUGS AND DRINKING CUPS	245
XXXI.	THE WILLOW PATTERN	252
XXXII.	TOBY JUGS	256
XXXIII.	A SHORT ACCOUNT OF OTHER ENGLISH POTTERIES (ALPHABETICALLY ARRANGED)	263
XXXIV.	OLD TOBACCO PIPES	313
XXXV.	CONCLUSION	318
	APPENDIX—SALE PRICES	321
	INDEX TO SUBJECTS	335
	INDEX TO POTTERS AND DECORATORS	339

LIST OF HALF-TONE ILLUSTRATIONS

ETRURIA HALL, WEDGWOOD'S HOME. A DISH FROM THE SERVICE MADE FOR CATHERINE II., EMPRESS OF RUSSIA, FOR THE PALACE OF LA GRENOUILLÈRE . . . . . *Frontispiece*

PAGE

SALT GLAZE WARE; SOME COLOURED, TORTOISESHELL WARE CANDLESTICK, AND LEEDS PUNCH KETTLE . . . . 16 a

ASTBURY WARE, WHIELDON WARE, LAMBETH DELFT, AND A SLIP-WARE CRADLE . . . . 24 a

WHIELDON AND ASTBURY WARE . . . . . . 32 a

SALT GLAZE WARE, SOME COLOURED . . . . . . 48 a

SALT GLAZE WARE, SOME COLOURED . . . . . . 56 a

SALT GLAZE WARE, BEAR JUG . . . . 64 a

EARLY EXPERIMENTAL JASPER-WHITE WEDGWOOD TERRA-COTTA. SOME OF THE FINDS . . . . 80 a

WEDGWOOD BROOCH AND EARRINGS. PLAQUE BY FLAXMAN—"SELENE VISITING ENDYMION" . . . . . 88 a

JASPER PLAQUES: WEDGWOOD—"ENDYMION" AND "DIANA" 96 a

WEDGWOOD WARE: TWELVE PIECES . . . . . . 112 a

WEDGWOOD CANDLESTICKS AND A VASE (FLAXMAN'S DESIGNS), WEDGWOOD JASPER WARE MOUNTED IN STEEL. NEALE AND PALMER VASE . . . . 120 a

TURNER STONEWARE JUG. JACKFIELD COFFEE-POT . . . 128 a

ADAMS COFFEE-POT, JASPER WARE. NEALE AND PALMER VASE . 144 a

ADAMS VASE, BLUE AND WHITE JASPER WARE . . . . 152 a

ADAMS TRANSFER-PRINTED DISH. VIEW OF REGENT QUADRANT, PICCADILLY . . . . 160 a

LIST OF HALF-TONE ILLUSTRATIONS

	PAGE
ADAMS TRANSFER-PRINTED DISH. VIEW OF BLENHEIM PALACE	176 a
LEEDS WARE. NINE PIECES	184 a
STAFFORDSHIRE FIGURES. BOTT'S SHAKESPEARE, AND QUEEN CHARLOTTE	192 a
STAFFORDSHIRE. QUAINT CUPIDS	208 a
STAFFORDSHIRE GROUPS AND FIGURES	216 a
STAFFORDSHIRE "ST. PAUL." WALTON WARE. STAFFORDSHIRE SILVER LUSTRE	224 a
STAFFORDSHIRE. "THE DEPARTURE INTO EGYPT," AND "ST. GEORGE AND THE DRAGON"	240 a
STAFFORDSHIRE SHEEP, LAMBS, AND DOGS. EARLY VICTORIAN	248 a
STAFFORDSHIRE. EARLY VICTORIAN COTTAGES. OLD "PIG-SPOTTED" COWS	256 a
ORDINARY COTTAGE STAFFORDSHIRE. LATE PERIOD	272 a
DOULTON WARE. NAPOLEON AND NELSON JUGS. BACCHANALIAN JUG, AND "REFORM" SPIRIT FLASK	280 a
"QUEEN CAROLINE" MUG WITH LIST OF DEFENDING COUNSEL. "ROCKET" ENGINE JUG, LIVERPOOL AND MANCHESTER RAILWAY	288 a
SUNDERLAND LUSTRE WARE, TRANSFER-PRINTED. OUTSIDE OF "FROG" MUG. FOUR PIECES	304 a
SUNDERLAND LUSTRE WARE, TRANSFER PRINTED. FIVE PIECES	312 a
TOBY JUG BY ENOCH WOOD. BACCHUS JUG BY VOYEZ	320 a
FAMOUS "SOLON" PLAQUES, FROM THE WILLIAM BEMROSE SALE, DERBY, MARCH, 1909	328 a

OLD POTTERY

CHAPTER I
INTRODUCTORY

THE origin of the potter's art is lost in the darkness that surrounds man's early history. The rain fell, the clay became moist; in the moist state it could be easily moulded. The sun shone, and its heat, in those countries generally dry and hot, gave hardness to the moulded form, which was retained until the damp caused it to fall to pieces. The moulded vessel was placed upon the fire, and the discovery was made that burning in the fierce fire gave such a degree of hardness that enough of vitrification or glazing took place to enable the domestic vessel to assume a permanent form and to hold water. Little by little this knowledge spread. The accidental discovery of clays containing more or less glassy materials led in the end to the gradual abolition of the horn and skin-bottle, as well as to an increasing demand for the products of the potter. "These were the potters, and those that dwelt among plants and hedges: there they dwelt with the king, for his work," is the Biblical description of a family of potters of the tribe of Judah, evidently held in high esteem. "And these are ancient things" is the statement preceding it, which shows that pot-making was known and practised in very early times. Though common natural clay supplied material suitable enough for common pottery, soon it happened that some clays were observed to be better than others even for this purpose; and whilst the methods employed, and the degree of heat secured, were somewhat the same, the advantage obtained by washing and mixing the clay marked the next step forward. Then followed the artificial preparation of clays for pottery, but this process was not employed in Europe until centuries after it was familiar to the Chinese, and indeed does not seem to have been adopted until early in the eighteenth century. It appears probable, too, that the potter's wheel was derived from China, but how and when it reached Europe is unknown. The first illustration shows a potter's wheel as represented on the tombs of ancient Thebes, and the second an Egyptian deity. The rotary motion of the wheel, on which the clay was thrown, was, by the action of the fingers, utilised in raising circular or cylindrical forms of various kinds from the shapeless lump.

POTTER'S WHEEL—THEBES, EGYPT.

Let us follow, for a moment, the processes through which modern pottery passes when it leaves the wheel. After being air-dried, the pieces of earthenware are placed in fire-proof *saggers* or pans, having flat bottoms and vertical sides, which are arranged in a kiln. The "biscuit" kiln is then "fired," and after three clear days "drawn," and its contents removed. In this "biscuit" state the pottery would readily absorb water, therefore it has to be glazed, unless decoration is to be applied under

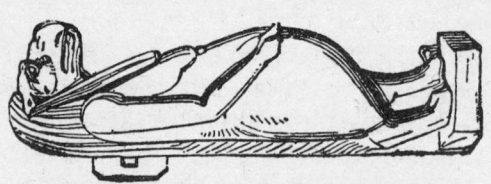

EGYPTIAN POTTERY—THE GOD TA-HUR (THOUCRIS).

the glaze, as in "printed ware." In that case the impression from an engraved plate is taken on paper, pressed on to the ware, and then dexterously removed. After printing, the pottery, still in its biscuit state, is placed in a "hardening kiln," where the oil in the colours applied

INTRODUCTORY

is driven off. Now comes the glazing process, which is really coating the ware with glass. The materials of the glaze may and do vary, but they are all reduced to powder which is mixed with water to form a creamy fluid. Into this the earthenware is carefully dipped, then again placed in "saggers" and fired at a lower temperature than before in the "gloss" or "glost kiln" for about one day. When it is withdrawn, it is ready for the market. If the potter wishes to mould the clay, he squeezes flattened pieces into plaster-of-Paris moulds and the air-dried parts are stuck

ROMAN POTTERY KILN, FOUND AT CASTOR, NORTHAMPTONSHIRE.

together with "slip," that is, clay in a creamy state. Another method of moulding is to run the slip into a plaster mould, so that the space between the inner and outer parts of the mould are filled with clay slip. When the drying is complete the objects are removed, finished by the lathe or by hand, and the handles and spouts stuck on with slip. Coloured glazes are formed by the addition to the ordinary glaze of the oxides of various metals; in fact, they resemble in their composition the enamel colours used for decoration over the glaze. These enamel colours would be spoilt by the temperature of the "glost" kiln, so they are submitted to further firing at a lower temperature. Gold, for gilding, is fired at this temperature too, but the various enamels may demand many visits to the kiln before the ware is finished.

Having rapidly described the modern process of manufacturing pottery, it may be well to indicate the lines of our chapters about it. A short sketch of the classical vases and ware of Greece will be followed by some description of Roman pottery found in England, compared with that found elsewhere; then Mediæval pottery, including early English pottery found in London; Staffordshire pottery, and the products of the other English potteries, with many illustrations.

And here it will be advisable to state frankly, that the difficulties of collecting are due to the existence of immense quantities of pieces quite modern and entirely fraudulent which are produced as required from the factories of France, Germany, Holland, and England. Not only does this apply to the commoner Staffordshire figures and Toby jugs, to the Leeds ware, and the ordinary old pottery—which is worth collecting only when it is old—but we have seen the finest coloured salt-glaze ware, the gems of the potters of the late seventeenth and eighteenth centuries, reproduced in soft colouring, correct form, and in every particular of pattern, and, when necessary, of mark, so that the beginner is heavily handicapped if his own prudence and knowledge do not safeguard his start. No collector troubles about idle or artful tales; he depends upon his eyes, so highly trained that they seldom fail to carry conviction; and therefore, to beginners and others buying *pottes and figgars*, we commend the words of Solomon: " They are all plain to him that understandeth, and right to them that find knowledge."

SALT GLAZE WARE, SOME COLOURED, TORTOISESHELL WARE CANDLESTICK, AND LEEDS PUNCH-KETTLE IN CENTRE OF TOP SHELF.
Lent by Mr. G. Stoner.

CHAPTER II

ETRUSCAN OR GREEK VASES AND TAZZAS

THE most striking glaze applied by the Greeks in their scheme of decoration was a black one which, it is said, is due to the dust of volcanic ashes spread by the brush over the selected part of the surface. Fusion took place when the vases were exposed to a high degree of heat. But it is certain that the same glaze could have been made artificially by mixing glass containing much soda with oxide of iron. This is rather technical, but the main point is that the black glaze was used for painting. The first illustration

shows an early Greek vase with a reddish body, on which the figures were sketched in red and then coloured with the black glaze before firing in the oven or kiln. The other decoration used upon these vases in white or red or other colours was painted on by coloured clays—that is, coloured slips. The name " engobe " distinguishes this form of painting, so that, as sometimes happens, when the engobes have peeled off, the clever designs sketched upon the vases

reveal a facility which recalls the latest Americanism, "Never take two strokes when one will do." We talk about our pottery—well, this vase was made about 700 B.C.! The lines showing red through the black glaze were scratched out with a point. The second vase is not so old by two or three hundred years, but, like the first, the body is reddish, the design is drawn with black glaze, and the details of the figures are worked out by scratching through this glaze with a point. Some persons think that they know because they read; but reading is assisted by illustrations. Our illustrations are meant to send our readers to the British Museum or to South Kensington, where fine specimens are to be seen. Collectors have an

occasional chance of "picking up" genuine vases, if they know! Our next specimen shows two views—top and

ETRUSCAN OR GREEK VASES AND TAZZAS

bottom—of a tazza in which the figures are left in red by painting with black glaze. All of the above specimens were found at Vulci, in the Roman Campagna. The second tazza, also in two illustrations, was found at Ruvo, Naples. It dates about 270 B.C., and has a red body in which the figures in red are left on a black ground, the outlines being in black. The making of the next vase took place about 300 B.C. As before, the body is red, and the black glaze leaves the figures in red. Perhaps the sketches given will form a real help to the collector, but personal experience only can

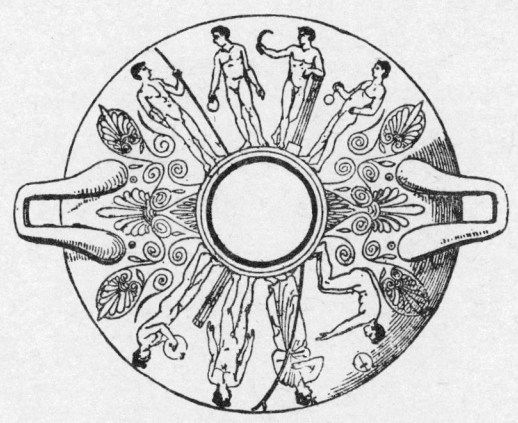

be a trustworthy guide. Imitations and forgeries are common. In 1848 or 1850, Mr. Dillwyn introduced, at Swansea, an imitation of Greek vases. This ware had a fine rich red body on which was printed, in black outline, Etruscan figures, borders, etc., copied from the examples in the British Museum or from Sir William Hamilton's "Antiquités Etrusques, Grecques, et Romaines." Sometimes the figures were left in the original red of the body, the groundwork being in black. The mark, DILLWYN'S ETRUSCAN WARE, is found now and then, but the ware did not pay, and very little was produced. These were honest imitations; but forgeries—impudent attempts to foist false specimens upon eager buyers—have to receive, and ought to receive, the careful attention of the law in every European country.

OLD POTTERY

Another potter who was attracted by the classical designs of the Greek vases was Josiah Wedgwood, who, in this phase of his work, was very materially helped by John Flaxman.

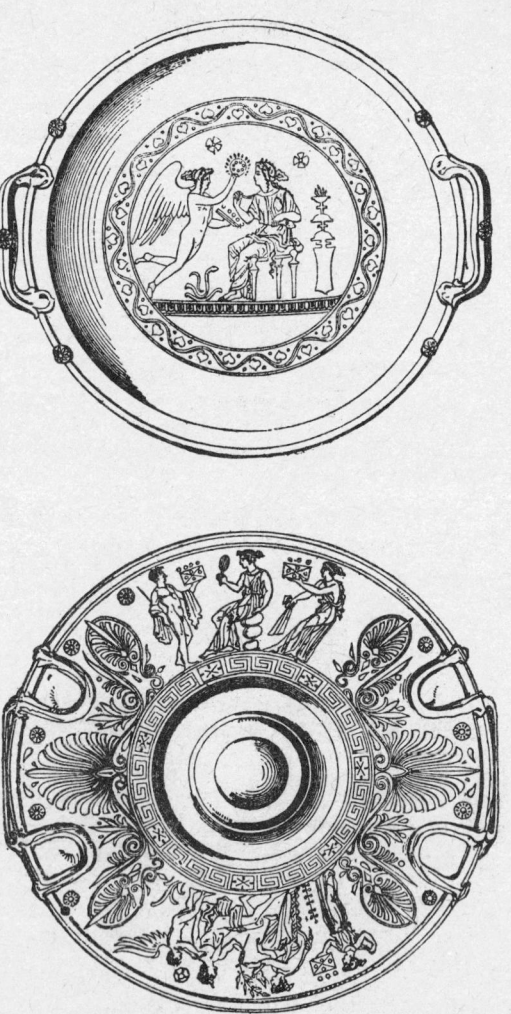

The result of this collaboration was to make Wedgwood ware famous all over the world; and it is remarkable that these two men, both crippled, brought together—one as

ETRUSCAN OR GREEK VASES AND TAZZAS

a master of the potter's art, and the other of classical decoration—so much fine feeling and artistic excellence that it is

doubtful if anything more beautiful has ever had a greater influence in directing public taste. Wedgwood broke away entirely from the traditions which had guided Staffordshire

GREEK AMPHORA.

factories, and took Greek art for his model in form as well as in decoration. We give three illustrations of classical designs followed by him. We show how the beautiful Etruscan and Greek productions, even at a vast distance

CYPRIAN VASE.

GREEK VASE.

of time, impressed themselves upon later work to such a degree as to make it always distinctive. Mr. Gladstone, in the course of his speech at the laying of the foundation stone of a museum and library in memory of Wedgwood, sixty-three years after his death, said : " England has long taken a lead among the nations of Europe for the cheapness of her manufactures, not so for their beauty. If the day shall come when she shall be as eminent in taste as in economy of production, my belief is that the result will probably be due to no single man in so great a degree as to Wedgwood."

CHAPTER III

ROMAN RED LUSTROUS WARE

ROMAN pottery had but little influence upon the British potter in later times. Indeed, after the Romans quitted England, early in the fifth century, the pottery which they left behind seems to have continued in use amongst the principal inhabitants of the country, as is shown by fragments of vessels of red lustrous and other ware found in graves of early Saxon date. This red lustrous ware marked the settlements of the Roman people as they came, and saw, and conquered. Its manufacture extended from the first century B.C. to the third century A.D. Some friends of mine were strolling across the Sussex Downs, near Brighton, on a lovely summer's day, when they flung themselves down to rest at the edge of a chalk pit. One of them felt a stony substance just projecting from the top of the turf, and soon two fine red lustrous amphora-shaped vases were unearthed before their delighted eyes. How and when they got there must ever remain unknown, but the old camps of the Romans are not uncommon on the Downs. The paste of this ware is commonly of a fine sealing-wax red colour, worked with unusual skill into vessels of various forms, and the glaze is generally brilliant. M. Brongniart praises this pottery. He says that "it was worked in the most perfect manner and with the aid of the greater part of the processes and means now employed in the most perfect manufacture." Plain pieces seem to have been turned on the lathe, and stamps of different kinds produced a great variety of patterns. Although all of this ware does not show potters' marks, a large proportion of it is found carefully stamped with them. Roman red ware is sometimes known as Samian, from Samos, where a fine red pottery was made; but it is doubtful if any true Samian ware has ever been found at the Roman stations in Britain. The illustration gives a

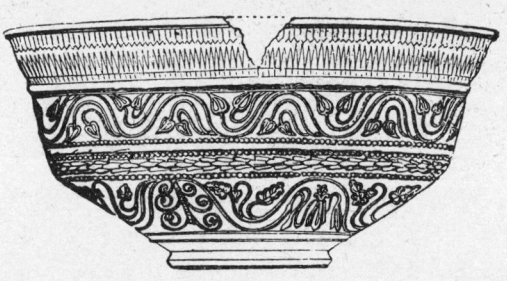

large elegantly formed vase, 9½ in. across the top, having the red paste or body and the lustrous glaze. The potter's mark OFVITAL is to be seen on the bottom of the vase. This was found in St. Martin's-le-Grand in 1845 during excavations, and further examples will be given of such Roman pottery found in England—in fact, quite a large number were unearthed in London.

In the history of ceramics the question of marks plays a large part, and Roman pottery, as will be seen from our illustrations, was often marked. The first mark is on a fragment of a cup, just over 3 in. in diameter, which

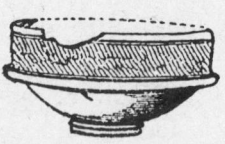 

was found at the Greenwich railway terminus in 1841. The footprint was a common potter's mark at Aretium—modern Arezzo. The next specimen is a mortarium or mortar, in which substances were ground or pounded for domestic use. Up to a certain height inside it was lined with grains of hard stone forced into the paste before the piece was fixed

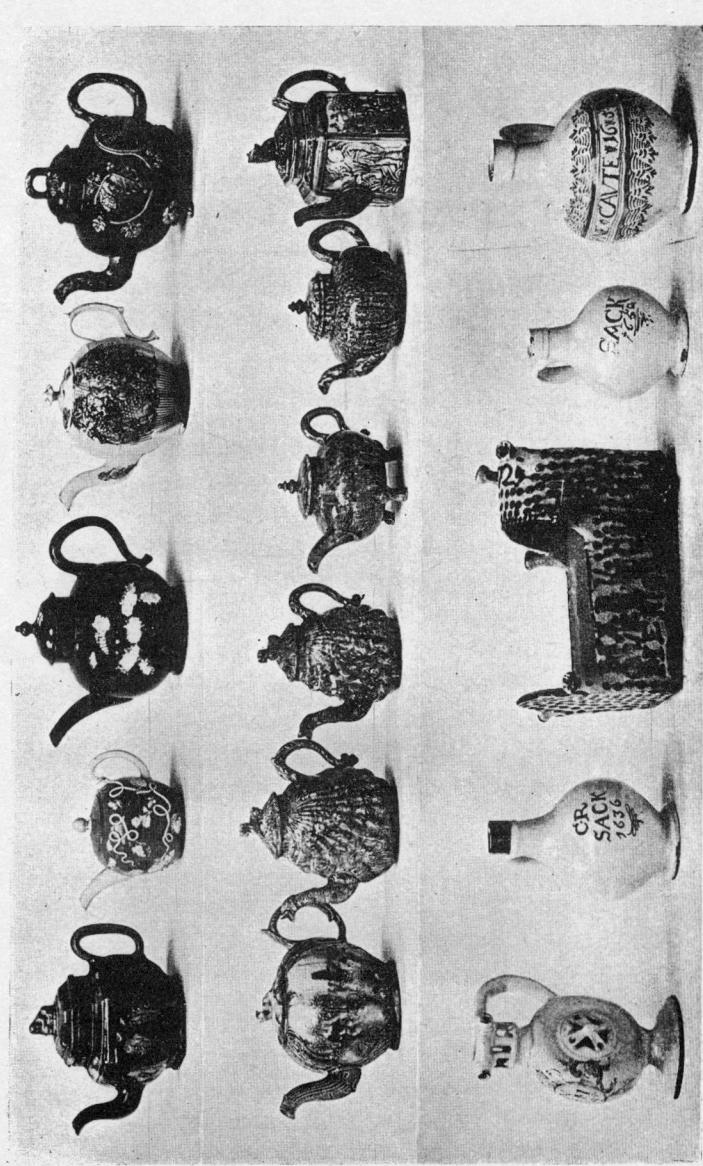

ASTBURY WARE, WHIELDON WARE, LAMBETH DELFT, AND A SLIP-WARE CRADLE.
Lent by Mr. G. Stoner.

in the kiln. Notice that the mask in front is pierced by a hole through which the substances, which had been ground and mixed with some liquid, were poured. This example was found in London, and it had the potter's mark VLIGGI·M by the side of the mask. The three lamps with yellowish

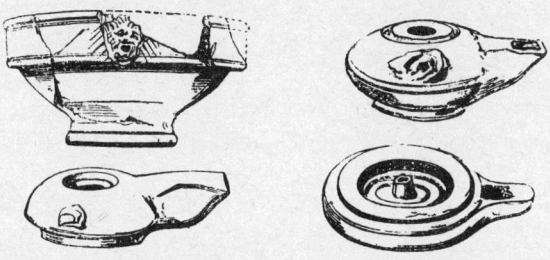

brown bodies were found, too, in the City. Other marks shown on fragments—MICCIO, found in Creed Lane, London; AISTIVI·M, found at the same spot; CELSINUS·F, unearthed in Staining Lane, London, 1845—are interesting because they show the importance of London as a station in Roman times. In this relation it is strange that the excavations which have recently taken place in the City

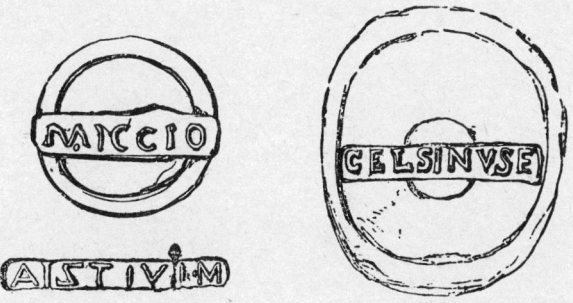

and in Aldwych and the Kingsway have been so barren in "finds" of this character.

The stratified section shown, prepared while works were in progress in Cannon Street, illustrates the approximate position where discoveries may be looked for during the digging process, and we venture to suggest that the authorities should pay special attention to this subject in every case where old buildings are being displaced by new, and where the foundations have to be dug deep down into the earth. It may well be that treasures have been smashed

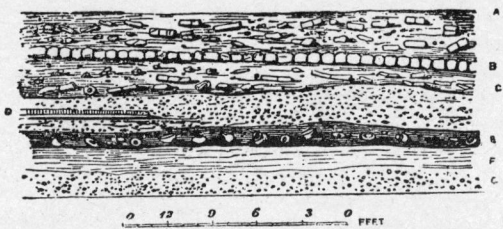

A, present level of the street; B, roadway, previous to the Great Fire of London, 1666; C, ground in which the Norman and Early English pottery is found; D, Roman pavement; E, ground in which the red lustrous and other Roman ware is found; F, clay; G, gravel.

beyond recovery by the steam devil or steam navvy, whose iron teeth have but little regard to anything except the shifting of the greatest amount of soil in the smallest possible time. Yet an inspection before the digging operations are in full swing might reward the archæologist, and furnish rich treasure-trove for the museums of the Metropolis. The

Roman terra-cotta toy, with a reddish brown body, of a boy on horseback, was found in the Borough in 1840, and another figure of a boy, partly clothed, was also a London

ROMAN RED LUSTROUS WARE

find. Naturally, after the discovery of Roman kilns at Castor, we should expect to find many fragments illustrative of the style of decoration employed by the Romans, who must be reckoned amongst our ancestors—for when Julius Cæsar, in his own "Commentaries on the Gallic Wars," describes the invasion of Britain, 55–54 B.C., he shows the beginning of a process by which, in Britain, the foundations were laid of a cosmopolitan people. Romans, Britons, Picts, Scots, Saxons, Normans, and other races practically disappear as separate races, and their further history becomes the history of England. It is to Castor, then, that we turn for information on Roman pottery and its style of decoration, and the illustrations show that there were no local existing influences to divert the potter from the patterns which he brought with him from the banks of the Tiber. The large fragment of a vase with upright sides was found at Castor. It shows several cracks, and these

have been ingeniously mended by means of lead rivets. The two pieces, one with a hare and the other with a dog, came from the same place, to which must also be ascribed the three vase shapes in the next illustration. Of these the third is curious, because it has ribbed corners, apparently

made by the overlapping of cut pieces of the clay, before glazing and firing.

Before the Romans quitted Britain, in 410 A.D., they drew their supplies of pots and pans mainly from Castor, near Peterborough; New Forest, Hampshire; Upchurch, Kent; and from the Rhenish district, by water-carriage, through the mouths of the Rhine. London, Winchester,

and Colchester have furnished a large number of specimens. Now we will examine a few more, of differing shapes and decoration. The shape and decoration of the first vase indicates that it is a Castor piece. It is 8 in. high, and its decoration is in white slip on a pale yellowish-brown paste, with black glaze in the larger and upper portion and red glaze on the stem of the vase. It was found at Winchester. The next vase, 5¾ in. high, has a pattern produced by toolmarks in bands; after turning on the lathe the sides were depressed into seven compartments. This was dug up in Lothbury, London, and has a red paste where most fused,

ROMAN AMPHORA.

with a darker colour inside. The glaze is black, with the red tint of the paste showing through. It is Upchurch ware. The third vase, 4½ in. high, was found at Cateaton Street, London, in January 1845. The paste is white, with a dark glaze, and the decoration—hounds hunting a stag—was laid on in slip after the vase was turned. Tool work is shown at the bottom. Generally the Castor ware is grey or yellowish brown with a dull black or slightly reddish glaze; it is thin, hard, and well potted.

The vases, unguentaria, and jars of the New Forest

are made of local clay furnishing a smooth porous body in shades of grey, buff, pale red, and brown, whilst the glaze is either purplish or reddish, and washed on in bands, or stripes, or circular ornaments. Upchurch ware, also made of the local clays, is of a dark ash-grey or slate colour, with a blackish hue on the surface caused by the imperfect oxidation when the supply of air was almost cut off and the smoke could neither escape nor burn. The decoration consisted of raised

dots or bosses and incised lines. After the Roman conquest we expect to find evidences of the knowledge and skill of the Southern potters, and we do find the accuracy of the potter's wheel, which does not seem to have been known in England before the first century B.C. We have evidences of the use of the lathe; there are slip patterns and moulded ornaments on graceful shapes, and, sometimes, the surfaces are glazed. The Roman pottery found in London includes some fine amphoræ. The figure in the illustration on the last page was not intended to stand like a vase—the two arms were used for suspension.

ROMAN RED LUSTROUS WARE

The next amphora was found in digging the foundation of London Bridge, and the following one in Old Broad Street in 1850. The decoration on this last is a plain band with a zigzag edge at the height of the base of the handles. The others have no decoration. The dish or mortarium has a light brown, somewhat coarse body, and is unglazed. 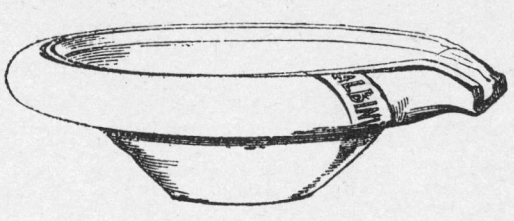 The potter's mark is ALBINVS. This was dug up in Cock Lane, Smithfield, London, in 1844.

The next examples were chiefly obtained from Cologne, having been discovered in that city or in its vicinity. They are important for the purposes of comparison, showing that Roman ware—even the red lustrous ware—was introduced into Britain from the Rhenish provinces, being manufactured at Heilegenberg, about five leagues from Strasburg, where some of it was found in a Roman kiln similar to that already pictured from Castor. The remains of several Roman kilns have been

unearthed in the Rhine district, at Tabernia Rheni (Rheinzabern). No less than fifteen kilns were discovered in a small area. A perfect bowl, consequently very rare, was found at Cologne, and is shown in the illustration. It is Roman red ware, lustrous, like red sealing-wax in texture, 6 in. high and 10 in. in diameter. The design shows a soldier in

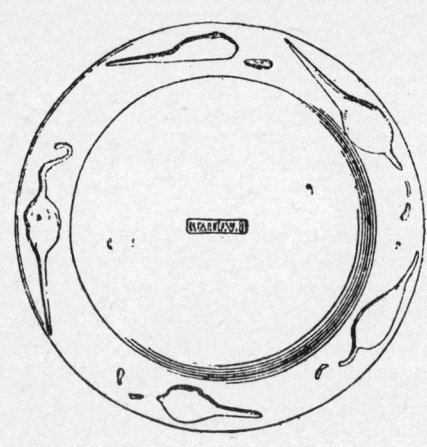

armour, with sword and shield, engaged in combat. A retiarius, his opponent, holds in his left arm a net, and in his right hand a trident or three-pronged spear. This may well be a scene from the arena, for the fighting figures are by the side of an Emperor seated on a throne. What memories does this evoke? The thumbs down or thumbs up —Death or Life—which?

The character and manufacture of this bowl are so closely allied to the specimens found in England that there is but little doubt that much of this ware came from Southern Germany, or that the potters from Germany came to England and made the pottery here. Plates and dishes are rare. A patera of red lustrous ware, 8 in. in diameter, has been figured very often, and our illustration shows it with the ivy-leaves in relief, laid on in slip or *barbotine*. The potter's mark is VRSVLVS. The two-handled vase shown next is 7½ in. high, and differs in style from the amphora previously described. The whole form differs, and the design, laid on in slip, represents a peacock amid ivy-leaves. In this case the ware, the manufacture, and

WHIELDON AND ASTBURY WARE.
Lent by Mr. G. Stoner.

the kind of ornament are similar to fragments which have been dug out during excavations in London. The deduction is obvious : they came from the same kilns, and these London pieces were imported from Germany.

As a contrast, we might take the vase of Upchurch ware, with raised bosses or dots and the blackish hue before referred to. The pattern is in raised dots or bosses, laid on in a slip similar to the body, after that had been turned on the wheel. A short time since, a friend in digging the

ROMAN LAMP WITH EIGHT BURNERS.

foundation for his new house at Portsmouth, was lucky in finding a pitcher of New Forest ware, deep down in the earth, and still more fortunate in getting it out absolutely sound. Other examples of a later period have been unearthed in the same way, and in a following chapter we give an illustration of a small greybeard pitcher which was found when the excavations were being carried out for the foundations of the Hotel Metropole at Brighton. The mark made by the pick is plain, but otherwise it is uninjured. A really fine example of a Roman lamp with eight burners is shown above. The lamp was suspended by the aid of three loops upon an interior circle ; but what a contrast is this in lighting—the best of that past—to the worst of the present day! The higher style of art employed in ornamenting the red lustrous ware, the most beautiful product of Roman ceramic art, is shown in the small bowl, $2\frac{1}{4}$ in. high, 5 in. wide,

which gets its name from Arretium, or Aretium—modern Arezzo, in Tuscany. The moulds were made of terra-cotta, and the pottery—Arretian ware—seems to have been made with success as late as the seventh century.

CHAPTER IV

EARLY ENGLISH AND MEDIÆVAL POTTERY

VASES were often used as cinerary or sepulchral urns, and in the British and South Kensington Museums are specimens of ancient British ware, which were first sun-dried and then burnt in an open fire, as is shown by the partial blackening, resulting from such an imperfect firing process. These urns appear to have been used for sepulchral purposes only, simply to hold the ashes of the dead. An illustration shows an ancient British urn of this type. Contrast this with the much more elaborate Romano-British urn, or vase, of glazed slip ware, and it can be easily seen that the British products, both before and after the Roman occupation, suffered by comparison. Anglo-Saxon pottery was poor in quality, made of local clay, with very simple designs. At the most a twisted cord was impressed in the soft clay; or a zigzag design, scratched by a point into a variety of combinations, usually in straight lines, was produced, but this pottery was never highly fired; in fact, it is wonderful that examples should have survived to our times, because some of it was scarcely more than sun or air-dried.

The pottery used in Britain before the Norman times (1066 A.D.) is not easily placed with regard to age. It is, in this respect, like old Chinese. One says, "This is a Ming piece or a Ch'ien-Lung piece," and who can refute the expert's statement ? So in the British section it is difficult to state the exact date of any old piece. Consult the early illuminated pictures, and certain pottery forms will be noted. In early manuscripts references are found to " La Potere " or " Le Squeler," a seller of pots in the first case, and porringers, dishes, and basins in the other. Orders are noted to the "pitcher house" for "pottes"; and, later, "that erthyn pottes be bought," or "earthen potts for red wine and ipocras." Even Pepys, in 1663, in his Diary—what a delightful, garrulous old man he was!—mentions drinking out of "earthen pitchers" at a Lord Mayor's feast. All

ANCIENT BRITISH AND ROMAN URNS.

of this shows that ordinary pitchers and pots were used at the tables of important persons; were mentioned, in the inventories of royal households, in which the black-jack, made of leather, was commonly used as a drinking vessel, together with smaller cups all made of "ledder." These earthen vessels, many of which were made in this country, continued in use down to the sixteenth century.

There is, however, much reason to believe that German and

EARLY ENGLISH AND MEDIÆVAL POTTERY 37

Flemish wares—notably Cologne ware—were still imported. Cologne ware had a great reputation. A curious and interesting petition was addressed to Queen Elizabeth by William Simpson, merchant. "Whereas one Garnet Tynes, a stranger living in Acon (Aix-la-Chapelle) in the parts beyond the seas, being none of her ma^{ties} subjecte, doth buy uppe all the pottes made at Culloin (Cologne), drinking stone pottes, and he onlie transporteth them into this realm of England and selleth them: It may please your ma^{tie} to graunte unto the sayd

LEOPARD WARE TANKARDS.

Simpson full power and onelie licence to provyde, transport, and bring into this realm the same or such-like drinking pottes; and the sayd Simpson will . . . . sell them at as reasonable price as the other hath sold them from tyme to tyme." This ware and the Flemish ware were very popular from 1540 to 1620, when it is supposed, though the evidence is slight, that Chinese porcelain was introduced into Europe. The earthen pots were often "garnished with silver." This introduces a very debatable point. Was there, then, no manufactory of such pots in England? It is quite probable that the drinking-vessels known as "grey-beards" and "Bellarmines," so much used in the inns of the sixteenth and seventeenth centuries, "were made in Germany," but we must not forget that stoneware, ornamented with designs in white clay, was made at Fulham and Lambeth in the seventeenth century, and a little later in Staffordshire.

It is only recently that the Fulham stoneware of Dwight, who began his experiments as early as 1640, and took out a patent in 1671, has been properly appreciated. Who made the so-called Elizabethan "leopard or tiger ware" tin-glazed tankards, three specimens of which are in the Gold Ornament Room of the British Museum? The second one, in the illustration, has the hall-mark 1549–50 on its English silver-gilt mount. The others have similar mounts unmarked. They are valuable, and fine specimens with early dated silver mounts are worth two or three hundred pounds. The ware has a coarse body, a glaze usually spotted with purplish black, reddish yellow, and an impure blue, or streaked with a purplish brown or splashed with a bolder colour.

ELIZABETHAN TANKARD.

Apropos of "tiger ware" tankards, a provincial dealer had heard of one in Newcastle, and, through an agent, bought it for £45. The London experts often visited him, notably two, who always came together. One sometimes bought a few pieces, the other bought nothing. When asked why, he replied, "Oh, you have never got anything good enough for me!" Whereupon the Elizabethan tankard was produced. "How much?" was the instant question. "A hundred guineas," was the reply. "Make it pounds," and "pounds" it was. The two companions left the shop, and the tankard was "put up" on the return journey to London, and the last bid was £280!

But to return to early English pottery anterior to this. Our first three jugs, or pitchers, are, probably, thirteenth century. The first is unglazed, but the other two are covered with dull green glaze upon a light brown clay, either in patches or over the whole surface. It is almost im-

EARLY ENGLISH AND MEDIÆVAL POTTERY 39

possible to fix the dates of these specimens, but some of them have been excavated with coins, so that, approximately, we arrive at a rough conclusion. For instance, the

first jug was found with coins of Henry III. and Edward I. In reality, it is a matter of no great importance, considering how rude is the fictile art they represent. In the fourteenth century, when artistic skill was shown in stonework, metalwork, and in missal-painting, it is only in one product that

we find fine ceramic art—that is, in the tiles, which will be the subject of a future chapter. Up to the sixteenth century the wares were coarse, red, buff, or grey clay, unrefined, and, generally, ill baked. The translucent lead glaze was often coloured green, but sometimes it has a yellowish tone, and, occasionally, purplish black. The next group consists of two jugs and a costrel, all of which were found in London. The first is a pitcher with a double swell; the body is of light-coloured clay, partly covered with a yellow glaze. The second jug has a cream-coloured body, and the upper part of the outside is covered with transparent glaze, spotted with black. The third, the costrel, has projections—two on each side—pierced for a cord or strap for suspension in the manner of a pilgrim's bottle. The body of the costrel is red, and it is glazed in a marbled pattern of mixed red and white. Speaking of pilgrims' bottles gives

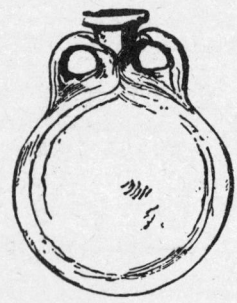 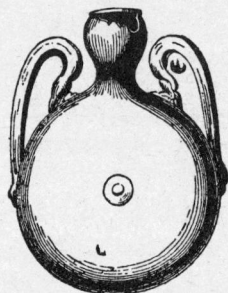

ROMAN.   PILGRIMS' BOTTLES.   EARLY ENGLISH.

an opportunity for a contrast between a Roman and an early English bottle. Possibly the first might have been the bottle of a Roman soldier, yet the same general idea of suspension is carried out in the present time, although pottery is not used. The body is the light straw-coloured ordinary Roman pottery as distinguished from the red lustrous ware, whilst the early English bottle has a cream-coloured body, much less flat than the other.

It will be noted that the common ware was usually plain, without decoration, and it is unlikely that such pieces would have been found at the tables of the rich in an age when the metal-work was so beautiful. The common pottery was for everyday use by menials. When it was more highly ornamented it reached a higher social status. Really, the best of the decoration consisted of hand-moulded reliefs of animal

EARLY ENGLISH AND MEDIÆVAL POTTERY 41

and plant forms, masks, and rudely incised drawings or patterns impressed with the notched end of a stick. Rarely were the designs stamped, but applied strips, discs, or leaf-shaped pieces of clay were not uncommon. The use of " slip " or " barbotine " decoration seems to have been known from an early period. The highest development of the potter's art at this time consisted in the excision of certain parts of the body in accordance with a design, and, as it were, inlaying a coloured or black clay, which, when rubbed down, made a pattern which was practically everlasting against reasonable wear and tear. This was the principle underlying the celebrated Henry Deux ware, priceless specimens of which are to be seen in the South Kensington Museum and at the Musée Cluny at Paris. The private collections of the Rothschilds are said to hold wonderful pieces of this ware, unfortunately " caviare to the general." The few examples belonging to the nation were extremely costly, yet, considering their rarity, they are of inestimable value. Passing along the streets, how few are they who would recognise a piece of this famous faïence!

Grotesque drinking cups were amongst the productions of

the potteries of England in mediæval times, which however consisted chiefly of pitchers and jugs, cups and bowls, bottles and dishes. The term "pottes" referred to the drinking-cups then in general use. From them, and from the Bellarmines, grey-beards or long-beards, the ale-houses, using them as ale pots, derived the expression "a pot of ale." A pot was a quart; a little pot, a pint; the pottle pot, two quarts; and the gallonier, a gallon. As a rule, they were glazed, but plain, except the larger jugs or pitchers, which were sometimes decorated with heads or foliage in more or less high relief, and sometimes they took the form of a mounted knight or other figures. The illustration on the previous page shows a mounted knight of very primitive workmanship. Note the handle and the long pointed toes and "pryck spurs," which indicate the reign of Henry II. The figure measured 10½ in. long by 13 or 14 in. high, when perfect. It was made of coarse clay, glazed green in the top as usual. The next example is a mounted knight

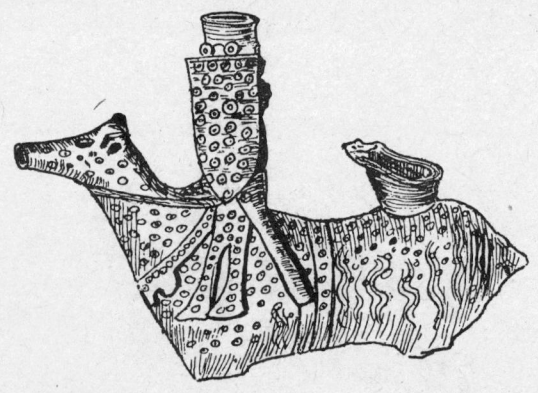

in armour. It is badly damaged, yet it very much resembles the figure of Richard I. as shown on his Great Seal. The eyes of the knight are seen above the shield, and the round dots represent chain armour. The handle is broken, though the circular hole at the bottom of the handle can be seen. Through this hole, as in the previous specimen, the vessel was filled, and the drink was taken from the animal's mouth. Curiously, the same idea seems to have been adopted in the

EARLY ENGLISH AND MEDIÆVAL POTTERY 43

far-off East, the next illustration, of a horse saddled, being decorated in front with the chrysanthemum, and having

a dark green glaze splashed with a lighter green. The legs and feet are very unusual, not to say comical, in shape: in fact, the modelling of the whole of the three suggests much to the imagination. The same remark applies to the animal with a twisted horn, which we will call a cow, which has the same green glaze as the first two described. It is in Scarborough Museum, and possibly was made in that town, where a potter's kiln was discovered in 1854. Notwithstanding Iago's dictum, " your Dane, your German, and your

swag-bellied Hollander, are nothing to your English" in powers of drinking, no nation has bestowed more skill

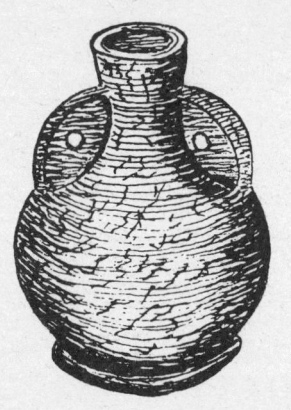

in quaint designs for drinking-cups than the Germans, who, perhaps, should occupy the place above assigned to the English. The old silversmiths of Augsburg and Nuremberg made the most grotesque figures of men, animals, and birds, beside which the quaint rude pottery figures described here seem too feeble for words. Yet they have an interest all their own.

Costrels or Pilgrims' bottles were used for liquor to be carried slung on the person, and the Romans first adopted the form and material which were still used in the

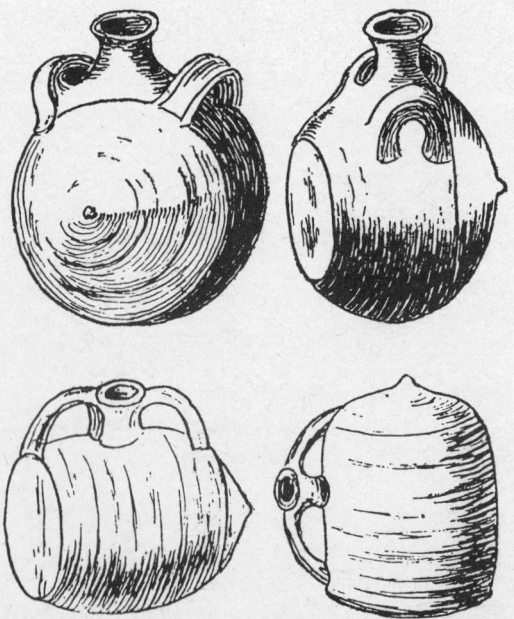

Middle Ages. The flattened amphora and the ordinary pilgrim's

EARLY ENGLISH AND MEDIÆVAL POTTERY

bottle have been illustrated side by side. Other examples are now given where the amphora form is modified and eventually displaced. The first example shows a modification. In this case the bottle is globular or gourd-shaped, not flattened at the sides, whilst the handles are simply flat pieces of clay affixed to the sides and pierced with holes for suspension. This may be ascribed to Tickenhall. Its surface is mottled all over with green glaze, like so many of the early pieces. The two other illustrations show the barrel and gourd shapes with one end flattened, so that when not in use the vessel could stand upon the flat end. Two views are given of each piece, so that the curious mammiform character of the other end may be clearly seen. Such small bottles would scarcely be very popular, for the small one is only $4\frac{1}{2}$ in. high and holds about half a pint.

CHAPTER V

OLD TILES

BALZAC has often remarked in his novels that the mania for collecting things is a primary symptom of madness. If this were true many collectors must long ago have been pronounced insane, for they began collecting when they were at school, and have gone on forming and improving their collections ever since. Indeed, the converse seems nearer the truth—the collector keeps ever young and need not die until he wants to. Such is the relief afforded by a hobby from the troubles and cares of business. It is not necessary to spend large sums of money in making a collection, provided that the collector is prepared to devote his leisure to collecting, and also is a specialist and has acquired knowledge by his special study which enables him to buy what he wants at a reasonable price.

The remarks that have been made as to mediæval pottery, which may have been common, but could not be called beautiful, do not apply to the so-called encaustic tiles. The tile-maker paved the floors and sometimes ornamented the walls of the churches and the monasteries, as well as of the houses of the nobility, and, coming into contact with the learning and refinement of the age, he rose above the mediocrity of the pot-maker, and became, in his craft, an artist. With no other materials than those we have described, the tile took its place in the scheme of ecclesiastical architecture, and did not suffer by comparison with the other details.

In a footnote of the British Museum Guide, the writer says, with much truth : " The ill-considered word ' encaustic ' has been widely adopted as a generic term for mediæval

OLD TILES

tiles. It has been rejected for the following reasons: In its literal meaning, 'burnt in,' if applied to the tile in the

CHERTSEY PANELS—(1) ISEULT WITH OTHERS IN SHIP; (2) KING RICHARD IN COMBAT WITH SALADIN.

sense of being burnt in the kiln, it is surely superfluous in any work that deals with pottery, a material which we may take for granted has been *burnt in a kiln*. If, on the other hand, it is applied to the slip ornament that is *burnt in* the intaglios of those tiles which have impressed patterns, it is not so suggestive a word as *inlaid*." As a rule, the tiles were of red clay, about four to five inches square and an inch in thickness. They were made, and had reached a high standard, as early as the thirteenth century, and the examples of this period, which we illustrate, are in the British Museum, having been dug out of the ruins of Chertsey Abbey.

It is quite probable that these beautiful tiles were made in the great religious houses by the monks, who were in-

PAVEMENT TILES—BITTON AND BRISTOL CATHEDRAL

fluenced by Continental and especially Italian art, and they kept the process of manufacture strictly secret. We can imagine these old craftsmen matching themselves with the sculptor and the carver, under whose hands the stone and wood seemed a new nature animated with angel and ghoul; grotesque and fantastic man in all his moods; animals and birds; trees, fruit, flowers, and things creeping innumerable. Then, too, the walls were bright with superb frescoes fresh from the hand of the master painter—perhaps a brother monk who, in his turn, saw the windows blush rosy red, as the perfect stained glass told the story of hope for evermore. In his cell, alone yet not lonely, the tile-maker designs the pavement, and marks the sizes and shapes of his tiles. Shall the surface be ornamented by incised or impressed designs, or by raised patterns? Shall they

SALT GLAZE WARE, SOME COLOURED.
Lent by Mr. G. Stoner.

GLAZED TILE—MONMOUTH PRIORY, 15TH CENTURY.

STOVE TILE—GREEN GLAZED, ELIZABETHAN.

be inlaid, or painted with slip-coloured clay ? Rightly he decides that, as the raised and the incised patterns will soon show signs of wear, he will adopt the inlaid design, and use white or coloured clay to fill the hollows made by the stamp on the clay, when it is dry enough. Then to the kiln; but first, before firing, powdered lead ore was dusted on, which combined with the red body to give a rich reddish-brown surface, and with the white slip to give a no less rich yellow tone. Thus, all working with a single aim, the house was finished, and the best gave their best to the best.

The earliest tiles were of one colour, the white inlaid tiles were succeeded by inlays of different colours, and the raised pattern seems to have been discarded at a very early period, but it reappeared in the baser work of the seventeenth century. Kilns for tile-making have been unearthed at Malvern, Droitwich, Farringdon Street, London, and various places in Worcester, Gloucester, Wiltshire, Staffordshire, and Shropshire. Amongst many other old churches, the Chapter House, Westminster, Malvern Priory Church, Bristol Cathedral, Gloucester Cathedral, and Chertsey Abbey show fine examples of these mediæval tiles. The illustration of a stove tile with letters of the Tudor period, 1485–1603, may be English, though the authorities are inclined to assign it to Germany rather than to England in the reign of Queen Elizabeth.

CHAPTER VI

GREYBEARDS OR BELLARMINES

WE have noticed the pots made at Cologne called *drinking stone pottes*, and we stated that the early pieces were without ornament of any sort. It was not until the fourteenth century that even the crudest human heads appeared on them. Later, in the second half of the sixteenth century, these German and Flemish wares were more highly decorated. They received the name of Bellarmine from Cardinal Bellarmine, who died in 1621. He was a determined persecutor of the reformed religion, and the Protestants seized upon this method of showing their hatred of him, so that his hard features and squat fat figure became the standing joke of the alehouse and the byword of the people.

FOREIGN BELLARMINES.

Ben Jonson calls the Bellarmine "A jug faced with a beard, that fills out to the guests," and again "A larger jug that some men call a Bellarmine, but we a Conscience." Many of the old writers make allusions to its general use at alehouses and homes. "Uds bud," says an actor in the play *Epsom Wells*, in a drinking scene, "my head begins to turn round; but let's into the house. 'Tis dark. We'll have one Bellarmine there, and then *Bonus nocius.*" From these same pots or mugs with "the hardmouthed visage" are no doubt derived the vulgar names for the human face, and for the man muddled with drink and therefore silly—each was a "mug."

In 1635 a patent was granted to David Ramsey and others " for a new method of heating boilers by means of sea coal, which invencion is alsoe very usefull for the Dryeinge of Bricke, all manner of Tyles, etc. . . . and alsoe that they

BELLARMINE CAROLIAN.   AN ENGLISH BELLARMINE.

have found out the Arte and Skill of Makeinge and Dyeinge of all sortes of Panne Tyles, Stone Juggs, etc., which nowe are made by Straungers in Forraigne Partes, etc." The parties concerned were bound to pay one-fourth of their profit yearly into the Exchequer! What were the products of this factory, or was the factory ever started? We do not know. Fulham and Lambeth have yielded "wasters" of uncertain age, and it is quite recently that we have been able to piece together John Dwight's history as a Fulham potter, and to identify specimens from his works. His patent for stoneware was granted

GREYBEARDS OR BELLARMINES

in April 1671, and the earliest products of Fulham are assigned to about ten years before that. This, then, is probably the date of the English salt-glazed Bellarmines; and the collector visiting the public museums will be able to compare the stoneware vessels of Raren, Cologne, and other German factories, not alone with the English, but with the Flemish specimens.

The old generic term for all of this ware was "Grès (stoneware) de Flandres." The price of these greybeards is still

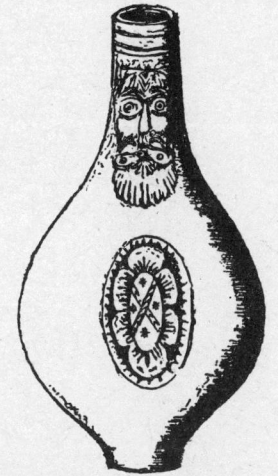

GREYBEARD, DUG UP AT BRIGHTON
WHEN THE FOUNDATIONS OF THE
HOTEL METROPOLE WERE LAID.

ALE POT.

moderate, unless they are mounted in silver, as is often the case with the "tiger" or "leopard" ware called Elizabethan, which bears a striking resemblance in texture and glaze to the stoneware Bellarmine. Some of my friends have picked up good specimens for a sovereign, but, like all really old pottery, the tendency is upwards, and three or four times this will soon be reckoned a fair price for a really good piece. Of course there is still a large field for any one who likes this early stoneware. The ordinary pint pots—"the ale pots" or "little pots,"—like the Bellarmines, were first imported, then they were copied in large numbers in the potteries of England. They were usually made of a light-coloured clay and turned on the wheel, the pattern being scratched in the soft clay with a sharp point—flowers, scrolls, and other designs. Sometimes a flower or initials was pressed on the front, just as the greybeard decoration was. These

FULHAM JUG—STONEWARE.

early pieces are thick, hard, and very durable. However, it is but little we know of the men and their work in the sixteenth century. Where, for instance, were the kilns of Gaspar Andries and Guy Janson, foreign potters, who established at Norwich, in 1570, a factory after the fashion of Flanders, and made decorative ware which was called " *les poteries gracieuses de la reine Elizabeth* " ? Did they make the " tiger " ware and the Bellarmines ?

CHAPTER VII

PUZZLE JUGS

THE village inn, besides using the greybeard, the stone jug, and the ale-pot, had its puzzle jug and puzzle cup, both of which were favourites with the villagers, who enjoyed the fun that resulted when the uninitiated spilt over themselves the good liquor that was drained at a draught by those who knew the secret of the jug. These jugs were perforated in the neck, as will be seen by the illustrations, and the rim had three, five, or even seven spouts, so that the ale could not be drunk in the ordinary way. One spout alone gave access to the contents. All the other spouts had to be closed by the fingers, as well as a hole hidden under the top of the handle. Then by suction at the spout the invitation often given, " Come, taste me if you can," was accepted. The late Mr. Henry Willett's old Staffordshire now enriches the Brighton Museum, where there are several of these jugs. Two are white, painted with an inscription in blue. The earlier one is ascribed to 1670 or thereabout, and the other was about 1750. The first is Lambeth delft, the second Liverpool. Another is Newcastle earthenware, printed with a fox-hunting scene, " The Find," and placed about 1820. Of the same date and place is a lustred,

NOTTINGHAM—C. 1700.

printed, and coloured jug, illustrating the "Friendly Society's Feast" and the "Club Day." So we may say that the

BRAMPTON BROWN WARE—DESIGN IN RELIEF.

ANOTHER BRAMPTON JUG.

jugs were first made in the seventeenth century, and at the beginning of the twentieth are still being produced *on*

THE WEDGWOOD PUZZLE JUG, 1691.

PUZZLE JUG—17TH CENTURY.

the old models. Brampton, or, as it is sometimes called, Chesterfield, ware—a brown ware of a remarkably hard

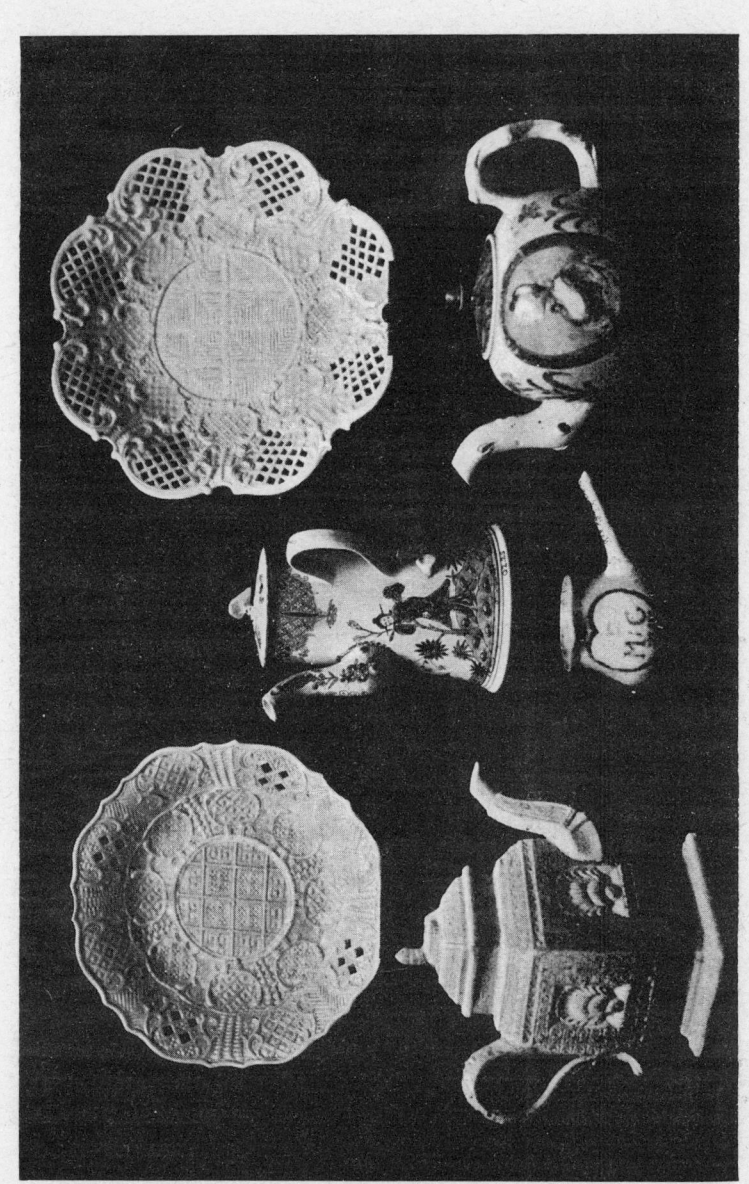

SALT GLAZE, SOME COLOURED.
Lent by Mr. A. M. Broadley.

PUZZLE JUGS

and durable quality—embodied the puzzle jug in a variety of shapes and sizes, sometimes with decoration of figures and designs in relief and sometimes quite plain. They were first made centuries ago. The earliest dated pieces are 1674, 1684, and 1691. The latter date is found on the jug with an inscription, "John Wedgwood," which is the earliest example of the celebrated name of Wedgwood occurring on pottery. John appears to have been born in 1654 and to have died in 1705, twenty-five years before *the* Wedgwood was born. His jug, like many examples by Thomas Toft, bears the name of the person *for whom it was made*.

In contrast to the Wedgwood puzzle jug is a puzzle cup of unusual shape of Lambeth delft, bearing the arms of the Drapers' Company, and dated 1674. This was two years before Van Hamme took out his patent with the object of making "tiles, porcelain, and earthenware" at Lambeth; but more will be said on this in the next chapter. It is probable that, years before, pottery had been made in London, if not at Lambeth. To the same period in the seventeenth century belongs the jug with a snake-handle and a bird for a mouth. The slip-ware of this was clay, reduced to a wash by adding water, and applied in the last two cases as a wash for the whole vessel. Sometimes, however, it was dotted on or trailed from a spout—the common method of decoration—at other times it was combed with a tool such as grainers use in imitating various woods, though wire, or even leather, was used to produce the marbled appearance. Lastly, the ground was

PUZZLE CUP—LAMBETH DELFT, 1674.

coated with one colour-slip, and then the surface wash was applied and the design scratched through. The last illustration dates from the early part of the last century. It is a fine example of the hard compact *white* earthenware of Leeds, and is most elaborate in design and careful in execution. Jewitt thus describes it: " The upper part is ornamented with punched perforations, and the centre of the jug is open throughout, having an o p e n flower — conventionally treated—on either side, between which is a swan standing clear in the inside. The jug is painted with borders and sprigs of flowers, and is marked with the usual impressed mark, ' LEEDS POTTERY.' " Of course it is well known that Leeds ware is generally cream-coloured, but the collector should remember that the *white* Leeds ware is deserving of special attention. Black transfer-printed pictures, such as " The Vicar and Moses," with the old ballad having the same name, are found on this white earthenware, which often has the golden fleece—the arms of the borough of Leeds—as a mask, dependent from the spouts of the jugs. Transfer printing is said to have been adopted in Leeds as early as 1780.

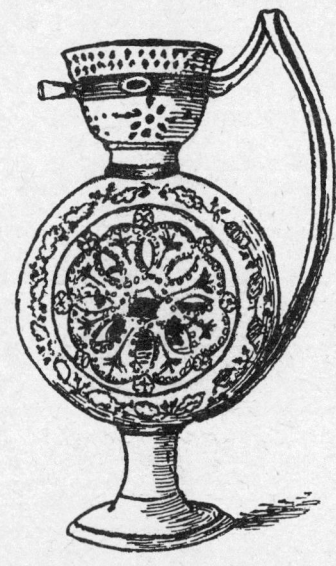

LEEDS WARE—MARKED LEEDS POTTERY.

Many of these old jugs have other inscriptions, such as:

    " Here, gentlemen, come try your Skill *
    I'll hold a wager if you will * *
    That you drink not this Liquor all * *
    Without you spill or let som fall * "

CHAPTER VIII

LAMBETH DELFT WARE

WE have said something about slip-ware—a purely British product—and shall return to it later. We also noted the characteristic green-glazed brown ware, and brown-glazed red ware, pitchers, pans, tygs, and pots of mediæval times, which, like the stoneware, owed much to foreign influences. The delft ware of Lambeth, and, indeed, all English delft, borrowed everything from abroad —the name included. Early in the history of pottery, Lambeth appears to have been actively associated with pot-making, though no date can be given to the beginning of any of the pot-works. It was about 1600 when the Dutch, in their efforts to imitate the Chinese blue-and-white, discovered an opaque tin enamel which effectively covered the buff earthenware body, and, at the same time, formed a fine ground, on which blue or coloured decoration could be applied.

TUDOR PERIOD GREEN GLAZED PITCHER.

The earliest dated pieces of Lambeth, where the process was imported from Holland about 1630, range onwards from this time to about a century later. The British Museum and South Kensington show specimens: the first a mug dated 1650; the second, a candlestick with the Fishmongers' Arms, 1648, and a mug, 1631. No doubt the

Dutchman, Van Hamme, who took out his patent in 1676, was the successor of a line of local delft-workers. These

TUDOR PERIOD GREEN GLAZED PITCHERS.

had made the Lambeth wine vessels, which are even now not rare. Many of them have dates earlier than Van Hamme's

COLOURED LAMBETH DELFT, 17TH CENTURY.

patent, and this early ware is in a special family, having a pale brown or buff body, covered with a white enamel, and being altogether harder than the common foreign specimens. Besides the white wine-pots, or sack-pots as they are named, tiles, plates, jugs, mugs, and dishes were made, also apothecaries' labels, wine-bin labels, and pill slabs. All of them were painted in blue, and covered with a thin transparent lead glaze. Shortly described, the process of manufacture was this:—The prepared clay was shaped and baked into a biscuit state, resembling in colour a pale red ordinary flower-pot at this stage. Then it was dipped into a vessel containing tin enamel ground to powder, and stirred up

MAJOLICA DISH—EARLY 17TH CENTURY.

in water till it could hold no more. The water having dried out, a fine coating of the white powder was deposited over the entire surface. The painting, in blue, was done on this soft, dusty, non-adherent coating of tin enamel which would scarcely bear touching—a fact which may account for the crude painting on the English specimens as compared with the fine Dutch work, in the latter case skilful and artistic, in the other, coarse drawing or a clumsy imitation of imported designs. After the painting was completed, a thin coat of vitreous, and therefore transparent, lead glaze was applied either by a second dipping or by spraying. Most of the painting was done in blue, but coloured delft had also received attention.

A Royal Proclamation, before 1672, declared that the importation of "coloured earthenware" to compete with the native product, "but lately found out in England," was unlawful, and should not be permitted. So delft—English delft—is found with coloured decoration, sprinkled manganese purple and yellow being the commonest, then black, green, puce, and a poor brownish red. Three dishes are given as illustrations for comparison. The articles

LAMBETH DELFT DISH, 17TH CENTURY.

made were mainly things in everyday use; ornamental pieces such as the puzzle jugs are rare. The dish with the Pewterers' Arms, dated 1655, about $16\frac{1}{2}$ in. in diameter, now in the British Museum, is well worth seeing; so, too, is the remarkable specimen by Palissy, oval in shape, and about $18\frac{1}{2}$ in. long. It is held by some that the delft ware made in England, in various localities, is not to be distinguished from the ordinary kind of Dutch delft. The latter is often marked with a factory or maker's mark. Lambeth delft is never marked. In addition to what has been said of the painting, comparisons, carefully drawn, show that

LAMBETH DELFT WARE

the Dutch body is composed of a finer and more carefully prepared clay, that it is softer, that it rings more clearly, and that it is whiter, and has more lustre. Lambeth delft is characterised by a rosy tint due to the paste showing through the thin glaze; by the common English fault of the cracking or crazing of the glaze; by the greyish tone of the blue; and by unusually quaint inscriptions, which are worth studying in the museums, not only in London, but in the provinces. Here are a few specimens of these

LAMBETH DELFT DISH, 1655.

inscriptions in the British Museum. On a set of six delft plates each has one line of inscription and the date, 1738 :—

1. What is a Merry Man?
2. Let him do What he Can
3. To Entertain his Guests
4. With Wine and Merry Jests.
5. But if his Wife do frown
6. All merriment Goes down.

This is another, "BEE MERRY AND WISE, 1660." A third has "RICHARD BIRCHET, 1641," on the neck of a jug, with the motto round the middle, "DRINK TO THY FREND, BVT REMEMBER THY ENDE."

The simplest forms of Lambeth pottery, as shown by sketches from actual specimens, were the apothecaries' pots, which are, even now, dug up in various parts of London. The forms are simple but varied, and the decoration is quite simple too—a conventional scroll in manganese purple. The most interesting is the one with the inscription in French, Pâte à La Reine, which has the crossed L's, the well-known Sèvres mark; the glaze is a slightly bluish-grey white, and the paste a very light red, just like all the others. These may be worth only a few shillings each, but they indicate quite the beginnings of Lambeth pottery as contrasted with the elaborate forms and decoration before described.

The drinking-vessels vary in size and shape from the cruskin to the posset cup and sack-pot. The cruskin, cruse, or cruske had one handle like a cup. Usually they were quite plain earthenware, and the common shape was like that of ordinary basins. The pipkin or porringer was very similar.

The early cruse had two handles, but it was always a bottle, flask, jug, or cup for holding liquids. Bickersteth wrote: "For God, let David witness, puts His children's tears into His cruse and writes them in His book," from which it may be inferred that the cruse was allied to the tear-bottle of simple vase shape. The "cruisken of whisky" is a usual form of expression in Ireland, where, however, they are made of wood. The godet or goddard—another drinking-cup much in use—was a large cup or bowl in which spiced liquor was mixed and drunk by "gossips" and friends, boon companions.

64 a

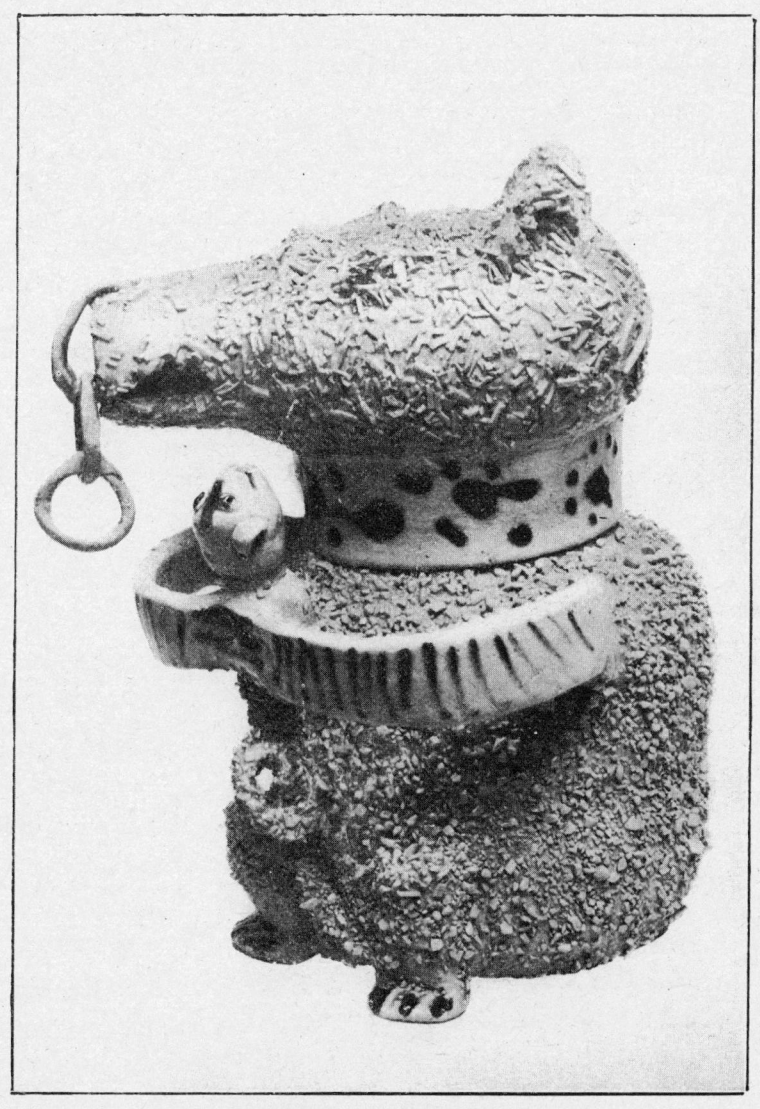

SALT GLAZE WARE BEAR JUG.

Originally a gossip was a sponsor in baptism, but later, a tatler or tale-bearer. The posset cup was a form common enough from the later part of the seventeenth to the early nineteenth centuries. It had two handles and a cover. The posset was made either with spiced ale or other liquor, or with hot milk, sweetened, spiced, and often thickened with bread. The posset had its dangers. An old preacher speaks

APOTHECARIES' POTS.

of a man "drugging his conscience with a posset." More will be said about these cups when we deal with slip-ware.

Sack jugs or pots were used for drawing wines from the barrel. The examples given are interesting. One has the early date 1653. A plain bottle was brought to me by its owner, who wanted a valuation. It was valued at £2. "Oh," said he, "there is a dealer in the West End who has one on sale for £25, and one was sold by auction some years ago for £14 or £15." "It may be so," was the reply; "we will try another valuer." The other valuer was on the premises. Said he, " Well, I would not give you a penny more than two guineas for it." Common specimens are worth about that, fine ones £10 to £15 ; but if they are mounted in pewter with a lid they are worth more, and they are very valuable when mounted in silver of an early date. The word " Sack " is painted in blue on the pot, with just a few curves below. This is the usual decoration, though the second one shows a crown with the letters C.R., and it is mounted in pewter. Sack meant, at first, the light-coloured Spanish wine; afterwards it was applied during the seventeenth century to all the strong, white, Southern wines, distinguishing them from the Rhenish and other red wines. These latter were served in pots exactly similar, except for the substitution of CLARET for SACK. Originally, claret was made in Médoc, France, but the name, first given in England to any Bordeaux or other red wine, has been extended to such as Californian claret, but is not used in this sense in France.

POSSET CUP, 1632.

Before leaving Lambeth delft a few words would not be amiss regarding the dishes on which were portrayed distinguished persons standing, or enthroned, or mounted on horseback. Charles I. and II., James II., William and Mary, Queen Anne, Prince Eugene, the Duke of Marlborough, and a few other portraits are the usual subjects. They show more of the home—the purely English—work than the other dishes we have previously illustrated, being rough pieces enamelled on the face only, the back being simply lead-glazed, or only smeared over with the glaze, which may occasionally be found tinted with such colours as are used on tortoiseshell ware. The drawings are quaint but not artistic ;

LAMBETH DELFT WARE 67

the colours are dull, on a somewhat dirty greenish-white enamel; blue is largely used, and is found in dash decoration on the rims.

No doubt in the early development of Lambeth some pieces of foreign origin were copied and re-copied. But it is still more likely that advantage was taken of the services of Italian and Dutch workmen who were able to manufacture,

SACK JUG, 1653.   SACK BOTTLE OR POT, CHARLES II.

at the works, pieces which resembled those produced in their own countries. So that the Lambeth pottery family was really the product of the several London potteries which were working for a period extending from 1637 to 1702 specially, and onward from then till now. Staffordshire claimed to have made these dishes, but Simeon Shaw, whilst producing evidence to that effect, discounts it by stating that delft was introduced into Staffordshire by Thomas

Heath, at Lane Delph, about 1710! The claim of the Cockpit Hill Pottery, Derby, cannot be substantiated, because its history cannot be followed farther back than the eighteenth century. The artistic excellence of the celebrated Doulton products at "The Lambeth Pottery," established in 1818, and those, too, of Messrs. Stiff & Son at "The London Pottery," established in 1751, deserve the highest praise.

LAMBETH DELFT MUG.

Barrel-shaped, 5½ in. high, painted with birds, insects, and flowers in blue. Around the rim is inscribed "William and Elizabeth Burges : 24th August, 1631," and dated under the handle 1632. Although the white-glazed surface of this mug somewhat resembles salt-glaze, it possesses qualities which mark it as Lambeth of early date. Other mugs with inscribed names such as "John Leman, 1634," and "John Williamson, 1645," if in earthenware, come into the same class of Lambeth delft.

CHAPTER IX

BRISTOL DELFT

IN the laws of Shotoku Taishi, Japanese era 2371—our era 1711—the seventeenth law says: "Important matters should only be settled after due conference with many men. Trifling matters may be decided, because they are not so material in their effects; but weighty matters, on account of their far-reaching consequences, must be discussed with many counsellors. It is thus that the right way shall be found and pursued." Applying this to the early history of pottery in England, one would like to hold a conference of collectors with the custodians of the chief museums, and to have their opinions on the many specimens which are, at present, doubtfully classified. The comparisons between Lambeth, Bristol, and Liverpool delft would be edifying. We need not dwell on the buff lead-glazed ware, nor the dark grey or brown stoneware made at Bristol, because such ware was without means of special identification; but it must be noted that in Edward I.'s reign, under date 1284, a reference occurs in the archives, *pro terra fodienda ad vasa fictilia facienda*, which places beyond doubt the fact that Bristol had fictile works at a very early period.

The delft industry began at the close of the seventeenth century, and continued until lead-glazed pottery became popular. Two factories, both producing an earthenware body having a coating of white tin enamel, were in operation at the same time, one belonging to Richard Frank, which was founded by an unknown potter and acquired by Frank in the early part of the eighteenth century, and sold by Joseph Ring, in January 1788, when delft ceased to be made; and the other was founded by Joseph Flower, who in 1777 removed from No. 2 on the Quay to 3, Corn Street, where Michael Edkins painted a sign-board for him, " Flower, Potter." Now, Michael Edkins, who, in 1761, manufactured Bristol glass, was a painter of delft ware in Frank's works, and the plate given as an illustration has the initials M. B. E.

(Painted by Michael Edkins.)

for himself and his wife Betty. It is dated 1760, when he left Frank's. This arrangement of initials, where the upper letter was the surname and the lower ones those of the husband and wife, was quite common.

The grandson of the painter, William Edkins, was a collector of Bristol pottery, china, and glass, and his collection was dispersed years ago at Sotheby's. The next plate,

BRISTOL DELFT

bearing the words "Nugent only 1754," made by Frank, commemorated the general election of that year; another for Tewkesbury election, from the same works, bore the words "Calvert and Martin For Tewkesbury 1754. Sold

ELECTION PLATE.   CHINESE PATTERN PLATE.

by Webb." The earliest dated example was a plate marked on the rim S M B 1703, in the same way as the mark given, with B on the top. Other dated pieces were a delft high-heeled shoe marked M. S. 1722, just like two sold at the Bernal

D	Elizabeth	B	H
T × H	Barnes	S · E	S × H
1716	1738	1744	1751
17 P 40 R S	P B M 1706	P J · B 1763	E F · G 1767
U · t · D 1760	IOHN SAUNDERS	Bristd 1752	I A G
R S October 27 1735	1754 F. E 1721	P W M 1711	Bristoll 1741 1761

sale, having an earlier date, M. I. 1705. Some more are shown in the list. They will serve as a guide to pieces having similar initials and dates.

Bristol tiles were common. A slab composed of twenty-four tiles, painted in blue, with a view of St. Mary Redcliffe

Church, Bristol, was formerly in the Geological Museum, Jermyn Street; and the Willett collection had the "March to Finchley" similarly painted on seventy-two tiles. Tile pictures for the fireplace, representing a cat and dog, in sets of nine tiles, were at one time frequently found in Bristol houses. Besides these and plates and dishes, delft teapoys and punch-bowls may often be safely ascribed to either Frank or Flower. The bowls, seldom dated, show various designs, commonly in blue, but also in red, yellow, and purple. The outlines are sometimes in this last colour, which was applied as

(Painted by Bowen.)

a mottled ground, leaving compartments which had Chinese figures, flowers, or conventional ornament in blue. Professor Church says: "Approximate dates may be assigned to some of the extant specimens of Bristol delft, by noting the form and fashioning of the pieces. For example, in the case of plates, those of the earlier period, say 1706-1735, resemble their Dutch prototypes, being without any flange beneath, and having either simple curved sides and a nearly flat bottom, or a steep sloping ledge and then a sharp curve. During the second period, 1735-1745, the outer ledge or brim was nearly level, the circumference was frequently cut or lobed in six divisions, the area of the central portion was reduced and a flange was added beneath. Some intermediate and transitional forms occur, but, about 1755, the final form was reached, which is seen in the majority of the extant examples, and which closely resembles that now generally

DELFT PLATE—WHITE UPON WHITE.

adopted for dinner plates." The body of Bristol delft is generally a light buff colour, darker and redder than the Dutch delft. The enamel has often a greenish blue tint, thinner and more opaque than the Dutch, very uniform in colour and texture. It is claimed that Flower's ware was thinner and neater in make than most Bristol delft; the glaze good, and the colour clear and brilliant in tone—indeed, in no respect inferior to the Dutch. Usually the Bristol blue employed under the glaze was rather a dull blue, and the decoration was either copied directly from Chinese patterns or from the Dutch, who themselves imitated the Chinese.

One kind of ornament is said to be peculiar to Bristol delft: this is the use of pure white enamel as a pattern upon the greenish-white body of the ware. This white upon white is known as "*bianco sopro bianco*." The same decoration is found on bowls, about seven inches across, with the outside painted in Oriental style, and the interior with characteristic *bianco sopro bianco* decoration and inscribed "Success to the

BRISTOL DELFT BOWL.

British Arms." These would be worth about £4 to £5. Approximate prices for other pieces would be:—Dishes from 12 to 16 in. in diameter painted in blue imitation of old Nankin, £3 to £4, if in good condition and of fine quality. The smaller plates from 7 to 10 ins. in diameter depend for their value largely on the decoration. Those coarsely painted in colour, say with a lady, gentleman, and trees, dated about 1740, are worth 15s. to £1 each, and the same value would be attached to those slightly sketched in blue, with the white-upon-white border. Smaller bowls are generally worth about twice as much as plates having the same decoration, and bottles about the same as bowls. Prices, however, are rising. The specimens in the British Museum, the Victoria and Albert Museum at South Kensington, and at Bristol Museum, deserve special attention.

BRISTOL DELFT

One of the most interesting points which a close inspection reveals is that the body of the seventeenth-century English green-glazed ware and that of the delft ware is the same. What happened seems to have been this. The Dutch or Italian potters, or both, brought with them to England the

POSSET CUP, $\frac{T}{A\ G}$ BRISTOLL, UNDERNEATH.

secrets of the tin enamel and the transparent lead glaze, which displaced to a large extent the earlier glaze. The delft bowl in the illustration has all the characteristics of the Bristol factories, of which it is a fine specimen. The posset cup in the British Museum has a very rare mark. Two other marks, "Bristol, 1752," and "A. G. T. Bristoll, 1741," should be noted.

CHAPTER X

LIVERPOOL DELFT

THE coarse wares of mediæval times, such as pitchers, jugs, dishes, and "muggs," were made, without doubt, in the pot works of Liverpool, but the records only commence with 1674, when entries appear in the town tolls: "For every cart-load of muggs shipped into foreign parts 6d." Was this delft? We do not know. Whatever the seventeenth century produced cannot be traced, but early in the eighteenth century a dated plaque, "A West Prospect of Great Crosby, 1716,"

EARLY LIVERPOOL PLATE.

now in the Mayer Museum, shows the buff-coloured clay, smeared with a fine white clay, then painted in blue and glazed. This came from Shaw's Brow works, where Alderman Shaw must have been working for years, if this piece is any test. "Every merchant of note" was concerned in the network of kilns which covered the " Brow." In 1790 no fewer than 374 persons were engaged at these potteries, so the output must have been very large. The early ware has a bluish tinge, and was *painted* in blue.

Many of the delft punch-bowls painted with a ship belong to the Shaw period. Oftentimes they have inscriptions, such as the one in the Mayer Museum, " made for Captain Metcalfe, who commanded *The Golden Lion*, which was the first vessel

LIVERPOOL HERALDIC PLATE.

that sailed out of Liverpool on the whale fishery and Greenland trade, and was presented to him on his return from his second voyage by his employers, who were a company composed of the principal merchants of Liverpool, in the year 1753." Not only were punch bowls and mugs made, but charpots or dishes for char, fish of the salmonoid family, plates, dishes, and drug-pots were delft, with the tin-enamel which distinguishes this class from other wares. Frank's Bristol delft was a buff-colour, and the Liverpool delft was also buff-colour. The factories followed after Lambeth in this order of time: Bristol, Liverpool. The early Liverpool tiles varied in thickness to as much as an inch and a half, which is the thickness of the plaque in old Crosby Church dated 1722. Other early dated pieces bear the dates 1728, 1753, 1758, and so on. The site of Shaw's works on the Brow was excavated in 1857, and the discoveries made indicated that Liverpool delft was made of a coarse clay, reddish or pinkish-white in tone, and *painted* in blue.

The next name is one nearly forgotten—Zachariah Barnes. He was born in 1743 and died in 1820. He was noted as the maker of wall-tiles and druggists' jars, or drug-pots. But many of the large round dishes, octagonal plates, and dishes for dinner services and potted-fish pots were from his factory in the old Haymarket. The large round dishes were mainly used in Wales, where the household fed from the common dish by dipping their spoons into the food.

DRUG-POT OF LIVERPOOL DELFT.

These large coarse pieces were plain thick white delft. Liverpool delft is decidedly inferior to early Lambeth in its tin-enamel, but immensely superior to all other factories in its transfer-printing decoration. Barnes's tiles, about five inches square and about a quarter of an inch in thickness, are better potted and harder than the Dutch ones. Again, the edges of the backs of the Dutch tiles are quite square, whereas the Liverpool tiles have the edges bevelled so as to give a better hold on the cement. The early tiles made by Barnes were used for lining walls and fireplaces, for chimneypieces, and they were *painted* in the Dutch style with flowers, landscapes, ships, groups, etc., usually in blue, but other colours were used too. The reference to transfer-printing revives an old difference of opinion. Was transfer-printing first discovered at Liverpool or Battersea, Worcester or Caughley ? At Battersea, Janssen used the process in the decoration of Battersea enamels as early as 1750, and his work was quite independent of the Liverpool printers, Sadler & Green. At Worcester, the earliest dated example is 1757, and Caughley practised transfer-printing about the same time. Liverpool furnishes a fine sharp specimen with the date 1756. Note, both of

TRANSFER-PRINTED LIVERPOOL EARTHENWARE.

these dated pieces, the Worcester and the Liverpool, had the celebrated portrait of Frederick the Great of Prussia. Whether Battersea was earlier at this work than Liverpool is not yet definitely settled, but in 1790 *Moss's Liverpool Guide* stated that—" Copper-plate printing upon china and earthenware originated here in 1752, and remained some time a secret with the inventors, Messrs. Sadler & Green, the latter of whom still continues the business in Harrington Street. It appeared unaccountable how uneven surfaces could receive impressions from copper plates. It could not, however, long remain undiscovered that the impression from the plate is taken first on paper and thence communicated to the ware *after it is glazed.* The manner in which this continues to be done here remains still unrivalled in perfection."

The John Sadler, the engraver, was a kindly soul. When waste or soiled impressions came from his engraved plates he used to give them to the children, who stuck them upon the broken fragments from Shaw's Brow pottery and made ornaments for dolls' houses. This evolved the idea of decorating pottery with printed pictures. Sadler invoked the assistance of Guy Green, a studious youth who frequented his shop, and

BOWL, LIVERPOOL DELFT.

together they succeeded, and entered into partnership. They had found out how to transfer a print to an enamelled tile, just as Janssen had found how to transfer it to an enamelled metal, but their method seems to have been very expeditious. There is a record showing that the two partners, without assistance, printed within the space of six hours no less than twelve hundred earthenware tiles of different patterns. The printing colours were black, red, and purple, or puce, with green sometimes added by hand. Alderman Thomas Shaw and Samual Gilbody certified on August 2, 1756, to this effect, and stated further that Sadler & Green " have been several

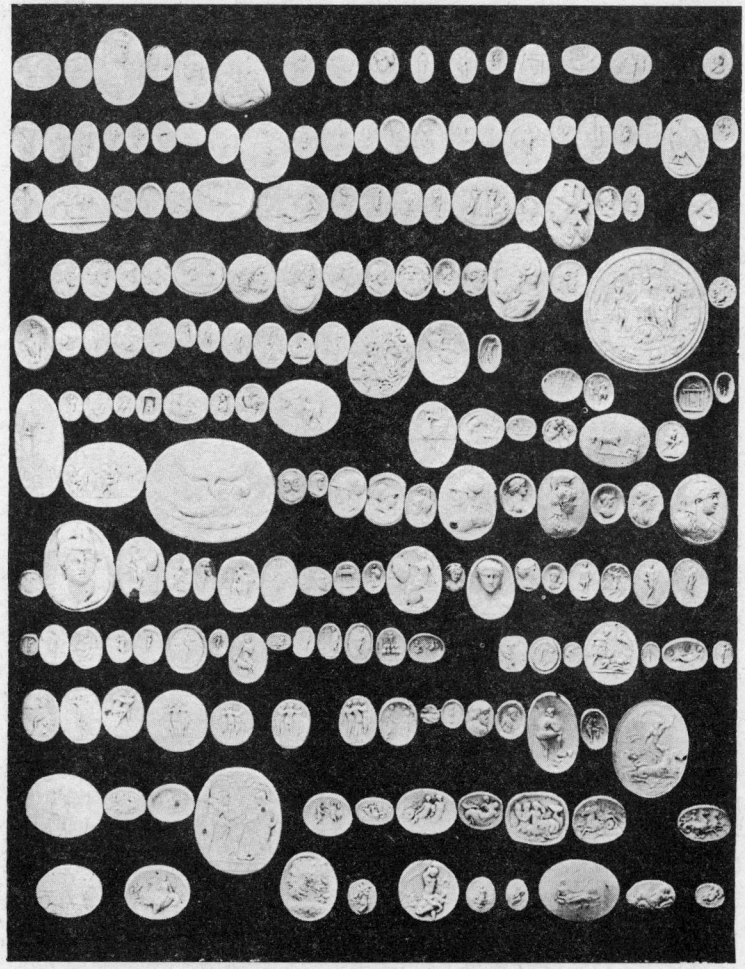

EARLY EXPERIMENTAL JASPER-WHITE TERRA-COTTA.
Some of the "Finds." Lent by Josiah Wedgwood & Sons.

LIVERPOOL DELFT

years in bringing the art of printing on earthenware to perfection." Sadler retired about 1774, and Green continued the business until 1799.

LIVERPOOL TILE—ÆSOP'S FABLES.

LIVERPOOL TILE.

The subjects on the tiles were actors and actresses, chiefly from the prints in Bell's "British Theatre," Æsop's fables and caricatures, etc. It was not likely that other potters would neglect such a novel and effective means of decoration. Besides, it was very cheap. Therefore we find Josiah Wedgwood packing his wares in waggons and carts, and even using packhorses to convey his goods, notably his cream ware, to Sadler & Green for transfer printing. Other Staffordshire potters did the same, though Wedgwood at a later period carried on this kind of work himself. Specimens of this Liverpool printed Wedgwood ware are rare. The transfer printing is remarkable for the sharpness and clearness of the engraving, which gave beautiful transfers ; for the excellent quality of the printing ink ; and for the superiority of the glazes. Though tiles furnish the greater number of the pieces now in existence, transfer-printed mugs, jugs, teapots, etc., are not uncommon ; some of them were made by Sadler & Green, who had an extensive business as potters.

LIVERPOOL PRINTED WEDGWOOD MARK.

Apropos of Wedgwood ware printed by Sadler & Green, a curious teapot is in the Brighton Museum—Willett Collection —which bears on one side an engraving of a mill *to grind old people young again*, and on the other, within a border of foliage, a ballad entitled " The Miller's Maid grinding Old Men Young Again " :

> " Come, old, decrepit, lame, or blind,
>   Into my mill to take a grind."

Visitors to this museum will be keenly interested not so much

LIVERPOOL DELFT

in the fineness of the pottery, as in the illustrations of history and social events. The teapot is marked Wedgwood. Other designs of this printing include a lady pouring out tea for a gentleman, and on the opposite side a verse:—

> "Kindly take this gift of mine,
> The gift and giver I hope is thine,
> And tho' the value is but small,
> A loving heart is worth it all."

Passing from the consideration of the printed decoration to

TILE, LIVERPOOL DELFT.

the other potters who worked at Liverpool, it is to the Mayer Museum there that we must look for authenticated examples of the work of George Drinkwater, who had a pottery in Duke Street.

Another interesting name is that of Richard Chaffers—who, about 1752, after serving an apprenticeship to the famous Alderman Shaw, took some small works at Shaw's Brow, and made, at first, the ordinary delft—blue-and-white—for some years. He succeeded in placing his ware amongst the best of his time. Curiously, it is America which supplies fine old specimens of Chaffers' delft. He "exported a very large portion of his manufacture to the then English colonies." Chaffers carried on his works for many years, making both china and earthenware; and on his death, which was the result of his affection for his foreman—Podmore—from whom he caught the fever, some of his workmen emigrated to America, though a few of the best hands were employed by Wedgwood and other Staffordshire potters.

W. Reid formed a company in 1753, or thereabouts, and founded pottery works, which in 1756 were known as " The

REVERSE OF THE LIVERPOOL WOLFE JUG, SHOWING A LANDSCAPE:
PERIOD ABOUT 1770-75.

Liverpool China Manufactory," and made all kinds of ware. His work is little known, but from his advertisement in the last-mentioned year, in the *Liverpool Advertiser*, he seems to have possessed an uncommon and enterprising spirit :— " Samples sent to any gentlemen or ladies in the country who will pay carriage." Another name, which stands out more prominently, was that of Seth Pennington, who, with his brothers, James and John, had each his own pottery. James, the eldest, produced only the common kinds of ware. He seems to have been somewhat of a fool, for he gave away

Seth's discovery of a secret in the mixing of colour. In the making of blue Seth Pennington eclipsed all other potters of his day. It is stated that a Staffordshire manufacturer offered him a thousand guineas for his recipe, but was met with a refusal. Pennington said, " It is a source of great profit to me, being kept so secret that none ever mixed the colours but myself." James was a hard drinker. So, having got from Seth the secret of the making of the blue, he could do no better than blab it to a boon companion in one of his

THE DEATH OF WOLFE, ON A LIVERPOOL JUG.

bad days. At once the false friend went off and sold it to a Staffordshire house. Seth, the youngest, is the only one we need to consider further. His works at Shaw's Brow were very extensive, and he produced a remarkable ware, rivalling the Oriental in glaze, decoration, and colour.

His fine punch-bowls—collectors please note—were not only delft, but also earthenware *and china*. They were sometimes very large; specimens have been known to measure as much as $20\frac{1}{2}$ in. in diameter by 9 in. in height. Some of these were painted by John Robinson, who was employed

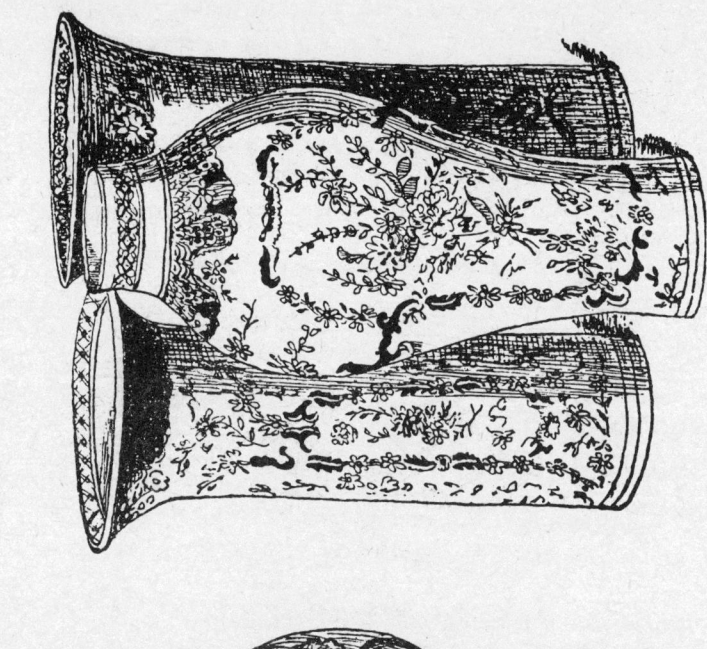
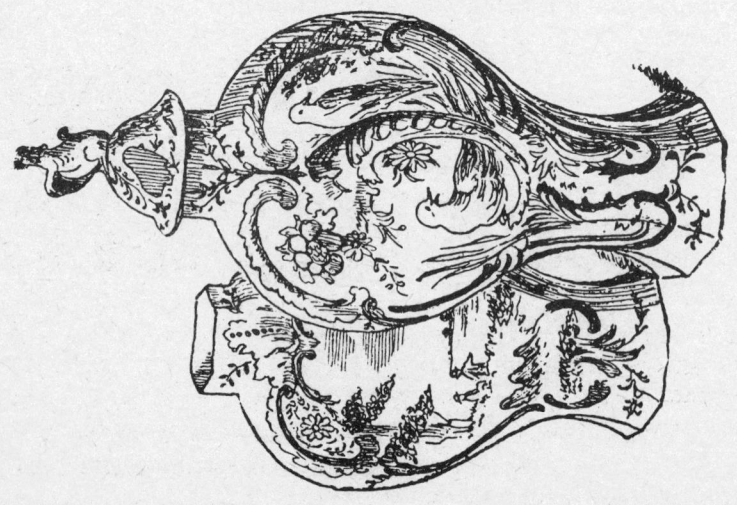

SETH PENNINGTON'S VASES.

LIVERPOOL DELFT

by Pennington after he had served his apprenticeship with him. A remarkable delft bowl, having the dimensions

A "GARNITURE COMPLÈTE"—DUTCH DELFT.

stated above, was given by Robinson to the Potteries Mechanics' Institute at Hanley. This was painted outside with a Chinese landscape, and inside with a group of ships and boats, having the inscription beneath, "Success to the Africa trade. George Dickenson." The inside part of the bowl, above the centre, was decorated with trophies, separated by various kinds of shot. A similar bowl in the Museum at South Kensington is of the same size. "Success to the *Monmouth*, 1760," "1770. Success to the *Isabella*," are types of other inscriptions. The fine vases and beakers, given as illustrations, were bought from Seth Pennington's only daughter, and though they are not delft, they serve to show to what excellence he had brought his work. A group of Dutch delft vases

are set out for comparison. The plate is probably Liverpool delft, with a portrait of Dr. S., that is, Henry Sacheverell,

LIVERPOOL (?) DELFT.

who was impeached by the Whig Government before the House of Lords for preaching against the *Act of Toleration* He attained immense popularity; died in 1724.

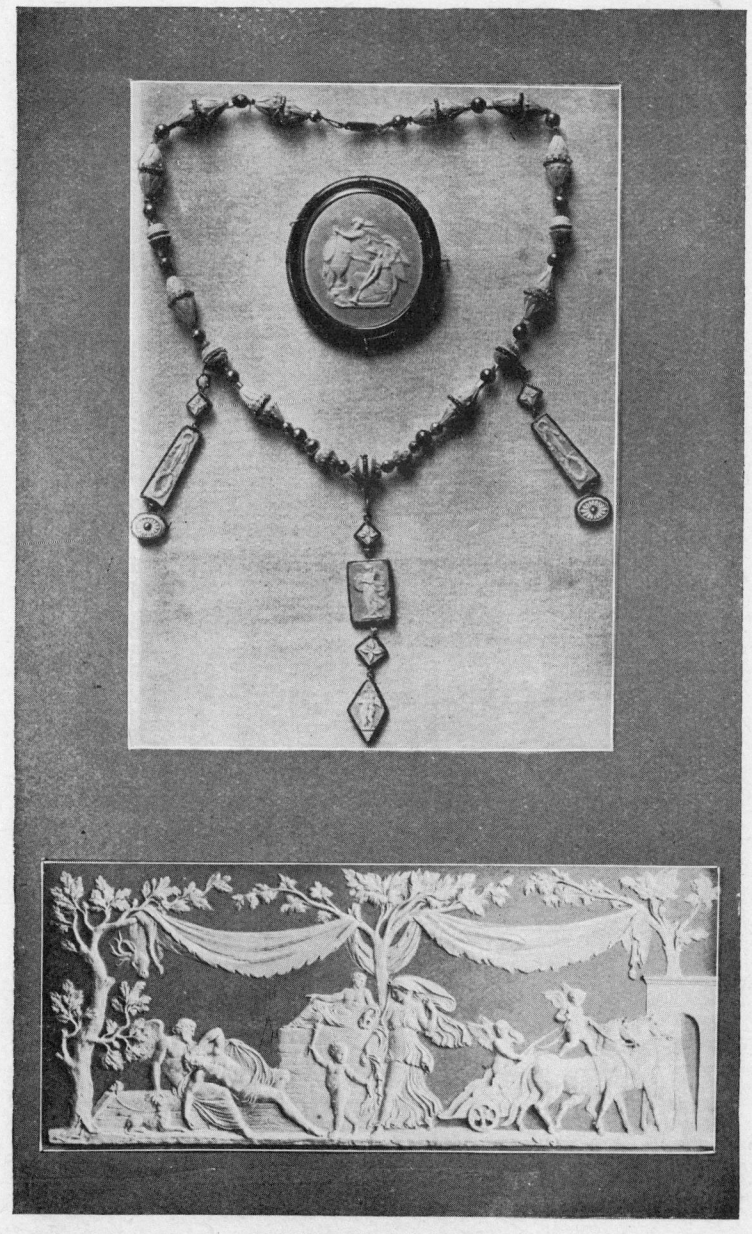

BROOCH AND EARRINGS.
Plaque by Flaxman: "Selene visiting Endymion." Lent by Josiah Wedgwood & Sons.

CHAPTER XI

SLIP WARE

WE saw that delft differed from the green-glazed Tudor ware mainly in the substitution of a tin glaze; the body underwent but little change. So with slip ware, the style of decoration changed, but the materials—the clays—were simply more and more refined. In 1722 Thomas Billin invented a method of making " the most refined earthen-

TYG—WROTHAM WARE.

ware, with help of clay and other materials found in this kingdom." We know nothing more of him, but we do know that in the twenty-seven years from this date no less than nine patents were taken out. They seem, however, to have had but one good effect, which was the general improvement in the decoration, mainly seen in pieces ordered for special functions—to commemorate a birth, a marriage, Christmas, or some other event.

The common ware was manufactured from clays in the vicinity of the works, blunged, or mixed in water by means of a blunger or wooden instrument like a shovel. The pug-mill for grinding, mixing, or tempering clays was not yet invented. The plain red ware which was produced from this clay was decorated with slip at the end of the sixteenth century, but this is not dated. Slip ware ornament was not confined to England, but seems to have been used at about the same period by the Flemish, French and Italian

TYG—WROTHAM WARE.

potters, and even by the Portuguese. What is slip? It is simply *any* coloured clay reduced to the thickness of cream, and applied by means of a spouted vessel, upon the surface to be decorated, being sun-dried *before* it was glazed and fired. Slip is commonly white, applied to a dark body, but dark and coloured slips may be found on a light body. If used as a wash the body was hidden; if the body was then combed with a toothed tool, a marbled effect was produced. Again, when the body and the overlying slip wash were dry enough to be handled, designs could be scratched through the thin layer of slip—a process termed *graffiato*. When, as sometimes happened, the slip wash was applied as a paste for ornamentation in low relief, it was known as barbotine.

The collector will have some difficulty in assigning the

TYG WITH THREE HANDLES AND A SPOUT.
ANOTHER VIEW.

TYG WITH THREE HANDLES.

early specimens : two counties, Kent and Staffordshire, each claim a large number of pieces, but the information available is very slight. Wrotham in Kent, between Sevenoaks and Maidstone, had a pottery in the middle of the seventeenth century which produced the ordinary red or brown ware ornamented with white and coloured slip. This was applied in patches or bosses, sometimes stamped with a flower, a spread-eagle, a swan, or with rosettes, fleurs-delis, crosses, etc. The usual slip and dotted patterns were

WROTHAM DISH, 1699—INCISED PATTERN.

dropped or trailed upon it, and over all was the yellowish lead glaze. The examples in the British Museum are dated from 1627 to 1717, though the initials accompanying the dates, such as E.W.E., WROTHAM ; T.E., WROTHAM, 1703 ; WROTHAM, W.R.S. C.R., 1659, have not been identified.

The Staffordshire slip generally has not so great a variety of decoration as the slip ware of Wrotham, neither is it so elaborate. At the same time it is equally interesting, dating as it does from about 1660, when Thomas and Ralph Toft, with other potters, made the well-known large, somewhat irregular, round dishes—17 to 18 in. in diameter and nearly 3 in. deep—which bear their names in large letters,

SLIP WARE

and have both decoration and name put on in coloured slips. Their style was adopted by the following—that is, if the names on the dishes are those of the makers, which is sometimes questionable:—Ralph Turnor, c. 1681; Robart Shaw, 1692; T. Johnson, 1694; William Chaterly, 1696; William Talor, 1700; W. Rich, 1702; John Wright, 1707; Joseph Glass, Thomas and William Sans, Ralph Simpson, and George Taylor. Two names—Margere Nash and Mary Perkins—are on two dishes in the British Museum.

The body of the Toft ware is the common coarse reddish or buff-coloured clay—firebrick clay—washed over with white slip when a *light* ground was wanted. On this the border, usually a lattice pattern, and the chief features in the ornamentation were laid in a reddish or black-brown slip. Then orange-slip completed the colouring, dots of white slip were added to the trailed slip pattern, and the whole was glazed with the lead glaze that gave a yellowish tone both to the ground and to the decoration.

WROTHAM—GLAZED RED WARE.

One cannot assume that these dishes were made for domestic use. It seems much more likely that they were bought as curiosities and used for ornamenting the home. The London museums have quite a number. Three at South Kensington have the name Thomas Toft below the design, on the rim. Toft's works were at Tinker's Clough, near Shelton. The name is supposed to be derived from the fact that the clough or dell was noted in olden times as a resort of gipsies and tinkers. Toft ware is a rough ware, but it shows nothing of foreign influence. The English potter of the period is seen in it at his best. It required no small amount of skill to trail a pattern with a free hand on a large piece of pottery.

The old pot works existed in various parts of England

and Wales, and we have seen that the artist was none the less an artist because at the time when the Court of Charles I. was singing the praises of Van Dyck, he, in his village hamlet, rendered to the best of his ability the King, the lion and the unicorn, the double-headed eagle, or the portrait of a lady holding a flower. Later, the same sentiment of loyalty prevailed, so we have C.R., W.R., or G.R. for Charles II., William or Gulielmus Rex, in quaint effigy, it is true, but

PITCHER IN "SLIP WARE," 1618.

in thin, even delicate lines. Before the potter stands the coarse dish of reddish clay, with a coat of finer white clay covering the inside. Now, with the vessel filled with slip, having a spout in which a quill was inserted when fine work was necessary, he lines out rapidly the pattern which he has before him, or, possibly, the design exists only in his mind. Gradually the surface is covered. The trellis border became almost conventional, but the *pièce de resistance*, the attempt to realise "The King," or some kindred subject, the evident desire for something which should be the best of its kind, deserves commendation. Though we may smile at the result, we should do well to remember that the brothers Toft—Thomas, Ralph, and James—the

EARLY "TOFT" DISH.

THE PELICAN IN HER PIETY.

two Taylors—George and William—and Ralph Simpson had, in their day, just such copyists as had Wedgwood at a later period.

The materials used for colouring the slips were few. The rich yellow tint was due to the galena or lead glaze, and the slip colours were those in use by the delft manufacturers as well, though these applied them with a brush, as may be seen in the coloured delft. The red was ochre; manganese ore furnished the curious purple, whilst a more or less vivid yellow came from ochre. Collectors of English pottery value specimens not alone of slip-ware dishes, but also of the tygs, posset-pots, pitchers, and fountains of the same period having similar decoration. From about 1660 to the close of the eighteenth century, slip ware, though rough, held a high position amongst potters, not perhaps such elaborate forms as are presented in the illustrations except for presentation pieces, but as a staple manufacture in brown ware with yellow traceries, which was gradually superseded by the finer and more serviceable tin-enamelled delft ware of Lambeth, Bristol, and Liverpool.

Barbotine or moulded decoration is not usually associated with the Toft school. The slips were applied from moulds, so that many raised outlined patterns could be taken from the same mould. Professor Church thus describes a piece of this ware: "The rough brownish body, the white clay slip, and the yellow glaze do not differ from the specimens of the Toft school, but the piece has been made on a form or mould, whilst the design is quite original. The dish on page 98, which is $16\frac{1}{2}$ inches across, has a border of small detached scrolls in brown, on the white slip-ground. The central, or main decoration, represents a plant with a single stem from which spring some leaves and three large flowers, the centres of which resemble human heads; on either side of the uppermost flower is a dove. An oblong label bearing the letters S. M. occupies the middle of the dish. The details of the design are slightly sunk in the white slip, but they are bordered on either side by a ridge, the sunk space between being filled in with an ochre-yellow or a deep brown clay." See page 98.

The British Museum and the Victoria and Albert Museum

96 a

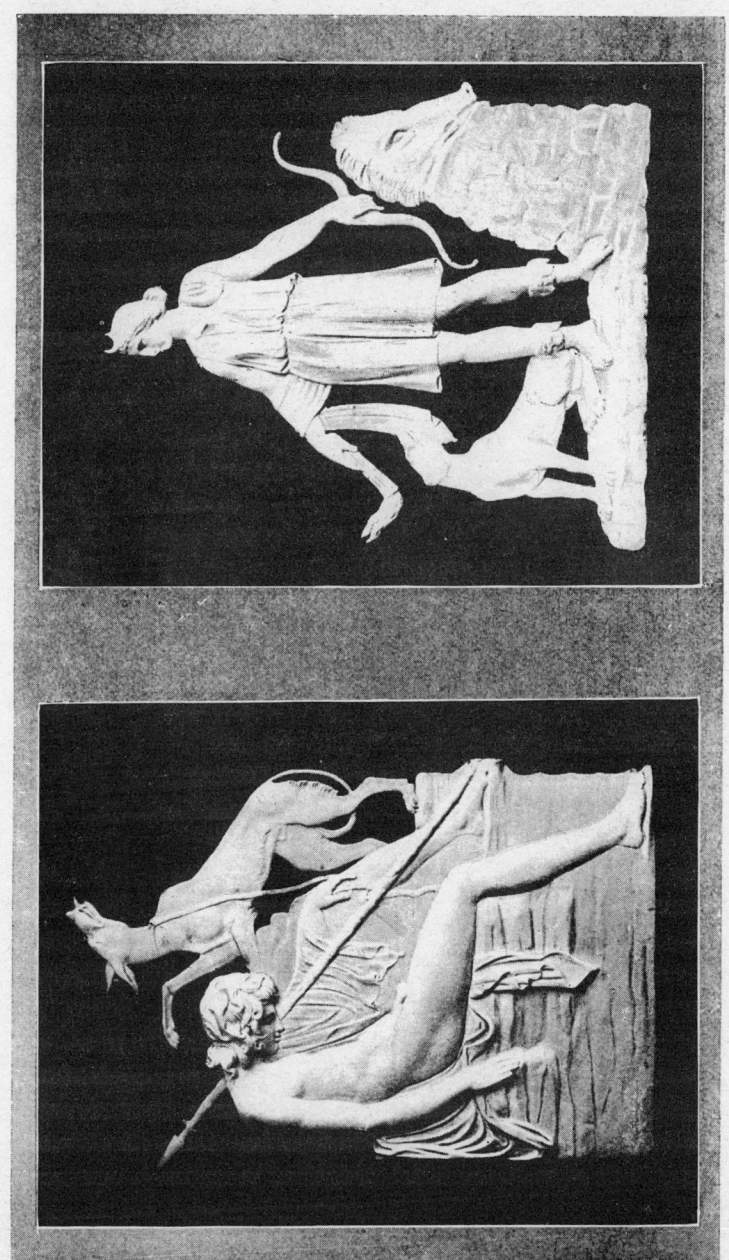

ENDYMION. JASPER PLAQUES. DIANA.
Lent by Josiah Wedgwood & Sons.

SLIP WARE 97

at South Kensington have specimens of this pottery. The date of a fine piece at the British Museum is 1726. The

THOMAS TOFT—"THE MERMAID."

RALPH TOFT—ANOTHER "MERMAID."

authorities seem inclined to ascribe this class of slip ware to John Meir, who worked at the Cockpit Hill Pottery in 1721; but whether the dish dated 1726 and marked S. M. was made by Samuel Meir or for him by W. Meir of Cobridge is uncertain. There seems to be no reason why the slip potters

ANOTHER "PELICAN IN HER PIETY."

MOULDED DECORATION—SLIP WARE.

of Burslem and Hanley should not have progressed from the somewhat irregular wheel-turned dish to the mould for form, and from the slip-pot to the mould for barbotine decoration.

SLIP WARE

This is all the more probable because, as in the Wrotham ware, so in the Toft ware, there are examples showing the two methods of slip decoration on the same piece.

When John and David Elers came into Staffordshire, as we shall see presently, and worked there from about 1690 to 1710, the decoration they used was largely relief ornament formed of applied pads of wet clay from metal stamps, or it may be, as Wedgwood stated, from alabaster moulds. A natural result of the revelations of the Elerses' secrets by John

MOULDED DECORATION—R.S.

Astbury and Twyford would be that the neighbouring potters soon learnt to apply their ornament by means of moulds. The coincidence of dates is remarkable, for Thomas Astbury, son of John, commenced business in 1723, which is quite close to the 1726 on the dish with the S.M. initials. On all grounds, therefore, it appears safer to ascribe the barbotine slip ware to the Staffordshire potteries, rather than to set up an unknown Derby potter, a mythical Samuel Meir, Mayer, or Mare, as the maker of these pieces in a Derby pottery.

Contemporary history seems to point in the same direction. In Plot's " History of Staffordshire," published in 1686, he says :—

"The greatest pottery they have in this county is carried on at Burslem, near Newcastle-under-Lyme, where for making their several sorts of pots they have as many different sorts of clay, which they dig round about the towns, all within half a mile distance, the best being found nearest

JAMES TOFT—DOUBLE EAGLE.

the coals, and are distinguished by their colours and uses, as follows :—

"Clays for the Body of the Pottery

"1. Bottle clay, of a bright whitish-streaked yellow colour.
"2. Hard fire-clay, of a dullish whitish colour, and fuller intersperst with a dark yellow, which they use for their black wares, being mixed with the
"3. Red blending clay, which is of a dirty red colour.
"4. White clay, so called, it seems, though of a blewish colour, and used for making yellow-coloured wares, because yellow is the lightest colour they make any ware of.

"All of which they call throwing clays, because they are of a closer texture, and will work on the wheel.

SLIP WARE

"Clays for the Slip Decoration

"Which none of the three other clays, they call slips, will any of them doe, being of looser and more friable natures; these mixed with water, they make into a consistence thinner than a syrup, so that being put into a bucket it will run

SLIP-WARE CRUSKIN.

through a quill; this they call slip, and is the substance wherewith they paint their wares; whereof the

"1. Sort is called the orange slip, which before it is worked is of a greyish colour mixt with orange balls, and gives the ware (when annealed) an orange colour.

"2. The white slip; this before it is worked, is of a dark blewish colour, yet makes the ware yellow, which being the lightest colour they make any of, they call it, (as they did the clay above) the white slip.

"3. The red slip, made of a dirty reddish clay, which gives wares a black colour.

"Preparation of the Clay

"Neither of which clays or slips must have any gravel or sand in them; upon this account, before it is brought to the wheel, they prepare the clay by steeping it in water in a square pit, till it be of a due consistence ; then they bring it to their beating-board, where with a long spatula they beat it till it be well mix't ; then being first made into great

TYG OR POSSET CUP.   SLIP AND MOULDED DECORATION.

squarish rolls, it is brought to the wageing board, where it is slit into flat thin pieces with a wire, and the least stones or gravel pick't out of it. This being done, they wage it,

SLIP-WARE POSSET CUP.

i.e., knead or mould it like bread, and make it into round balls proportionable to their work, and then 'tis brought to the wheel, and formed as the workman sees good."

The description of the various processes of the slip-ware

SLIP WARE

manufacture and decoration, glazing, and burning is both interesting and instructive.

"Application of Ornament

"When the potter has wrought the clay into either hollow or flat ware, they set it abroad to dry in fair weather, but by the fire in foule, turning them as they see occasion, which they call whaving: when they are dry they stouk them, *i.e.*, put ears and handles to such vessels as require them.

SLIP-WARE POSSET CUP, 1690.

These also being dry, they then slip or paint them with their several sorts of slip, according as they designe their work, when the first slip is dry, laying on the others at their leisure, the orange slip making the ground, and the white and red the paint; which two colours they break with a wire brush, much after the manner they doe when they marble paper, and then cloud them with a pencil when they are pretty dry. After the vessels are painted, they lead them, with that sort of lead ore called smithum, which is the smallest ore of all beaten into dust, finely sifted and strewed upon them; which gives them the gloss, but not the colour; all the colours being chiefly given by the variety of slips, except the motley colour, which is procured by blending the lead with manganese, by the workmen call'd magnus. But when they have a mind to shew the utmost of their skill in giving their wares a fairer gloss than ordinary, they lead them with lead calcined into powder, which they also sift fine and strew upon them as before, which not only gives them a higher gloss, but goes much further too in their work, than lead ore would have done.

"BURNING IN THE KILN

"After this is done, they are carried to the oven, which is ordinarily above 8 foot high and about 5 foot wide, of a round

SLIP-WARE BOWL, 1755.

copped forme, where they are placed one upon another from the bottom to the top; if they be ordinary wares such as cylindricall butter pots, etc., that are not leaded, they are exposed to the naked fire, and so is all their flat ware though it be leaded, haveing parting shards, *i.e.*, thin bits of old pots put between them, to keep them from sticking together: but if they be leaded hollow wares, they do not expose them to the naked fire, but put them in shragers, that is, in course metall'd pots, made of marle (not clay) of divers formes according as their wares require, in which they put commonly three pieces of clay called bobbs, for the ware to stand on, to keep it from sticking to the shragers; as they put them in the shragers to keep them from sticking to one another (which they would certainly otherwise doe by reason of the leading) and to preserve them from the vehemence of the fire which else would melt them downe, or at least warp them. In twenty-four hours an oven of pots will be burnt, then they let the fire go out by degrees, which in ten hours more will be perfectly done, and then they draw them for sale, which is chiefly to the poor crate men, who carry them at their backs all over the country, to whome they reckon them by the piece, *i.e.*, quart, in hollow ware, so that six pottle or three gallon bottles make a dozen, and so more or less to a dozen,

COMBED-WARE POSSET POT.

as they are of greater or lesser content ; the flat wares are also reckoned by pieces and dozens, but not (as the hollow) according to their content, but their different bredths."

Reverting to the consideration of the moulded slip ware, of which we have given an illustration marked S.M., collectors are again advised to study and compare the dishes in the nation's museums, for though in a previous statement they have been ascribed to the Staffordshire potteries rather than to the Cock Pit Hill pottery in Derby, it may be that further investigation will definitely assign them to one or the other, or even to Tickenhall pottery, which seems to have some claim to recognition. But, bearing out the contention for

Staffordshire, we may note that in some of the Staffordshire churchyards slip-ware headstones are to be found with the usual red or brown pottery, ornamented with slip either of the same colour—that is, red or brown—or with white. Some are even inlaid. One most interesting piece in the British Museum should not be missed. It is either a tombstone or an " In Memoriam " wall-tablet, with somewhat elaborate designs in slip, and incised. On it will be found the old distich :

> " When this V. C.,
> Remember Mee."

There are just a few other considerations which must be borne in mind when seeking the place from which slip ware originated. One is that the poorer slip ware, without involved patterns, could have been made at any pottery. The second is that the artists who drew the various ornaments in slip probably migrated from one pottery to another. The third is that, whilst Wrotham ware may occasionally show some signs of the influence of foreign potters who are said to have settled in Kent in the sixteenth century, old Staffordshire was English all through, and the later Staffordshire—Toby jugs and figures—were English too. The slip ware made in Sussex at the end of the eighteenth and early in the nineteenth century is chiefly remarkable for minute inlaid ornaments.

CHAPTER XII

WHIELDON WARE

FOLLOWING the slip decoration and the scratched *graffito* or *sgraffiato* ornamentation comes the combed, tortoise-shell, marbled, or agate wares, which are of such interest to the collector. The last—the agate ware—had a solid body of clays of a different colour. For example, red veins in a yellow clay, or *vice versa*. This process is an old one, and can be traced in early pieces of Japanese pottery. It consisted in thoroughly refining each clay by itself, and then placing a sliced-off piece of one colour upon a similar sliced-off piece of another, so that the result showed the two-coloured clay all through. Early pieces of *solid* agate are uncommon. The same result was aimed at in the marbled ware by means of tinted slips. The brush by which the thin clay was applied was dipped into one colour and ap-

WHIELDON CLOUDED WARE.

plied to the piece, to be immediately followed in a similar way by a brush dipped into another colour. The result was quite a good marbling. The surplus slip was usually wiped off the base. When this was not done, an accumulation—tears—formed at the base, which in old specimens will be found very much rubbed, owing to the weight of the piece upon it. In combing, the same result was produced as when

WHIELDON AGATE WARE.

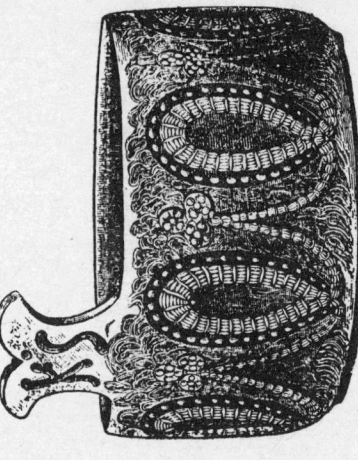

MARBLED WARE PIGGIN. K'S ON THE HANDLE.

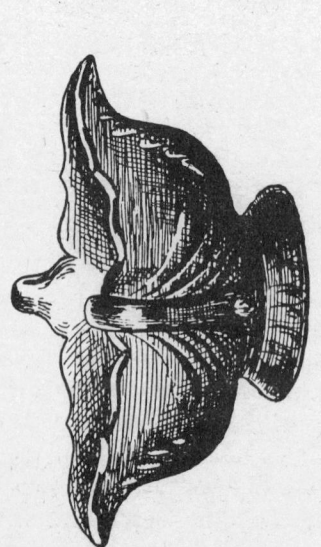

AGATE WARE SAUCE BOAT.

MARBLED WARE POSSET POT.

WHIELDON WARE

the painter grains the door, and in the same way. Tortoise-shell and similar patterns depended upon the instrument with which the coloured slip was treated: it may have been dabbed with a cloth or with a sponge, or even with a brush.

John Dwight, of Fulham, in 1684, applied for a patent for "white gorges, *marbled* porcelain vessels, figures, etc." We shall deal with stoneware and Dwight later. In 1729 Samuel Bell took out a patent for making "a red marble stone with minerall earth, which being so firmly united with fire will make it capable of receiving a gloss as to imitate, if not to compare with, rubie." That very litigious person, Ralph Shawe, or Shaw, potter, of Burslem, adopted all the improvements of Whieldon, Astbury, and Twyford, and then took out a patent for employing "various sorts of mineral earth, clay, and other earthy substances, which being mixt and incorporated together, make up a fine body, of which a curious ware may be made, whose outside will be of a true chocolate colour striped with white, and the inside white, much resembling the brown china ware, and glazed with salt." Salt glazing is a later story. It is sufficient to emphasise the difference between the solid agate or solid marble ware and that which was produced by combing or similar operations.

WHIELDON WARE DOVECOTE.

By common custom all of those early variegated wares are called "Whieldon ware," partly because of the difficulty of identifying early pieces made by Dwight, by Place of York, or by John Astbury, and partly because Whieldon appears to have been the most skilful and noted potter of his time, until Wedgwood, his assistant, partner, and rival, outdistanced him. He had a pottery at Little Fenton, or Fenton Low, from 1740 to 1780, where he produced much fine ware; but he was indebted to Thomas Astbury, John Astbury's son, whose body or paste included new elements, ground flint with Devon and Dorset clay, roughly potted at first, but improving later, and giving a great variety of fine sharp work. The collector will find considerable difficulty in assigning dates to examples which are earlier than 1720. From that date onwards for twenty years the progress just described had been going on, whilst during the next twenty years extensive use was made of scratched blue and other designs.

Josiah Wedgwood and Astbury, Spode, Aaron Wood, Garner, and Greatbach were associated with Whieldon's work, not alone in the early production of knife-handles for the Sheffield cutlers and snuff-boxes for Birmingham factories to finish with hoops and hinges, but also in the early figures, now so much in request. Wedgwood was a partner from 1753 to 1759, and it may be assumed that when he left Fenton Low he only continued the manufacture of agate and tortoiseshell ware till such time as his experiments resulted in the discovery of his cream-ware, which practically destroyed these wares, and soon also took the place of salt glaze and delft. This assumption opens up a wide field. How many of the unmarked figures ascribed to Whieldon were really made by him? The chapters on Staffordshire figures and Toby-jugs make further reference to Whieldon's productions.

TORTOISESHELL WARE GROUP.

TORTOISESHELL WARE BUTTER BOAT.

TORTOISESHELL WARE BOWL AND COVER.

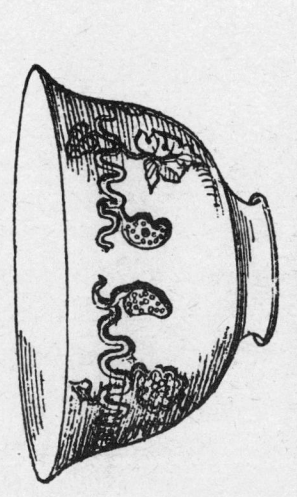

TORTOISESHELL WARE BOWL—MOULDED ORNAMENTS GILDED.

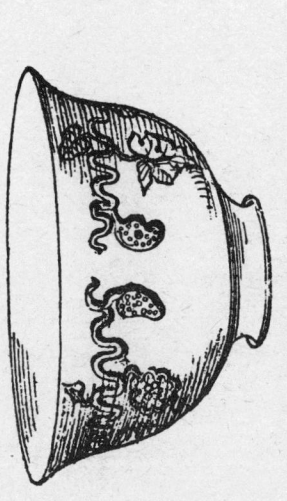

TORTOISESHELL WARE—OUTSIDE PIERCED.

CHAPTER XIII

FULHAM WARE

JOHN DWIGHT, M.A., of Christ Church, Oxford, was an artist in clay—that is, if he was his own modeller. His two patents, taken out in 1671 and 1684, give but little information as to " the mystery of transparent earthenware, commonly known by the names of porcelaine or china, and of stoneware, vulgarly called Cologne." Practical potters declare that his actual recipes would not produce transparent, or even translucent china, but only a fine opaque stoneware. This contention seems to be borne out by the specimens which have been recognised as the production of the Fulham works.

The Chinese made no distinction between true porcelain—that which is translucent—and the grey or red bodies which in England would be classified as stoneware. Even enamels are included in the term they use for porcelain. Dr. Plot, who wrote of pottery in his " History of Oxford," tells about Dwight's discoveries. The Cologne ware ; the Hessian ware ; earth, white and transparent as "porcellane " ; statues or figures of the said transparent earth, are all mentioned. " The figures were diversified with a great variety of colours—iron, copper, brass, and party-coloured, as some Achat-stones (jasper)." Other wares specified in the patent are marbled, blue and mouse-coloured stonewares. Dwight was born about 1637, and died at Fulham in 1703. As his first patent was taken out in 1671, he must have made his trials and experiments some considerable time previously, for Plot's account, written in 1678, states that " he (Dwight) hath set up a manufacture of the same which in three or four years' time he hath brought to greater perfection than it hath attained

WEDGWOOD WARE.
From Mr. A. M. Broadley's Collection.

where it hath been used for many ages." Indeed, the statuettes are quite deserving of all praise. "Triumphs of the modeller's and the potter's art," says Professor Church. "Undoubtedly the finest and most original productions of any English potter; indeed, it would be hard to find their equal among Continental wares. It is nothing short of

"PRINCE RUPERT," FULHAM—BRITISH MUSEUM—BOUGHT FOR £39 18s.

astounding to see this sudden and brilliant outburst of the potter's genius at a time when the greater part of the country had not advanced beyond the crude, if picturesque, slip wares." Such is the verdict of the British Museum.

In 1684, the first patent expired, and it was renewed for another fourteen years. When did Dwight come to Fulham?

It must have been long before 1684, because the patent recites as follows:—" CHARLES THE SECOND, by the grace of God, etc., to all to whom these presents shall come, greeting. WHEREAS John Dwight, Gentl., hath represented unto us that by his owne industry and at his owne proper costs and charges, hee hath invented and sett up at Fulham, in our county of Middx., SEVERALL NEW MANUFACTURES OF EARTHENWARE," etc. For about forty

DWIGHT STONEWARE, "FLORA," FULHAM.

STATUETTE, FULHAM.

years Dwight must have carried on his investigations; and, though few collectors have any specimen of his work, there must be many pieces which have not been identified, still in existence. This is the more likely because his son Samuel kept at the business till he died in 1737. After this, in partnership with Thomas Warland, his widow continued till 1746, when the business failed; to be revived when, at his

FULHAM WARE

death, she was again married, this time to William White, in whose family the works remained till 1862. In 1864 they passed to Mr. C. J. C. Bailey. We have now, approximately, fixed the date of the birth of the Fulham works. Corroboration is found in the "Letters on Husbandry and Trade," written by Houghton in 1694 (1693 old style). He says: "The best sort of mugs are made with it (Dorset clay), and the ingenious Mr. *Daught* of *Fulham* tells me that 'tis the same earth chinaware is made of." And again in 1695 he remarks of chinaware: "'Tis a curious manufacture, and deserves to be encouraged here ... and Mr. *Dowoit* of *Fulham* has done it, and can again in anything that is flat, etc." From this it appears that Dwight had not yet overcome all his difficulties, yet the ultimate results were absolutely beyond any that had been previously attained; they stand unequalled as specimens of pottery in this country—and more, they were the work of John Dwight. So much is conceded by the expert.

BROWN STONEWARE, FULHAM.

He must have been a singular and eccentric character. Old notebooks show how he hid his money in all sorts of places, noting them in his book and crossing them out when the deposit was withdrawn. In like manner it is believed that he buried or hid all his models, tools, moulds, etc., so that his children could not continue that branch of the business which was unremunerative. Indeed, he seems to have had a passion for hiding things. Some years since, the old buildings were put into the hands of the housebreaker because of their dilapidated condition. During the excavations for new foundations, a vault or cellar was discovered, in which there was found quite a number of greybeards or Bellarmines, ale-pots, etc. These were "the fine stone gorges made in England" to displace the old Cologne importations. This object was attained.

The immense number of stoneware bottles, jugs, noggins, and other measures made for everyday use displaced the pieces "made in Germany." Dwight was clever. He

"LYDIA DWIGHT," 1673-4.—VICTORIA AND ALBERT MUSEUM.
BOUGHT FOR £158.

made a contract with the glass-sellers of London, who covenanted to buy only his English-made stonewares and to refuse the foreign. We repeat the statement that there must be many of these specimens in existence only waiting identification. It may well be that some of the readers of this book have pieces in their possession worth a pound or more, which are lying unknown, and neglected because unknown. In 1862, a Mr. Baylis obtained at a sale about twenty-five extremely interesting specimens of the Dwight factory which had been kept in the family. The *Art*

FULHAM WARE

Journal had an account of them as follows : " The first is a dish, said to be one of a dinner set manufactured for the especial service of Charles II. It is of round form and large size, being 64½ in. in circumference. The groundwork is a rich blue, approaching to the ultramarine ; it is surrounded by a broad brim nearly four inches wide, formed by a graceful border of foliage and birds in white and shaded in pale blue. The whole of the centre is occupied by the

"LYDIA DWIGHT," FULHAM.   STATUETTE, FULHAM.

royal arms, surmounted by its kingly helmet, crown, and lion crest. The arms themselves are encircled with the garter, on which is inscribed the well-known motto, *Honi soit qui mal y pense*. The arms and supporters rest upon a groundwork of foliage, in the middle of which is the motto, *Dieu et mon Droit*. The workmanship of this piece of crockery is of a very superior character, and a dinner set of similar ware would make many a modern one look poor." There may be other examples of this magnificent dinner service extant, and the owners do not know that this is by far the finest early English work. Other specimens of the same period include brown-ware figures. Saturn is shown with a child in his arms, which he is devouring, in accordance with his agreement with his brother Titan. Jupiter, Neptune, Mars, Adonis or Meleager, according as the boar is conqueror or conquered, are types of the classical figures which were made. Charles II., his wife Catherine of Braganza, James II., his queen Mary d'Este, are amongst the contemporary figures, which include gentlemen and ladies of the Court of Charles II.,

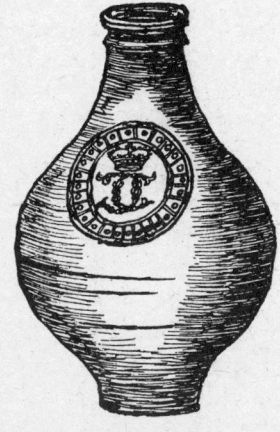

ONE OF THE GORGES FOUND
IN THE CELLAR.

FULHAM, IMPRESSED
ORNAMENT.

Flora, and the curious figure of one sleeping or lying upon a pillow, inscribed "Lydia Dwight, dyd March the 3rd, 1673." In the old notebooks John Dwight refers to Lydia Dwight, his daughter, who was born in 1667 and died in her seventh year. This little figure, now in the Victoria and Albert Museum, is unique, an exquisite gem of ceramic art. The opportunity of the collector is to study specimens which have been acquired by the nation; then the pieces which are now neglected will be appreciated. There are many opinions with regard to the ware itself. The truth is that it resembles the common grey hard porcelain from China, varying from pure white to a greyish white. Then there is the glaze. From careful

FULHAM WARE

observation we should say there was no glaze, as we understand it—that is, there was no application of a covering surface. The glaze looks like a smear, but really it seems the natural covering of a body that had the elements of opaque porcelain all through. Examine the specimens referred to for yourselves, and try to trace a glaze. Of course, salt-glaze will be uppermost in the mind. But there is no evidence that Dwight used any salt-glaze. No trace of it is found in the patents referred to, and history has no record of the nuisance caused by the salt-glazing process—the fumes and smoke.

All of this seems to indicate that neither the stoneware jugs, nor the statuettes, nor the commoner pieces, had any outside glaze either by dipping or by salt-glazing. Dwight's own recipes give directions how to make " porcelane or china cley, red porcelane cley, bright red cley, stone cley, fine white cley for gorges and cans, China glasse, blew porcellane, light grey cley," and many others, but only one has any reference to salt. That is " To make Porcellane by Salt,—Take eighteen pounds of fine white earth, etc., etc. This is a strong hardy cley, fit for garden pots, teapots, dishes, etc." Dwight discovered by experiment a porcellanous clay, possibly containing pounded flints, which when burnt was self-glazed. The later productions of Fulham were the brown stoneware vessels similar to those produced about the year 1700 at Lambeth, Bristol, Chesterfield, Brampton, and Nottingham—though the last had a very characteristic glaze.

CHAPTER XIV

PLACE'S WARE

WALPOLE gives some notice to Francis Place, who "discovered an earth for, and a method of making porcelain, which he put into practice at the Manor House, at York, of which manufacture he gave Thoresby a fine mug. His pottery cost him much money—he attempted it solely from a turn for experiments; but one Clifton took the hint from him, and made a fortune by it." Thoresby, in his book "Ducatus Leodiensis," 1714, mentions Place and his wares several times. Writing about a white clay found at Wortley, he cites his friend, Mr. Houghton; "he tells us that the finest mugs, and even chinaware, are made of this sort of earth, of which we may make as good in England as any in the world," and then he remarks, " and this I am fully convinced of, having a specimen in this museum made of English materials in the Manor House at York by the very ingenious Mr. Francis Place, who presented it to me with one of the outer coverings purposely made to secure them from the violence of the fire in baking." The only known specimen of this kind of earthenware is now at South Kensington. It is a cup with a handle, of thin glazed greyish or drab ware with streaks of brown and black, about $2\frac{1}{2}$ in. high, and nearly as wide at the top. There is a narrow raised band around it some distance from the top. Was this Thoresby's cup, or another which came into Walpole's possession and was sold at the Strawberry Hill sale? Walpole described it as "a coffee-cup of this ware; it is of gray earth, with streaks of black, and not superior to common earthenware." An old pasteboard label, probably in Walpole's writing, is

120a

WEDGWOOD.   FLAXMAN'S DESIGNS.

WEDGWOOD, WITH STEEL MOUNTS
BY BOULTON AND WATT.

NEALE AND PALMER.   JASPER WARE.

PLACE'S WARE

attached bearing the words "Mr. Francis Place's china." It is well worth seeing. The thought naturally arises, where are the other pieces of Place's ware? Some are said to remain in the possession of his family. Well, then, where are the products which made the fortune of that "one Clinton"? Being drab and plain, though elegant, have they escaped

PLACE'S WARE—THE UNIQUE SPECIMEN.

the collector's eye, or are they all gone? The ware, in texture, resembles Dwight's, and it may be that pieces of early origin attributed to China ought to be assigned, as we have before noted in Dwight ware, either to Clifton or Place. And there is only one precious example on which a judgment may be founded, one authenticated specimen, made by Francis Place, clerk to an attorney in London until 1665. Porcellanous it may be, but not more so than Dwight's Fulham ware.

CHAPTER XV

ELERS' WARE

WE must now take the story of old pottery to Staffordshire, where two Dutch potters, in 1690, erected kilns not far from Burslem, at Bradwell Wood. Here they made a fine red ware in imitation of the red Oriental. The clay used was dug on the spot, and the production of a hard compact body of a good colour was enhanced by the excellence of the designs, in both form

ELERS' WARE—CUP AND SAUCER IN RELIEF.

and decoration. From the clumsy liquor-pots of the seventeenth century to the elegant teaware of 1690–1710 made by John Philip Elers was not a step, but a leap. True, tea-drinking, though denounced, was becoming common. Pepys sent for a cup of tea, a China drink of which he had never drunk before, on September 25, 1660. *Rugge's Diurnal* tells us that, in 1659, tea was sold in almost every street in London. Two pounds of it was thought a gift worthy of the acceptance of the King. But, in 1678, we are told by Mr. Harry Saville that some of his friends " have fallen into the base unworthy Indian practice of calling for tea after dinner in place of the pipe and bottle," and that

"Arabian tea
Is dishwater to a dish of whey."

The World (1753), giving a description of a model country rector, said : " His only article of luxury is tea, but the doctor says he would forbid that if his wife could forget her London education. However, they seldom offer it but to

ELERS' WARE—SAUCER EMBOSSED OUTSIDE.

the best company, and *less than a pound will last them a twelvemonth*." This shows that Elers seized the opportunity and met the demand for small, delicately finished tea and coffee services ; for coffee, curiously enough, came into vogue about the same time as tea, and met with similar opposition. In fact, in 1675, a proclamation was issued for shutting up and suppressing all coffee-houses. But coffee, like tea, soon became a favourite drink, and the shops, where it was sold, places of general resort. This may be a diversion from our immediate subject, but it has this connection : the tea-services had been imported from China, and Elers made the Chinese or Japanese fine dry red porcelain, with ornaments, his model. His tea-ware was not cheap, for the red teapots sold for ten to twenty-five shillings each, at the London warehouse in the Poultry where David Elers was manager. Of course, with such opportunities, J. P. Elers strove to keep his manufacture a trade secret. He did not patent it, though the first patent for pottery was taken out in 1626 by Rose & Cullyn, of whom we know nothing but that their patent was for " stone potts, juggs, and bottells."

ELERS' WARE—RED PIGGIN.

Their extreme precaution to keep secret their processes, and jealousy lest they might be accidentally witnessed by any purchaser of their wares — making them at Bradwell, and conveying them by night over the fields to Dimsdale, there to be sold, being only two fields distant from the turnpike road— gave them much trouble. They tried to keep all their operations secret, and only engaged half-witted men to do the rough work. These they locked up in their several rooms and examined closely when they left at night. Strangers were warned off; but soon John Astbury and Twyford—who gained admittance as workers by fraud—mastered all there was to learn, and gave their knowledge freely and fully to the Potteries.

The sequel came in 1710, when the Elerses gave up their Staffordshire factory and moved to Lambeth. Some say they left because of the emphatic protests of the inhabitants against the dense volumes of smoke caused during the process of salt-glazing, which brought all the master potters of Burslem —eight—in dismay to Bradwell. The Elerses left, but the work they had done had an immense effect upon the Potteries. The potters learnt the use of the lathe, which Elers had applied to turn out far thinner and more uniform ware than the wheel alone could produce. This he decorated

ELERS' WARE

with simple patterns, turned on the lathe, or with ornaments in relief. Although it is next to impossible to be certain that any piece is really Elers' ware, because there is neither name nor date on any that has as yet been found, yet "Elers' Ware" generally is applied to all the fine early red ware. Most of Elers' pieces have a raised decoration of flowers, leaves, sprigs of so-called mayblossom, interlaced curves, fleurs-de-lis, birds, and figures. The method of decoration was entirely different from those hitherto practised in the district. A small piece of clay was stuck to the pot, and a metal die used to stamp the pattern on, the superfluous clay being scraped off by a small tool. The handles and spouts

ELERS' SCHOOL—RED WARE. LATE.

of the teapots were made entirely by hand, and were almost always simple in form and without ornament. Wedgwood stated that Elers brought alabaster moulds into use, so that assertion accounts for "almost always." To Elers, then, the Potteries owe the process of stamping and salt-glazing, as well as the use of the lathe. But they owe more. He practised the most careful levigation of his clays, reducing them to an impalpable powder, so that the body is beautifully soft and smooth, a really fine red stoneware. The later red ware, such as that made in the neighbourhood of Shelton, about 1750, was darker in tint than the earlier Elers' ware. So that Elers' ware would be defined as a fine red stoneware, comparatively light in tint, soft and smooth, with the designs sharply cut. Professor Church says: "The imitation Chinese mark in the seal character was used by other and later potters, though it probably was also employed by Elers himself. No fragments of red ware have been yet discovered near the site of his works at Bradwell Wood, nor at the store at Dimsdale. Systematic excavations at these two localities ought to clear up some of our doubts as to the true attribution of pieces now commonly given to Elers and his imitators and successors indiscriminately. At present, when we think we have identified an undoubted piece of the original ware, we are often suddenly disillusioned by finding a piece identical in form and decoration, but of a body which is known to have been devised after Elers' day, or with ornaments of historical character which refer to a time when Elers had left Staffordshire and abandoned the potter's art." Let us hope that this suggestion will be carried out, and that the work of investigation will settle the question of real Elers' ware once for all. In addition to the red ware of which we have written, and the salt-glaze, it may be that we shall find the common lead glaze with tortoiseshell mottlings, and even the black ware, the precursor of Wedgwood's black basaltes, were also produced at Bradwell Wood.

CHAPTER XVI

ASTBURY WARE

THE method by which John Astbury accomplished his object, and by improper means won from Elers the secret of his unique processes of manufacture, may be condemned, but Astbury gave away this knowledge to the Staffordshire potters. He also gave them the results of his own improvements, for, though he was an imitator, he was much more. He had sense enough to change, more or less, the character of the work of the Dutchmen. His imitations

ASTBURY WARE—ADMIRAL VERNON, 1739.

were inferior to theirs in the smoothness and fineness of the body, and still more in the clearness and sharpness of the ornament. There seems but little doubt that he, and perhaps Twyford, made at Shelton red, black, and salt-glazed ware. But *Astbury* ware is quite different from these. The mixture of clays, which formed the body of his earthenware, produced pottery of various colours—buff, chocolate, fawn, orange, red or yellow. The ornament was stamped and generally in pipe-clay, sometimes tinged with a purple brown. The coating applied was a fine lead glaze.

The elder Astbury—died 1743—seems to have made "crouch" and "white stone" ware, using salt-glaze for some of the pieces and lead for others. His ware was in its turn imitated by Dr. Thomas Wedgwood, Ralph Shaw, and other potters early in the eighteenth century, and these imitations continued as late as 1780. The other special features of John Astbury's work seem to have been marbled and scratched (or *graffiato*) ware, and, above all, the introduction of the use of ground flint, as a substitute for sand, and of the Dorset and Devonshire clays first as a wash, later as ingredients of the body.

ASTBURY WARE FIGURES.

Thomas Astbury, son of John, in 1725, started a factory at Lane Delph, where he became distinguished as a potter, and first produced "cream" ware. It may safely be assumed that most of these early pieces were unmarked, though now and again an example marked ASTBURY may indicate rather the work of the son than the father. Some few figures in different coloured clays with a very good lead glaze have been assigned to Shelton, but the evidence is slight, and the term *Astbury school* is certainly safer. Such figures, usually small, have splashes of green and brown on a red or brown clay, often with coloured slip ornament. The Admiral Vernon bowl is a fine specimen of Astbury ware.

JACKFIELD. COFFEE-POT.
From Mr. A. M. Broadley's Collection.

TURNER STONEWARE JUG.

CHAPTER XVII

SALT-GLAZE

A SHORT description of salt-glaze is that it is a pottery glaze formed by volatilising common salt in a kiln in which are placed the articles to be coated. Here, volatilising means turning into vapour by heat. So that pottery, when white-hot, is attacked by the vapour of salt thrown into the kiln, and a fine glaze is formed on the surface, which does not interfere with the sharpness of the designs. There appears, as we have shown, to have been some indication that Dwight knew something about salt-glaze, and that Elers practised it, but none of this salt-glaze can be identified. The early pieces are of a drab or buff colour, often known as "crouch ware." Possibly 1680–90 was the experimental period. Then follows Elers' ware until 1710, and in 1720 a variation was introduced in the paste by the introduction of flint and Devon and Dorset clay. The results were seen in the increased beauty of the potting, which became very fine and sharp.

The next period, till 1760, saw the adoption of scratched designs in blue. Later work in this period was the use of coloured enamels and gilded ornamentation on the salt-glaze surface, whilst during the next twenty years basket-work and pierced-work after the Oriental style made their appearance; but, as salt-glaze had displaced lead-glaze, so Wedgwood's cream ware, brought to perfection, was so popular that salt-glazed ware, though manufactured as late as 1820, ceased to be the rival of the finer earthenwares after 1780. The early improvements are ascribed to the Astburys. John Astbury tried to remedy the drab or buff colour in crouch ware by a wash of white Devonshire clay, afterwards used as an ingredient of the paste itself.

The story of the discovery of salt-glaze may be a myth, but it is interesting. "At Mr. Joseph Yates's, Stanley, near Bagnall, five miles east of Burslem, in Staffordshire, the servant was preparing in an earthen vessel a salt-ley (brine) for curing pork, and during her temporary absence the liquid boiled over, and the sides of the pot were quickly red-hot from intense heat; yet, when cold, were covered with an excellent glaze. The fact was detailed to Mr. Palmer, potter, of Bagnall, who availed himself of the occurrence, and told other potters." It is said that Adams, at Holden Lane, and Wedgwood, at Brownhills, devoted themselves to the manufacture of salt-glazed ware. The ovens were very large, and from the scaffold round them the firemen cast salt through holes, specially designed, into the interior, where the heat vaporised it. The ware itself was enclosed in perforated saggers, so that the vapour could easily circulate through them, and thus glaze the surface of the ordinary articles for domestic use, such as jugs, cups, dishes, plates, etc.

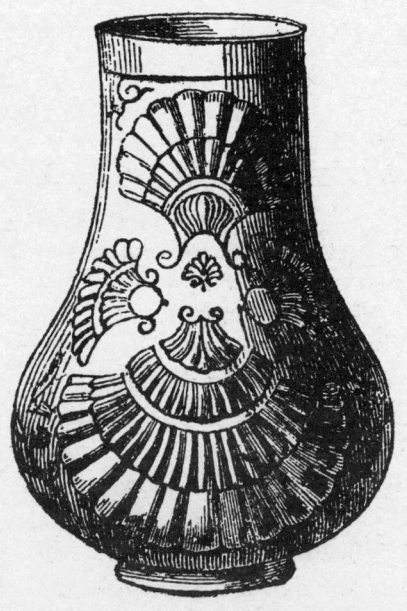

SALT-GLAZE—PATTERN MOULD.

There were only twenty-two ovens at this time in Burslem, and the special weekly "firing up" took place on Saturday mornings from eight to twelve. The dense white smoke produced was extremely disagreeable, and was likened to the fumes of Etna or Vesuvius. The decoration of this early ware was at first of the simplest form; engine-turned bands and lines were followed by similarly simple incised and scratched patterns, on the drab or ash-coloured body, which was, as we have seen, covered with a white clay wash, sometimes partly cut away in the pattern, and sometimes decorated with applied ornaments in white and blue clays, cast previously in moulds, or stamped on from metal moulds. It is most interesting to note how carefully the surplus clay was removed by tools from the moulded ornament.

SALT-GLAZE—VERY SMALL TEAPOT, WITH LID. IMPRESSED PATTERN.

The next step of progress is noted in the colour. Zaffre, a cobalt ore with silica, was used to impart a blue tinge, and manganese a copper-brown; both were used by powdering previous to glazing. The sharpness and delicacy resulting from the use of metal moulds was largely lost when plaster moulds were substituted—some time between 1740 and 1750. As usual, a great deal was lost when "cheap" displaced "good."

Another potter, Thomas Miles, made a white stoneware in 1685 at Shelton, similar to the "crouch" and "white" stoneware of Astbury and Twyford, also of Shelton. But though they all used salt-glaze for some of their productions, they applied lead ore to others. Indeed, there seems to be a consensus of opinion that the potters added a little red

SALT-GLAZE—BUTTER BOAT. IMPRESSED.

lead to the salt thrown into the kiln to make the glaze both smoother and thicker.

Joseph Cartledge, of Blackley, Yorkshire, doctor of physic, in 1783-4 took out a patent for glazing earthenware. In the application which he made he gives some information with regard to the glazes then in use: "All sorts of common ware are now, and have been heretofore at all times, both in this and all other countries I know, glazed either

SALT-GLAZE—DOUBLE-HANDLED BUTTER BOWL. IMPRESSED PATTERN.

by sea-salt, or by lead ore, or by some preparation of lead, or of lead and tin united to ground flints or clay or both." Tin enamelling on a blue ground will be found on white stoneware, to which transfer-printing in black, red, or violet was often applied for over-glaze decoration. Sometimes

SALT-GLAZE

oil-gilding and japanning were used; but generally the drab or white surface of salt-glazed ware relied upon its own beautiful impressed designs, and received no aid from colour. The distinguishing feature of the surface is a fine or minute pitting, which gives it the appearance of leather or orange-skin. This is due to the high temperature at which the glaze was fused, as well as to its having been formed upon the ware whilst in the kiln by the vaporised salt combining with the silica, one of the constituents of the clay itself.

The increased popularity of Wedgwood's Queen's ware —lead-glazed—was one of the causes of the decay of salt-

SALT-GLAZE—FOUR-LOBED SMALL TEAPOT. IMPRESSED.

glaze. Another was the roughness of the glazed surface for use with spoons, etc., of silver. A third was to be found in its tendency to crack when exposed to changes of temperature. But for many years Staffordshire, Liverpool, Swansea, and perhaps Leeds and Jackfield, were devoted to the manufacture of salt-glaze ware, which was sent in considerable quantities to the Continent, where it was again ousted by the cream ware of Wedgwood, and practically in 1780 it was dying. Many potters are said to have made salt-glaze ware and salt-glaze figures, but none of the latter have as yet been found marked. Indeed, with the exception of a few blocks which bear the signatures of the cutters, the early eighteenth-century ware had no mark. Aaron

SALT-GLAZE—SHELL-SHAPED TEAPOT.

SALT-GLAZE—HEART-SHAPED. THE LOVERS' TEAPOT.

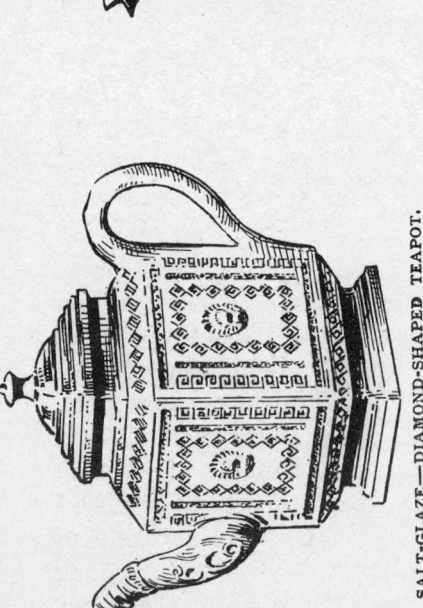

SALT-GLAZE—DIAMOND-SHAPED TEAPOT.

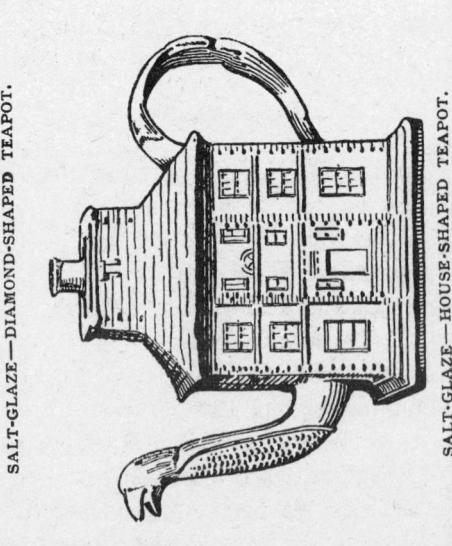

SALT-GLAZE—HOUSE-SHAPED TEAPOT.

SALT-GLAZE

Wood's signature is sometimes found, and his brother Ralph has left one signed mould.

Amongst the manufacturers who made white salt-glaze stoneware, as given by Simeon Shaw, were the two sons of Aaron Wedgwood—Thomas and John—of Burslem; R. and J. Baddeley, of Shelton; Thomas and Joseph Johnson, of Lane End; R. Bankes and John Turner, of Stoke; John

SALT-GLAZE VASE—IMPRESSED DESIGN.

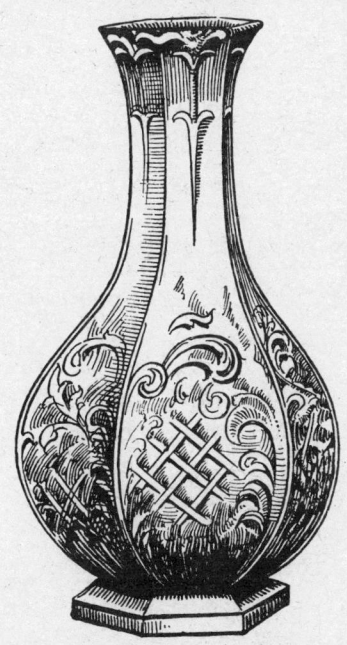

SALT-GLAZE VASE—IMPRESSED PATTERN.

Barker and Robert Garner, of Fenton; John Adams and John Prince, of Lane Delph; and Thomas Whieldon, the great manufacturer, of Fenton Low. Such is the number of names given that we may fairly assume that, between 1720 and 1780, all of the potteries in Staffordshire and elsewhere made salt-glaze as well as lead-glazed ware, except in the few, where delft lingered on.

Aaron Wood became a potter on his own account. He had been apprenticed to Dr. Thomas Wedgwood in 1731, but from 1743 to 1750 he worked for John Mitchell, of Burslem, as a mould maker. The making of the moulds was an intricate and difficult process, especially at first, when carved moulds only were used, to be followed later by plaster-of-Paris moulds brought from France by Ralph Daniel, at some time between 1743 and 1750. The carved mould had first to be cut in sections in some soft stone, usually alabaster, according to the shape of the piece to be moulded. Next came the *block*, which was a thick piece of clay in one piece, pressed when quite soft upon the outside of the mould, then dried and fired in the kiln. From these earthenware *blocks* other earthenware moulds or pitchers could be multiplied, and the seams which showed the sections 'of the original carving were utilised as borders for the different patterns. Handles, legs, and spouts were added, and the whole piece was placed in the kiln and glazed with salt.

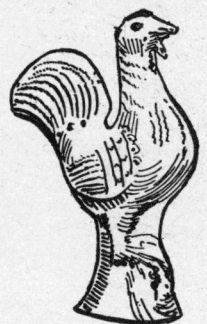

SALT-GLAZE FIGURE.

The decadence of salt-glaze ware began with the adoption of plaster moulds, which gave very inferior impressions, especially after they had been worn by frequent use. The poor character of these is emphasised by comparison with the earlier ones, which were made in metal moulds with designs apparently borrowed from the silversmith or wood-carver. The patterns were mainly shells, leaves, tendrils, various flutings, diapers, frets, and coats of arms; but the potter was not fastidious. He joyfully set a mythological subject by the side of a Chinese mandarin, or a homely English scene. Then, again, the shapes of the articles themselves are quite quaint—teapots shell-shaped, heart-shaped, lozenge-shaped, house-shaped, camel-shaped, and so on. The museums of the Metropolis show many striking specimens, which should be carefully inspected.

One feels inclined to agree with Professor Church: " The sharp archaic designs, the waferlike thinness, and the other characteristics of this ware are perhaps best seen upon the richly decorated sauceboats, teapots, and pickle or sweetmeat trays of this beautiful pottery. There can be no doubt that these things are far more worthy of preservation than many of the English porcelains and earthenwares which command high prices at sales and form the usual objects of worship amongst the devotees of bric-à-brac. They are original, but avoid meaningless extravagances of form and decoration. Duly displayed upon the shelves of a cabinet lined with puce-coloured velvet, they hold their own in competition with most of the highly esteemed wares of European origin."

The very finest and rarest pieces of salt-glaze ware, covered

SALT-GLAZE GROUP.

all over with a deep blue or pink ground colour, are now ascribed to W. Littler, the first man in Staffordshire to attempt the making of chinaware. He commenced business at Brownhills, about 1745, and a few years afterwards removed to Longton Hall, where he produced china of great beauty, having similar colours. His salt-glazed ware is sometimes enriched with black and opaque white tin enamels. His china has similar white enamel decoration. Specimens of this decoration on salt-glaze are very rare, and so are those with gilding and transfer-printing. Although Ralph Shawe, of Burslem, is not mentioned, there is scarcely a doubt that he made salt-glaze ware. He had adopted the improvements of Astbury and others, and was constantly threatening the neighbouring potters with lawsuits for infringing his *sole* patent rights, till, in self-defence, they, in 1736, supported John Mitchell, the employer of Aaron Wood, in a suit which Shawe brought against him. The verdict was against Shawe. The judge nullified his patent, and, addressing the manufacturers present, said, " Go home, potters, and make whatever kinds of pots you please," which, translated into the native dialect, became, " Gooa whomm, potters, an' mak wat soourts o' pots yoa loiken." This decision was hailed with joy in Burslem, and, indeed, was largely responsible for the enterprise and determination which ultimately made the Potteries the centre of the earthenware and china trade, and immediately set the manufacturers to improve the salt-glaze ware, which was perfected between 1740 and 1760.

About 1750 painting in enamels on the finished ware was introduced, the colours being fired in a muffle kiln, which required less than the kiln-heat used for glazing. Ralph Daniel, of Cobridge, employed workmen from Delft, and at Bagnall he started works for them so as to keep the process of enamelling secret; but soon other enamellers were at work elsewhere—Robinson and Rhodes, of Leeds, being especially prominent as advertisers till 1760. The earliest attempts to apply colour on the salt-glaze were simply dabs of blue or manganese, just like those found on pieces having a lead glaze. Occasionally black or brown slip was used, either in the details or inlaid. Scratched blue ware received its name from the patterns being first scratched on the surface and then the scratches filled in by the cobalt dusted on. Pottery figures in salt-glaze are very rare; usually they are small and sometimes modelled by hand, though the majority were moulded, some after the antique, others perhaps from china, and a few in the Oriental style. Animals—rabbits, cats, sheep, monkeys, swans, and hawks— are not so uncommon as the figures and groups. The well-known jug, the figure of a bear hugging a dog, with the head as the cup, has an unusual decoration, being

SALT-GLAZE

covered with fragments or chips of rough clay. The claws, teeth, eyes, and collar of the bear may be found touched with brown or white. Because salt-glaze ware is rare the collector is keen upon getting it—not alone for that, however, but for the merits of the ware itself. Indeed, the finest pieces are worthy of comparison with the best products of any other factories, and they show how great had become the skill of the potters in the few years which had elapsed since Daniel brought back the first plaster-of-Paris mould from France, when they got blocks of gypsum

SALT-GLAZE SWEETMEAT DISH.

from Derbyshire and carved them instead of burning the gypsum and grinding it to cast into plaster moulds.

The British Museum should be visited by any student of salt-glaze. Amongst the specimens will be found numerous tea and coffee pots, which are quite amongst the best of their kind. Notice the piece with Admiral Vernon's ship *Burford*. Two pieces of W. Littler's salt-glaze, with his successful blue ground, may be profitably compared with a similarly decorated piece of Longton Hall china, also Littler's. A few quaintly modelled figures are worth noticing, as indicating the rude type of figures not copied from porcelain models. A toy tea-service is almost unique, and its workmanship is excellent. Several ornaments, where the pecten shell is used with effect, should be noticed. A comparison may be made between two teapots from the same mould, one in salt-glaze and the other in marbled earthenware. The salt-glaze is the smaller, because salt-glaze, subjected to a fiercer heat, diminished more by shrinkage. The subject of the teapots is a squirrel holding a nut. Besides the several figures of Frederick the Great, King of Prussia, there are some others which aptly illustrate the fact that Whieldon made salt-glaze as well as tortoiseshell and the other articles which are known as Whieldon ware. The Victoria and Albert Museum has quite a treasure in a block for a small milk-jug cut by Ralph Wood, whose initials R.W., with the date 1749, it bears. There are also several other good moulds, including a very clear sharp one for a cup, and a cup taken from it. Note that the plain rim has been roughly decorated in "scratch blue." The

SALT-GLAZE. C. 1730.

Schreiber collection contains some good specimens. Attention is drawn to the facilities for seeing and closely examining fine examples, which are like object-lessons, for which we furnish the text. The public museums of Staffordshire contain some choice pieces, notably the Wedgwood Institute at Burslem, which has a block PORTO BELLO TAKEN, and the Mechanics' Institute at Hanley, which has a series of these blocks in hard stoneware. The subject of salt-glaze ware is a most attractive one, for though Fulham may have had something to do with the Staffordshire crouch ware—drab

SALT GLAZE, SCRATCHED BLUE, POSSET CUP.

WEDGWOOD'S FIRST TEAPOT.

SALT-GLAZE BOWL.

CAULIFLOWER WARE.

salt-glaze—the influence was but slight, if we judge by the wonderful superiority of Dwight's figure-modelling. The modelling of the Staffordshire figures in salt-glaze was not exactly poor—it was bad. Later, the coloured earthenware figures and groups made vast progress. So much, then, for the Fulham influence. The same cannot be said of the Oriental hold upon the English potteries. The embossed ornament was often copied directly from Japanese stonewares, though native talent added details. Still, with every allowance for this, and perhaps for a little help from the German stonewares, this salt-glaze ware must hold a foremost place amongst English decorative pottery.

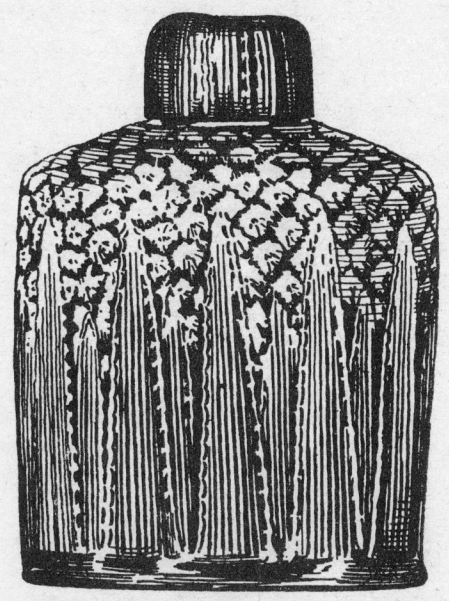

PINEAPPLE WARE.

Before leaving such an attractive branch of ceramics, the question as to what part the Wedgwoods took in it will lead naturally to Wedgwood's productions, which will be the subject of our next chapter. We know that Dr. Thomas Wedgwood was a celebrated potter, but he must not be confounded with Thomas Wedgwood, father of Josiah; nor Thomas Wedgwood, eldest brother of Josiah, to whom he was apprenticed. Josiah's relatives in another branch of the family, Thomas and John Wedgwood, were potters, who manufactured lead-glaze ware till 1740, when, though one was excellent in burning or firing the ware, and the other an excellent thrower, they for a time unsuccessfully attempted to make white stoneware, that is salt-glaze. Ultimately they succeeded, and in 1763 retired upon the fortune they had made by their industry. Whilst they were on the high road to success Josiah was serving his apprenticeship to his brother from 1744 to 1749, and for three years afterwards he still worked with his brother In 1752 he was partner with Harrison and Alders. Then, in 1754, he left them and joined Whieldon as a partner. This partnership continued till 1759, when, probably with the £20 left to him, twenty years before, by his father, he started for himself. Alders was a potter at Cliff Bank, near Stoke, and he made mottled ware, tortoiseshell, salt-glaze, shining black, and scratched blue wares. And Whieldon also made these wares. What, therefore, was the natural outcome of Wedgwood's training? Certainly, it seems as if the young potter, just beginning business, could do nothing more nor less than make the same kinds of ware. Hence the conclusion is forced upon us that many of the fine pieces of the wares mentioned above, as well as many Staffordshire figures, were made by Wedgwood. "When he started i' bizness fust, he made spewnes, knife hondles, and smaw crocks at the Ivy hahs," " an' arter that he flitted to th' Bell Workhus."—*The Burslem Dialogue.*

CIRCULAR SALT-GLAZE PLATE,
With scalloped border, 9 in. in diameter, moulded with a diaper pattern, and the centre ornamented with a transfer print of the fox and the lion in red. This is an early example of transfer-printing upon salt-glazed ware, which is very unusual.

CHAPTER XVIII

WEDGWOOD

THE introduction to Wedgwood in our last chapter is sufficient for our purpose. We have noted the small beginnings of a great concern, and we are only unfortunate in two items. What ware did Wedgwood make before his

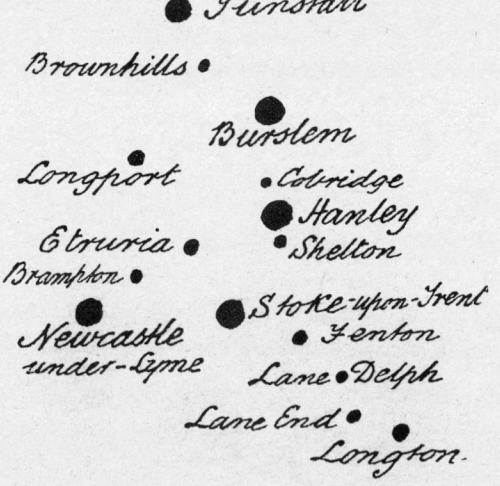

SKETCH MAP OF THE POTTERIES.

Since 1802 many of the smaller places have been absorbed by the larger. Hanley and Shelton became one market town—Hanley—in 1812. Lane End is merged into Longton; Lane Delph into Fenton. Hanley, Longton, Stoke, Burslem, Tunstall, and Fenton form the Parliamentary Borough of Stoke-upon-Trent.

Queen's ware came into fashion? When did he begin regularly to mark the products of his works? We can only surmise as to the first question, though we are certain that many

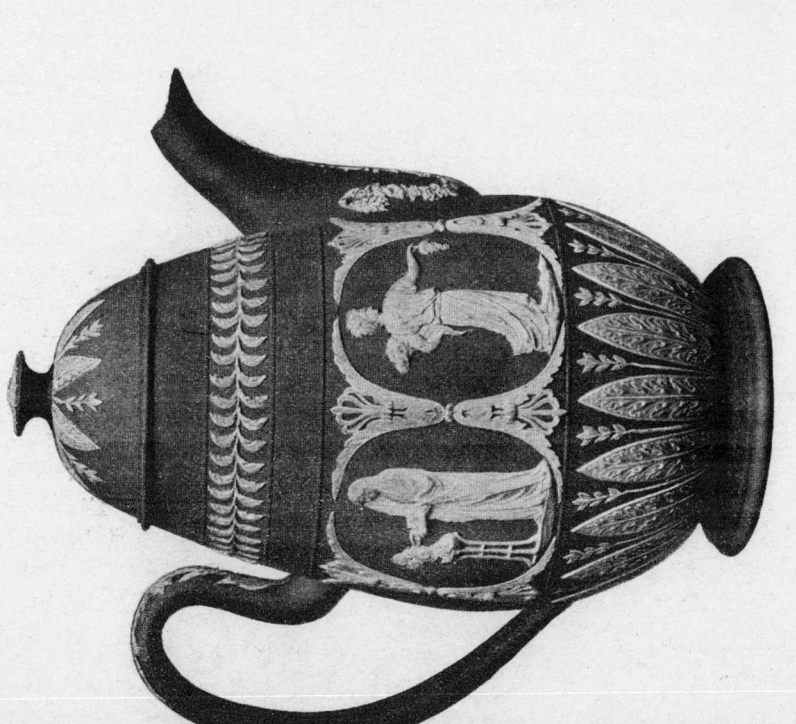

144a

NEALE AND PALMER. JASPER WARE.

W. ADAMS. JASPER WARE.

Staffordshire coloured and glazed figures were manufactured by him. The figure of "Charity," from the Willett Collection at Brighton, was modelled by Mrs. Landré, who was, in 1769, being paid for services rendered as a modeller of various Scripture subjects—"Moses and the serpent," "Joseph," "The Lord's Supper," "Christ and the Virgin," "A Magdalen," "Faith, Hope, and Charity," appear in her list, and the "Charity" before mentioned is marked WEDGWOOD. Other figures are also found with the same impressed

"CHARITY." STAFFORDSHIRE WEDGWOOD.

"FORTITUDE." STAFFORDSHIRE WEDGWOOD.

mark. "Fortitude" is one, which may, like "Charity," bear its name on the front of the base. "Venus with Cupid and a Dolphin" is a third. But the early potters rarely marked their figures. Now and then we meet with R. WOOD or ENOCH WOOD; WOOD AND CALDWELL or TURNER; WALTON or SALT; NEALE & CO.; LAKIN & POOLE; I. DALE; Hartley Greens & Co.; HALL; B. S. & T.

(Barker, Sutton, and Till); Dixon, Austin, & Co.; J. WALLEY; VOYEZ, and a few others; but marked figures are rare, in some cases very rare indeed. So that Wedgwood only followed the prevailing custom in sending out these wares without a mark. The set of figures "Faith, Hope, and Charity," which have been referred to, were also made upon square moulded bases with the names impressed in front by Robert Garner, another apprentice to Whieldon.

All the potters seem to have made figures after similar models, and in his early days Wedgwood's works were quite

STAFFORDSHIRE LION. WEDGWOOD.

on a small scale, and we can imagine that he gained his early success by the sheer superiority of his ware. The task of complete identification is difficult, but Miss Meteyard, who may be looked upon as *the* biographer of Wedgwood, expresses a strong opinion that the time will come when Wedgwood figures will be identified. She gives one hint: "the marbling of the plinth gives positive assurance of Wedgwood's workmanship." Whilst not altogether accepting this as the final word on Wedgwood's Staffordshire figures, it may be worth investigating. See "Fortitude"; at the base is the marbling, also at the base of the Lion. Other suggested tests are the piercing of the base or bottom by a hole, or in the case of large figures, say the Wedgwood lion, by three holes. Possibly the other test will be the superiority of the body itself. Ten years had elapsed since Wedgwood started for himself, and Mrs. Landré was working for him. But Theodore Parker also appears on the list as a modeller. Amongst his works at the same date, 1769, are "Milton," "Shakespeare," "Ceres," "Juno," "Prudence," and others. This was three years later than the period when Wedgwood produced his "basaltes" or "Egyptian" fine black ware, which, though famous, neither in his own time nor since

WEDGWOOD. TRANSFER PRINTED BY SADLER AND GREEN. "OLD PEOPLE GROUND YOUNG AGAIN."

has been subject to any considerable appreciation in price; there is little demand for it.

Let his catalogue description of his various wares prepared by himself in 1787 come before any attempt is made to analyse them:—

"1. A *terra cotta*, resembling porphyry, granite, Egyptian, pebble, and other beautiful stones of the silicious or crystalline order.

"2. *Basaltes* or black ware; a black porcelain biscuit of nearly the same properties with the natural stone; striking fire with steel, receiving a high polish, serving as a touchstone for metals, resisting all the acids, and bearing without injury a strong fire—stronger, indeed, than the basaltes itself.

"3. *White porcelain biscuit*, of a smooth, wax-like surface, of the same properties with the preceding, except in what depends on colour.

"4. *Jasper*; a white porcelain biscuit of exquisite beauty and delicacy, possessing the general properties of the basaltes, together with the singular one of receiving through its whole substance, from the admixture of metallic calces (oxides) with the other materials, the same colours which those calces communicate to glass or enamels in fusion ; a property which no other porcelain or earthenware body of ancient or modern composition has been found to possess. This

LORD CORNWALLIS AND LORD NELSON. STAFFORDSHIRE, 1799. IS THIS WEDGWOOD?

DEATH OF GENERAL WOLFE. STAFFORDSHIRE, C. 1780. CREAM WARE. WEDGWOOD?

renders it peculiarly fit for making cameos, portraits, and all subjects in *bas-relief*, as the ground may be of any particular colour, while the raised figures are of a pure white.

"5. *Bamboo*, or cane-coloured biscuit porcelain, of the same nature as No. 3.

"6. A *porcelain biscuit*, remarkable for great hardness, little inferior to that of agate. This property, together with its resistance to the strongest acids and corrosives, and its impenetrability by every known liquid, adapts it for mortars and many different kinds of chemical vessels.

"These six distinct species, with the Queen's ware already mentioned, expanded by the industry and ingenuity of the

WEDGWOOD

different manufacturers into an infinity of forms for ornament and use, variously painted and embellished, constitute nearly the whole of the present fine English earthenwares and porcelain which are now become the source of a very extensive trade, and which, considered as an object of national art, industry, and commerce, may be ranked amongst the most important manufactures of the kingdom."

A few words relating to the history of the works may be interposed here, before dealing with the various wares in detail. In 1766, the year in which his cousin, Thomas Wedgwood, joined him as a partner in making the useful

WEDGWOOD: QUEEN'S WARE BUTTER BOAT.

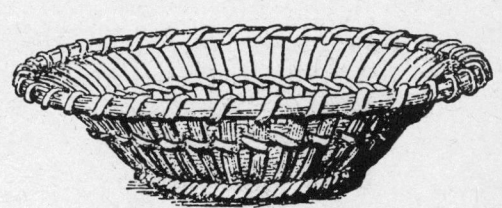

FRUIT BASKET, WEDGWOOD'S QUEEN S WARE.

wares, the Ridge House Estate, in the township of Skelton, was purchased, and, later, named Etruria. In 1768, Thomas Bentley was taken into partnership in the ornamental department, and the connection was most advantageous to the concern. Bentley mainly devoted himself to the development of the London business, though he was present at the opening of the Etruria works, and turned the wheel whilst Josiah Wedgwood acted as the potter and "threw" three Etruscan vases which bore the words:

JUNE XII MDCCLXIX
One of the first Day's Productions
at
Etruria in Staffordshire
by
Wedgwood and Bentley
Artes Etruriæ renascuntur

In 1770, the partners established works in Chelsea for the decoration of these encaustic vases, etc., and employed a number of workmen in painting and enamelling till nearly the close of the century.

In 1773, it is evident from the sale catalogue that in addition to the cream ware only three kinds of ornamental ware were made—*terra cotta, basaltes,* and *white biscuit ware.* To this period belong the vases and medallions of white figures, scrolls, etc., on a black ground. The oval, for instance, of the plaque was frequently made of the black ware, and the bust of the white terra-cotta. In 1774, a fine white *terracotta*, of great beauty and delicacy, proper for cameos, portraits, and bas-reliefs, was added. So that remained till 1787, when, as we have seen, *jasper* appeared, with its lovely blue and other coloured grounds. Was it merely a coincidence, or did Wedgwood avail himself of the opportunity afforded by Richard Champion's application for an extension of Cookworthy's patent to fight for freedom to use china stone and china (growan) clay? Champion obtained his patent in September 1775, but with an important modification, which is quite worth quoting: " Provided, also, that nothing in this Act (by which the patent was granted) contained shall be construed to hinder or prevent any potter or potters, or any other person or persons, from making use of any such raw materials, or any mixtures thereof (except such mixture of raw materials, and in such proportions, as are described in the specification hereinbefore directed to be enrolled), anything in this Act to the contrary notwithstanding." All of this indicates that the potters could make everything except hard paste translucent porcelain.

Wedgwood was keen, with an energy, perseverance, and ability rarely met with, and we can imagine that he made the fullest use of the liberty given under the Act. In any case, in 1776, about a year after its discovery, we have the first mention of the new white body, as jasper, and the catalogue of 1787 has his comment: " As these are my latest I hope they will be found my most approved works. . . . I must, therefore, beg leave to refer those who wish for information in these respects to a view of the articles themselves." This white jasper body was, after many experiments, coloured in the mass as solid jasper, and about 1785 (some say 1777) he invented the no less famous "jasper dip." In that year (1785) he wrote, "The new jasper, white within, will be the only sort made in future; but as the workmanship is nearly double, the price must be raised. I think it must be about 20 per cent." So it may be helpful to remember that till 1785 the jasper body was the same right through, and further, the colour of the body was almost exclusively blue. From 1785 to 1858 it was dipped—that is, its surface only was stained. The usual method, in fact, the universal method, was to have the ground in one of the colours—black, blue of various tints, lilac, olive-green, pink, sage green, or yellow. Pink and yellow are exceedingly rare. In 1858 "solid jasper" was reintroduced, and is continued at present. Jasper ware will be further described under its proper heading. Taking the usual classification :—

1. *Cream* or *Queen's ware* varied in colour. The white earthenware body, the same body which had hitherto received the salt-glaze, before the introduction of Cornish (growan) stone, was tinted cream, or straw, or saffron. Flint and lead glazing displaced salt glazing. The firing was exactly the process that had been used for the tortoiseshell, mottled, agate, and cauliflower ware. The progress made by Wedgwood seems to have been confined to the addition of flint to the lead as a glaze, and to improving the process of manufacture. In 1762 he had perfected the body and glaze of this fine cream-coloured ware, and he presented a caudle and breakfast service of it to Queen Charlotte. This service was painted by the best artists at the Bell Works— Thomas Daniell and Daniel Steele. The ground was yellow, with raised sprigs of jessamine and other flowers, in natural colours. The usual decoration of Queen's ware—for so it was called in 1765, after a complete table service had been approved by Her Majesty—was either painted in quiet colours or transfer-printed, at first, by Sadler & Green, at Liverpool. The royal patronage gave the "Potter to Her Majesty"

the opportunity of his life; quite fully did he avail himself of it. Orders poured in upon him at prices which made his fortune. This useful ware, and not the artistic and beautiful ornamental ware, drove him from Burslem to Etruria. Yet the table ware, at fifteen shillings for a dozen plates, had its own beauty. The body was perfection; carefully ground clays and flint lent themselves to an excellence of potting not often seen. A pile of plates fitted into each other as if they had been made only to fit each other. The "Trencher" pattern, the concave rim, and

SAUCEBOAT, WEDGWOOD'S QUEEN'S WARE.

other varieties had the same adaptation. The exportation to the Continent was enormous. Hosts of imitators sprang up, all making Queen's ware. Wedgwood did not patent his improvements. He relied solely upon the superiority of his productions. The admirable teapots were so shaped that the lids fitted and did not fall off, the spouts poured easily, the handles were comfortable. With the other pieces it was the same—no leaking from the lips of kettles or jugs. Then, too, the ware was light, the colour uniform, the glaze thin, and the general effect clean and refined. It deserved its popularity; but this is *not* the kind of Wedgwood ware which is valued by the collector unless it is decorated by painting of conventional foliage, flowers, etc., or by transfer-

152a

W. ADAMS. BLUE AND WHITE JASPER VASE.

printing in black or red. Sadler & Green's connection with Wedgwood has been noticed. The *Burslem Dialogue* has

WEDGWOOD COFFEE CAN AND SAUCER.   FINE PINK JASPER WARE.

the following:—" Oi'd summut t' doo t' get dahn t' L'rpool wi' eawr caart, at th' tevme as oi fust tayd Mester 'Siah

Wedgut's ware for t' be printed theer. Yu known as hâe ther wur noo black printin' on ware dun i' Boslem i' thoos deys."

WEDGWOOD PLAQUE, "GEORGE PRINCE OF WALES," BY FLAXMAN.

Another kind of decoration is found on some of this ware: that is, a pink lustre from gold, which was used at the end

WEDGWOOD VASE IN THREE-COLOURED JASPER. BLUE AND GREEN, WITH WHITE RELIEFS.
From the Collection of F. Rathbone, Esq. (pp. 153-5).

of the eighteenth century, and was more common later. Gold itself is seldom found, and, when used, the gilding is quite slight. As in Bristol and Worcester porcelain, so with Wedgwood, the pattern is frequently transfer-printed in outline, and with that outline as a guide (not an unimportant one) the enamel colours in the design were painted by hand; more accuracy, less art; more of the machine, less of the man.

2. *Black basaltes ware* or *Egyptian black* is a fine hard

CAMEO OF WEDGWOOD. BLUE AND WHITE JASPER.

BLACK BASALT MEDALLION OF JOSIAH WEDGWOOD, MODELLED BY HACKWOOD.

stoneware or black porcelain, which owes its colour to iron. But it must not be thought that all black basaltes ware is Wedgwood. Turner, Adams, Palmer, Neale, were only a few of the imitators of Wedgwood in this, as in other ware. Before me are two specimens very rich in tone, and smooth with a fine grain just like Wedgwood. One, a sucrier with cover, is marked SPODE, and the other, a vase, has SWANSEA impressed. The decoration consists of raised medallions of classical designs and engine-turned lines, again just like Wedgwood.

WEDGWOOD

Here it is necessary to insist once more on the difference between the "Old Wedgwood" and the "Wedgwood ware." The latter is the useful ware, the ornamental ware forms the former class, so that black basaltes is "Old Wedgwood," yet it is not the valuable type. Certainly in "all black" it has never been the collector's rage. Even the vases in large size of classical shape, decorated with medallions, all in black, have mainly a museum interest. It is quite different when the black background has a lovely cameo in white, undercut, and showing just a shade of black through the thinnest parts of the raised ornament. Plaques such as "The Nymph with Cymbals" are then valuable; so are medallion portraits similarly treated. Wedgwood made services—tea and coffee—in plain black, in black with raised modelled ornament in white; and he, in addition, sometimes decorated them with enamel colours, with slight gilding or silvering. They may be suitable for a museum, but one or two specimens in a collection would be enough. The same remark applies with less force to the "Etruscan," or "encaustic" ware, decorated with unglazed or dry enamel colours, in imitation of the ancient Greek vases. Sometimes another form of decoration is found, which is not nearly so attractive as the white on black—that is, the red on black, or these inverted, black on red. Such pieces are not convincing, though of the two the black on red is the more pleasing. Good examples may be seen in the London museums, and at Nottingham and Birmingham. The British Museum has the Franks Collection; Felix Joseph bequeathed his beautiful old Wedgwood to Nottingham, Sir Richard Tangye lent his to Birmingham. In neither of these museums will be found more than a very few specimens of *bronze ware*, which is amongst the rarest of the black basaltes. Seemingly it was dusted over with a fine metallic bronze before firing. Though rare, this too was imitated, as in the figure of a Triton with a shell horn or cornucopia which has the mark WOOD & CALDWELL

CHAPTER XIX

WEDGWOOD (*continued*)

IT is quite likely that Josiah Wedgwood gets credit for all the pieces that are marked "Wedgwood," though there were many Wedgwoods who may have marked their wares with their own name. Aaron Wedgwood, of Burslem, is mentioned as having made crouch-ware (salt-glaze) in 1690. He is said to have been one of the earliest followers of Elers in making this ware out of common potter's clay and grit from Mow Cop. Abner Wedgwood attested the indentures of Josiah. Carlos Wedgwood was a good thrower employed at the Chelsea works. Gilbert Wedgwood was the grandfather of Aaron Wedgwood mentioned above; he married Mary Burslem, daughter and co-heiress of Thomas Burslem. John Wedgwood was a potter of Burslem, too, and in an early chapter a puzzle jug, signed "John Wedgwood, 1691," was given as an illustration. Moses Wedgwood was the brother of Aaron and Gilbert Wedgwood's fifth son. Ralph Wedgwood (about 1790) was the son of that Thomas Wedgwood whom we have noted as Josiah's partner for the useful Wedgwood ware. He was a man of great ability, and at his "Hill Works" he took out at least three patents. His style was "Wedgwood and Co." In 1796 he removed to Yorkshire and commenced business again at Ferrybridge. He died at Chelsea in 1837. Richard Wedgwood was a son of the first Aaron Wedgwood. He was a potter at Burslem "in the middle of the town," and made stoneware. Samuel Wedgwood and Sarah Wedgwood were potters, the latter—Josiah's cousin—married him in 1764. Thomas Wedgwood we have already noted as being Josiah's partner in 1759.

WEDGWOOD

Dr. Thomas Wedgwood has been mentioned as a successful potter. He made black and mottled ware. William Wedgwood had a factory at Yearsley about 1700, to which the old distich refers,—

> "At Yearsley there was pancheons made
> By Willie Wedgwood, that young blade."

He belonged to the Burslem Wedgwood family.

Reverting to the composition of the other wares in their order, we take next:

3. *Red ware (rosso antico) terra-cottas, etc.* Wedgwood imitated Elers' ware, but we cannot say that his imitation was successful; it never reached the wax-like fineness of the Elers' red ware in colour and grain. The ferruginous clay of Bradwell was carefully levigated, passed through fine hair sieves, then artificially evaporated, so that a kind of red unglazed stoneware, in imitation of the red pottery of Japan, was successfully copied. Wedgwood used another process for his terra-cotta in many colours, red in combination with buff, cane, chocolate, cream, bamboo, grey, green, red with black reliefs, and *vice versa*. It should be remembered that the earlier cameos, such as seals and gems, were made of terra-cotta body, but it was nearly white, and also that some of the other terra-cottas appear in cameos; in fact,

LAMP, BLACK BASALTES, WEDGWOOD.

some of the so-called terra-cottas approach very nearly to fine white semi-porcelain or stoneware. A cane-coloured sugar basin with white figures in relief in the writer's posses-

WEDGWOOD MEDALLION, PEGASUS AND THE MUSES, GREEN GROUND, PINK BORDER, WHITE RELIEFS.

sion seems to be of this terra-cotta, as it has none of the qualities of the jasper ware, although it is marked with what Miss Meteyard describes as the mark of a fine period—Wedgwood, o 3 3, irregularly arranged.

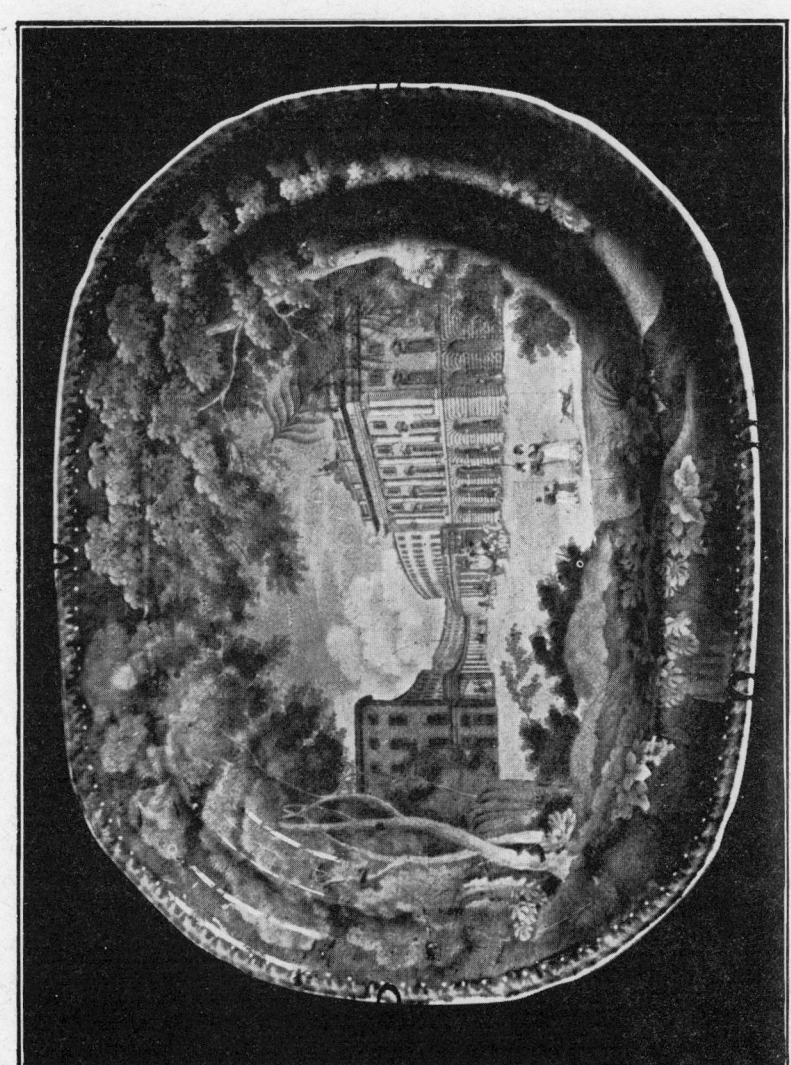

W. ADAMS. VIEW OF REGENT QUADRANT, PICCADILLY.

WEDGWOOD

4. *White semi-porcelain or stoneware.* This differed from the white terra-cotta in being of a waxy smoothness, and in having, as its name implies, a translucency in the very thin parts. This, too, was used for some cameos and medallions and for the slabs or plinths, either square or round, of his variegated vases. It is quite possible that many of the so-called poor medallions are made of this white semi-porcelain upon coloured terra-cotta. The objection to its use was found in its

JASPER WARE. WEDGWOOD NECKLACE AND BRACELET.

warping and cracking in the kiln. It differed from the jasper ware, which was a later invention. Jasper had barytes in its composition, and this barytes when used in excess produced an unpleasant chalky whiteness.

5. *Variegated ware.* We have already seen how solid agate ware was made by Whieldon, who blended different coloured clays in bands. Wedgwood improved this process, and made two forms of agate or marbled ware, one solid as in the solid agate ware of Whieldon, and the other cream ware mottled, spangled or marbled to imitate stones. In both

cases the surface colouring showed bands, stripes, twists, and waves; but the difference was that whereas the one was on the surface, the solid agate-ware pattern was in the clay itself. This variegated ware was perhaps good for decorative purposes, but at the best it was only a poor imitation of the real onyx or jasper or marble. Though Wedgwood's work was an improvement on anything of this kind before attempted, we must classify this ware as being merely

JASPER WARE PLAQUE, BY FLAXMAN.
"VIVE L'ENTENTE CORDIALE."

interesting and not very valuable. It is well to note, too, that both kinds were glazed, and the ornaments and reliefs were often in gilt.

6. *Jasper ware.* It is by this most valuable and artistic of all the wares ever produced in England that Wedgwood is distinguished above all other potters. In the first place the body was new, new ingredients were used to form a new paste in which barytes composed more than a half of its percentage, being no less than 57·1 per cent., and barium carbonate very nearly 5 per cent., so that the clay was only just about one-quarter of the whole body. The natural result of this combination was a clay with a yellow tinge,

which was overcome by adding a little cobalt for the white jasper. The coloured jasper was treated just in two ways, as we have described in variegated ware; that is, it was either coloured through by means of metal oxides used as stains for the whole body of the clay, or the white surface was covered by a "dip" colour. Solid jasper was so hard and so dense that it could easily be polished on the wheel. Jasper ware was only used for a short period, about 1774 or 1775 till 1780, when Bentley died. Solid jasper usually has the W. & B. or the "WEDGWOOD & BENTLEY" mark. When jasper dip was invented the white jasper body received a surface wash only of cobalt or other metallic oxides; the seven resulting colours have already been mentioned. "WEDGWOOD" only, appears on the jasper dip.

In some few cases a curious variation may be observed where the pale blue solid jasper has received a wash of the same colour, but deeper. This result is sometimes seen in cameos and medals; so in vases, one colour is found in front and another at the back of the vase. If we imagine, then, a plaque with a plain surface coloured by jasper

LARGE WEDGWOOD PLAQUE, SHOWING CAMEO WARE ON FLAT SURFACE.

dip, we can easily understand that when the reliefs in white were applied the colour could often be seen through the thinner parts of the applied ornament. A striking feature of many of the finest of these medals is the undercutting, which must have been done after the removal of the block by which the white medallion was applied; so, too, many parts of the drapery through which the undercolour appears

JASPER WARE: WEDGWOOD PLAQUE, GREEN GROUND, "AN OFFERING TO PEACE."

seem to be cut as if a tool were used for that purpose on the wet or dry clay before firing. The marks of Wedgwood will be given later, but it is interesting to note that some pieces have holes bored in the backs which were made to remove surplus substance in the piece itself, so as to prevent warping, to aid firing, and to avoid shrinkage. These holes are often found at the backs of cameos, medals, plaques and tablets. Some pieces not marked have these holes.

Some few hints may be of use to collectors:—First, the surface of old Wedgwood is always perfectly smooth and wax-like, there are no air bubbles or holes, and it may be said to be perfectly homogeneous and uniform throughout. Some portrait medallions in very high relief are exceedingly rare and very valuable. Amongst these may be mentioned Robert Boyle, Sir Joseph Banks, Benjamin Franklin, Sir William Hamilton, J. Lock, Sir Isaac Newton, Joseph Priestley, Dr. Solander. All these are about $10\frac{1}{4}$ in. by $7\frac{1}{2}$. We notice in this connection the prices received by Flaxman

OLD WEDGWOOD JARDINIÈRE. WHITE ORNAMENT ON CHOCOLATE GROUND.

for modelling these and similar portraits: Sir Joseph Banks, 42s.; Dr. Solander, Lord Chatham, Rousseau, and Sterne, 16s. each; Dr. Herschel, 42s.; Captain Cook, Dr. Johnson, C. Jenkinson, the same price; Governor Hastings, £3 3s; Mr. and Mrs. Meerman, £5 5s. Other portraits by Flaxman were Sir Joshua Reynolds, Josiah Wedgwood and his wife, and Sir William Hamilton. The most delightful and pleasing works of Etruria were the three-colour cameos with classical subjects, such as the

"Sale of Cupids"; they are called three-colour, although usually there are two colours with white. These little plaques are about 2½ in. by 1¼, oblong in shape with the corners taken off. Vases in jasper ware with *bas reliefs* are very much sought after, and secure good prices. The first of these were produced about 1781, though the finest period was 1786–95.

In 1781, the year after Bentley had died at Turnham Green, that part of the stock in the joint names of Wedgwood and Bentley was sold by Christy and Ansell. The prices paid for what we should now term " Old Wedgwood " were comparatively small. The chief purchasers were Flaxman, who bought largely, as did Sir Harbord Harbord, the Duke of Devonshire, Sir Thomas Rumbold, and others. Black seals fetched 8s. a dozen, black busts 30s. to 70s. each, and vases in imitation of marbles only 40s. to 60s. the set of five. The remarkable feature of this sale was the small prices fetched by large cameo medallions. From 15s. to 30s. were the usual prices paid, whilst teapots fetched 42s. a dozen. Compare these recent prices :—

	£	s.	d.
Black basaltes ware :—			
Vases and covers, pair with palm tops, forming taper-holders, supported by three partly draped classical figures on triangular plinths, 13 in. high, on circular marble plinths	30	9	0
Mercury on socle, 18 in. high	16	5	0
Vases with covers, pair, large	4	17	6
Bust of Fletcher, the dramatist, 15½ in. high	4	15	0
Jasper ware :—			
Cabaret with children and cupids in relief in white on *Pink* ground, consisting of teapot and cover, sugar basin and bowl, cup and saucer, and an oval plateau	21	10	0
Plaque, the Medusa in high relief, Wedgwood & Bentley	42	0	0
Plaque, large, of scroll foliage and convolvulus flowers, blue and white ; 29¼ in. by 5⅝ in.	33	0	0
Portraits, blue and white :—			
Sir Joseph Banks, grey-blue, and Matthew Prior, Wedgwood & Bentley	3	3	0
Lord Hood and Solander, Wedgwood & Bentley	8	17	6
Jonas Hanway and Joseph II., Emperor of Germany	5	15	0

OLD WEDGWOOD VASE. WHITE ORNAMENT ON BLUE GROUND.

	£	s.	d.
Chas. Townley, original black frame	8	8	0
Mr. and Mrs. Meerman	8	8	0
Marquis and Marchioness of Buckingham	15	10	0
Mrs. Siddons (pale blue)	30	0	0
Portraits on coloured grounds :—			
Bergman, green ground	3	3	0
J. Stuart, celadon ground	6	15	0
Sir Joseph & Lady Banks, a pair on yellow ground	25	10	0
Vases, pair blue and white with reliefs of women and children, white plinths 8½ in. high	20	10	0
Plaque, Duke of York, blue jasper, in ormolu frame	18	18	0
Plaque, Lady Auckland, dark blue and white, in gilt frame	10	10	0
Plaques, pair of blue jasper, by Wedgwood & Bentley, with figures in relief	21	0	0
Plaques, five dark blue, with subjects of "A Sacrifice to Flora," nymphs sacrificing, and figures emblematic of the Thames and the Severn, framed	67	4	0
Plaque, oblong, of blue-and-white jasper, with subject of a sacrifice in relief, 10 in. by 24½ in., framed	220	10	0
Wedgwood ware :—			
Tea service, French, with flowers in blue, red, and gold, consisting of teapot, cover and stand, sugar bowl and cover, basin, cream jug, three plates, a shaped dish, fourteen teacups, eleven coffee-cups, and fourteen saucers	8	0	0

It is very interesting to learn how the plaster casts were prepared, from which the models were taken. The design was usually made in wax of a reddish tint, and the medallion was then struck down on a slate bed. These formed the original subjects, from which the plaster casts were taken in intaglio. The cameos were exact reproductions of the original designs taken from the casts, and afterwards modelled and cut. The work of preparing and modelling a black basaltes bust, for instance, took about a fortnight. Haskins & Grant did the cast work for Wedgwood at a price varying from 6s. to £2 2s. for single objects, and £3 3s. for sets of four or five bas-reliefs.

The modellers were notable men; amongst them was Webber, who became Wedgwood's manager in 1782, after the death of Bentley. He modelled amongst other works the following bas-reliefs: Triumph of Mars; Cupid drawing his Dart; Apollo and Daphne; A Sacrifice to Hymen; A Sacrifice to Concordia; Hope Addressing Peace; Labour and Plenty. He also did vases, cups, chimneypieces. Flaxman, whom we have before noted as working for Wedgwood and Bentley in 1775, in addition to the portraits already given, modelled bas-reliefs—Muses and Apollo; Hercules and the Lion; Hercules and the Boar; Hercules and Cerberus; Bacchus and Ariadne; Jupiter; June; Juno; Justice and Hope; the Four Seasons. For a set of the English poets he received 10s. 6d. each in 1777. Other works of his were: A Sacrifice to Pan; Greek Heads; Dancing Hours; Marriage of Psyche; Apotheosis of Homer; Apotheosis of Virgil; Triumph of Ariadne; Homer and Hesiod; An Offering to Flora; A Bacchanalian Sacrifice. Two celebrated statuettes of Voltaire and Rousseau were modelled by Keeling, who was in Wedgwood's employ for many years.

In 1783 Flaxman was paid at the rate of a guinea a day. We find three bas-reliefs took him three days, and for his work he was paid three guineas. But with increased fame as a modeller came increased charges; for

WEDGWOOD BLACK BASALTES BUST OF THE MADONNA.

some models he received as much as £23. That price was paid for the model of Hercules in the Hesperian Gardens. The " Mercury Uniting the Hands of England and France " (p. 162) cost Wedgwood £13 13s. for modelling. It must be remembered that much of the modelling attributed to Flaxman was really the work of some of the Italian modellers, of whom the chief were: Dalmazzoni, John De Vaere, who afterwards succeeded Webber as manager of the ornamental works; Pacetti, Angelini, Fratoddi, Mangiarotti, Manzolini, Cades. The last two worked in Rome.

In 1790, Wedgwood's sons, John, Josiah, and Thomas, became his partners, with Thomas Byerley, and the name of the firm was Josiah Wedgwood, Sons, and Byerley. In 1793 Wedgwood retired, and died two years later. On the tablet erected to his memory in the chancel of the church at Stoke-upon-Trent are these words :—

" Sacred to the Memory of
JOSIAH WEDGWOOD, F.R.S., S.A.,
of Etruria, in this County,
Born in August, 1730, died January 3rd, 1795,
Who converted a rude and inconsiderable manufacture
into an elegant Art
And an important part of National
Commerce."

Before leaving Wedgwood ware, it will be well just to take one or two points which should be made clear. Take Wedgwood's inlaid ware, for example. Very little stress is laid upon this, although he made a variety of articles in it. The process was to impress a pattern on the wet clay from a metal runner. This pattern was filled up with a different coloured clay, and the surface was then turned or scraped level, after the style of the " Saint-Porchaire " ware, sometimes called " Henri Deux " ware, which is among the rarest faience ever made. To show the value of this French inlaid ware, we may note that a candlestick, which cost Mr. Fountain £1,000 more than a century ago, realised the enormous sum of £3,675 when offered at the sale of his collection. Wedgwood inlaid ware will one day be valuable. The firm also made Parian ware, but that was later, about 1848. The best modellers were employed for this ware, such as Wyon and Beattie. But Parian, whether Wedgwood, Minton or Copeland, beautiful as it is, has never been in demand. Still later, in 1858, we have the works of Emile Lessore, whose paintings are so fine that eventually they may reach a very high price.

WEDGWOOD BLUE AND WHITE JASPER.
From the British Museum.

The story of the "Portland Vase" is well known. At auction in 1787 this glass vase was put up, and Wedgwood bid up to £1,000 for it, but the Duke of Portland promised that if he would not bid further he should have the vase to copy, so the Duke bought it for £1,029, and Wedgwood kept it for twelve months experimentalising, until in 1790 he issued fifty copies at 50 gns. each, marked 1 to 50 in written figures; but £2,500 was the cost of producing the vases, so that Wedgwood's efforts here were to demonstrate

MARK REPRODUCED FROM THE BACK.

his art rather than to realise profit. The body of the vase was black jasper, or a mixture of blue and black, dipped in black. The figures were white, and cut by the engraver to the finest possible finish. The original blocks are still used, and copies of the vase are produced in black, deep blue, or light blue. The "Portland Vase" is now in the Gold Room of the British Museum.

We shall deal more fully with the potters who imitated Wedgwood, either the cream ware, black basaltes, or coloured jasper: W. Adams, Tunstall; R. & J. Baddeley, Shelton; W. Baddeley, Hanley; C. E. Bourne, Denbigh,

Derbyshire; also E. Bourne, Derbyshire; David Dunderdale, Castleford; Hartley, Greens, & Co., Leeds; Lakin & Poole, Hanley; I. Neale, Hanley; Sewells & Donkin, Newcastle-on-Tyne; Tomlinson & Co., Ferrybridge; J. Turner, of Stoke and Lane End; and many others of the Staffordshire Potters. Spode, for instance, copied the black basaltes ware, which was also done at Swansea. In other countries we find that Wedgwood was imitated at Sèvres, where biscuit plaques of blue and white, grey and white, sea-green and white, were made, in imitation of jasper ware. Bas-reliefs were designed by Boizot, and the tinted porcelain was largely used for the decoration of furniture. In Lisbon, jasper ware plaques in imitation of Wedgwood were produced. In Sweden, at Marieberg, it was also copied.

The last point in Wedgwood's work that we need consider is the celebrated green-frog service, made for the Empress Catherine II. of Russia, for the Grenouillère Palace, in which each piece was marked by a painted green frog, not underneath, as stated by Chaffers and others, but in a shield over

WEDGWOOD BLUE AND WHITE JASPER.
South Kensington Museum.

the middle of each of the views. Much misapprehension is caused by the mention of the green frog, and we only need emphasise the point that this splendid service had 1,282 views of the seats of the noblemen and gentlemen of England, and a green frog painted on each piece (*Frontispiece*). Porcelain was not made by Wedgwood himself, but Byerley, in 1808, did produce some Wedgwood porcelain, which showed certain characteristics of Spode, but was not otherwise distinguished, and the manufacture soon ceased.

Prices

It will be interesting to put on record for reference some prices of vases, etc., as sold by Wedgwood. Etruscan and Grecian vases were catalogued from 6s. or 7s. to 30s. (that is the ordinary kind of ware); with elaborate decoration from 18s. to 5 gns.; but the finely painted ones cost a large sum to produce, and were sold for 30 gns. or more. These prices are taken from the old invoices 1768–9. The 10-in. vases, for instance, with four serpents and festoons with vine pattern, were sold for £1 each; black urn-shaped vases, 12½ in. high, £1 4s.; blue vases, serpent-handled on marbled plinth with gold decoration, £1 11s. 6d.; plain marbled vases without plinths, 7s. 6d.; Etruscan vases ornamented with husks, 14½ in. high, 2 gns.; white biscuit vases, 24 by 11 in., 3 gns.; variegated marbled vases decorated with satyrs' heads and gilt ornaments, 1 gn.; vases with blue ground and shell shoulders, 10s. 6d. Bronzed vases ranged from 10s. 6d. to 2 gns.; those having a pebbled ground, satyrs' heads and horns, were listed at 2 gns.; Etruscan vases, 13½ in. high, with handles or shoulders in festoons of drapery, and covers, 2 gns.; others with leafage on neck, no handles, 2 gns.; smaller ones of same design, 1 gn.; Etruscan, with goats' heads and drapery in festoons, 3 gns. Others with a medallion of " The Sacrifice," £2 12s. 6d.; Etruscan dolphin-handled ewers, 2 gns.; Etruscan vases, 19 in. high by 10½ in., 4 gns.; Etruscan with festoons of drapery and laurel frieze, £2 12s. 6d.; vases with grey marbled base and gilt ornaments, 12s. 6d. to 18s.; others, blue, with satyrs' heads, laurel festoons and gilt ornaments, 12 in. high, £1 12s.

A comparison of these prices with those given previously as sale prices will prove that the value of old Wedgwood has not maintained a steady high level, though the tendency is always upwards. About the middle of the nineteenth century original copies of the Portland vase were sold for about £20, but the recent auction prices have averaged £160 to

WEDGWOOD BLACK EGYPTIAN OR BASALTES WARE. VASE SUPPORTED BY THREE LARGE FIGURES.

WEDGWOOD GREEN AND WHITE JASPER.

£180. The fine white upon black ware appears to be much more esteemed by collectors than even the Portland vases; but any fine old Wedgwood is worth securing, and collectors may be sure that it will be much more difficult and costly to obtain in future. Owners of good Wedgwood are advised to hold it, because the time will come when people will realise that, as Palissy, by many years of diligent research and patience, gave to the world the enamel which made his ware famous, so Wedgwood, by his intense devotion to his art and his determination to issue nothing but the best, has left a precious possession to the English nation, which for all time will keep old Wedgwood in the highest estimation.

FINE WEDGWOOD VASE.

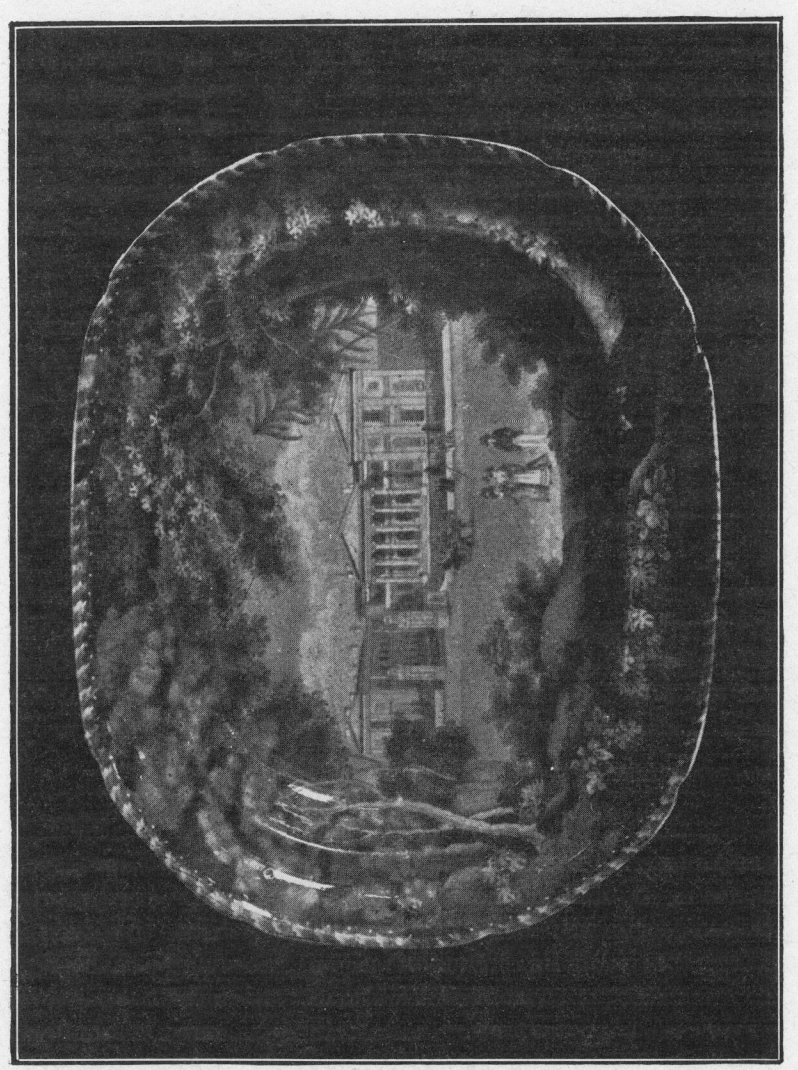

W. ADAMS. VIEW OF BLENHEIM PALACE.

176 a

CHAPTER XX

OLD WEDGWOOD MARKS

MR. Rathbone, whose gallery is in Alfred Place, South Kensington, W., has the finest knowledge not alone of marks, but of all the characteristics which distinguish "Old Wedgwood." Those who wish to buy really good pieces cannot do better than pay a visit to him. Our thanks are due to him for several illustrations.

The word "Wedgwood," as we shall see later, was always used as an impressed mark, and the "O's" in the stamp of the older pieces are always much rounder than in the later ones. It will be easily understood that the constant use of a stamp would tend to thicken the sides of the O's. Sometimes the letters "T.B.O." and "T.T.B.O." are used. "T." stands for top, "T.T." for tip-top, and "B.O." for biscuit oven, so that these letters were an instruction to the packer of the kiln.

The following additional notes are worthy of consideration. Every mark was impressed, except on the porcelain, the "and" was short "&"—"Wedgwood & Bentley," never "Wedgwood and Bentley." The good period has the mark clearly and evenly stamped, and except on glazed pottery and Queen's ware it is easily deciphered. Inscribed marks, letters, and figures are often found. Many of these are only workmen's marks, single letters, as H, G, and O; or pattern numbers, as 275, 496, usually scratched. Other marks indicate size, such as are found on teapots, etc.—18; 24; 4 x 4. "K" may be met with on busts by Keeling, and "W. H." on others which were the work of William Hackwood; o.3.3 has been found upon Wedgwood specimens of good quality teaware, salt cellars, etc. Pieces marked with O T W, A L X, and other three-letter signatures, are comparatively modern, being first used in 1846. Other inscribed marks refer to processes in manufacturing, as "L. Tub," "E. Wash," etc. Old vases, perfect pieces, noted for the beauty and accuracy of reproduction in blue or other colours, and jasper ware, are usually marked with "Wedgwood" only. The stamp, as shown in our marks, seems to be indiscriminately used as far as regards the size, for a big stamp may often be found on a small piece, as in the "Etruria" plaque already used as an illustration, and, as shown, the mark was $1\frac{1}{8}$ in. in length. As long as the piece was stamped, it seemed to be quite a matter of indifference as to the size of the stamp.

Taking the marks in order, the first is modern, the second, the earliest mark, is quite uneven. Each letter was stamped separately, but only a few specimens of this mark are known. The next group of three marks seems to belong to "Wedgwood" up to the time of Bentley's partnership, 1768–80. The circular stamp, without the inner and outer ring, and without Etruria, was the earlier circular stamp. The next mark, without the inner and outer lines, was applied as a wafer or bat, and may be found fixed in the corner inside the plinth of basaltes vases, busts, candelabra, and other large specimens. The well-known circular mark with inner and outer lines is often found round the screw by which the base of the basaltes vases was fitted up. The group of Wedgwood and Bentley marks may frequently be met with impressed on granite and black vases, busts, figures, plaques, medallions, and cameos, from the largest tablet to the minutest cameo, and also upon useful ware of the period. Intaglios were often marked with catalogue numbers, as in the one given 356. Very small intaglios are sometimes found marked "W. and B.," or with a number only. The oval W. and B. mark is met with on the chocolate-and-white intaglio portraits. After Bentley died, the "Wedgwood" mark given was again used, and was continued for a time after the death of Wedgwood. The dated mark of Josiah Wedgwood is the mark of Josiah the younger; the use of "Etruria" with "Wedgwood" dates from early in the nineteenth century, from 1815. The Wedgwood porcelain mark, printed in red, blue, or gold, was used, probably, from 1808 to 1815. The mark last on the list, varied in size, is still used, and the modern mark for china and tiles is placed first :—

WEDGWOOD
& BENTLEY
WEDGWOOD
& BENTLEY
Wedgwood
& Bentley
Wedgwood
& Bentley

Wedgwood

WEDGWOOD
Wedgwood
Wedgwood

Wedgwood
& Bentley
356

Wedgwood
WEDGWOOD

JOSIAH WEDGWOOD
Feb ℮ or 2nd Feby 1805

WEDGWOOD
ETRURIA
WEDGWOOD
ETRURIA
Wedgwood
Etruria
WEDGWOOD
(printed in red, blue or gold)

WEDGWOOD
WEDGWOOD

CHAPTER XXI

THE STORY OF THE WEDGWOOD "FINDS."

WE are able to give most interesting information regarding the "finds" at Etruria. Thanks to the kindness of Mr. Cecil Wedgwood, we give further particulars, which, as far as we know, have not before appeared in book form. The years 1905 and 1906 marked an epoch in the history of Wedgwood and its productions. Two momentous incidents occurred: first, the notable "finds" of old and experimental pieces; second, as a result of the first, the formation of a museum.

The present directors, whose courtesy we warmly acknowledge, are lineal descendants of the illustrious old potter. They had noted, with keen perception, that numerous interesting pieces were distributed over the works, and they consequently formed the resolution to bring them all together; hence the order was given for the collection of the old pattern pieces, and other fine old specimens, which had during long years accumulated, not alone in the present workshops, but also in the many old workshops, and in some unused rooms.

A further decision was made that these specimens should be stored in a place of safety, until order and method could be instituted in their classification, with a view to their further use in furnishing a museum. The result far exceeded expectations, for the "finds" included some hundreds of valuable basaltes and jasper vases, many original wax models of well-known subjects, numerous patterns ranging from the 1770 period onwards, which were unique in the fact that they were undoubtedly the shapes and decoration carried

THE STORY OF THE WEDGWOOD "FINDS" 181

out under Wedgwood's personal supervision. Amongst the more important and interesting "finds" were "the trials and experiments." Many of these probably dated back to the "Whieldon" partnership in 1754, when Wedg-

CHOICE OF HERACLES.

BACCHANALIAN TRIUMPH.

wood was busily experimentalising with the agate and crystalline body, or perhaps later, with the well-known jasper, which was invented about 1776, and which attained its great perfection probably ten years later. It was in 1773 that the fine white terra-cotta, of great beauty and delicacy, was discovered, which preceded the invention of the jasper ware. This became, by constant care and improvement, the most beautiful of all Wedgwood's productions. He pronounced it absolutely the best.

The " trials and experiments " were found in two old battered crates which had remained, unthought of and uncared for, in an out-of-the-way corner of one of the rooms, and of which no one knew the contents. These were carefully opened. It was found that practically the whole of the experimental works of Josiah Wedgwood were once again to see the light of day, and to form an object-lesson the importance of which must be invaluable to the student, who may be able to realise its full signification.

Collectors and connoisseurs are equally delighted with the specimens, now displayed in the fine museum, and they are amazed at the amount of time and labour that must have been bestowed upon the jasper ware before it reached its " absolute " state: thousands of carefully tabulated results of trials of the various coloured jasper in cameos, intaglios, portrait medallions, agate, etc., each one carefully noted with the number, and in many instances with abbreviated letters, showing where they were to be placed in the oven for firing, so as to secure the exact degree of heat for their perfect development. We repeat that in the firing " T.T.B.O." indicated the tip-top of the biscuit oven; " T.B.O.," the top of the biscuit oven, where the heat was most intense; " M.B.O.," the middle of the biscuit oven.

The first firing of most of the pieces was known as an " easy " firing, and was regulated so as to fix the shape. The second firing was " T.B.O." firing, used with the object of developing the colour and face; perhaps the best definition of " face " of the jasper ware is that it is like the surface of an eggshell.

It may be here interesting to note that in the ordinary course of manufacture it is often necessary that it should be passed through the oven twice—firstly in an " easy " place, so that the piece shall become set, preparatory to the second

THE STORY OF THE WEDGWOOD "FINDS"

and final fire, which is a more severe one, and which is necessary for the development of the colour, and also of the beautiful surface of the white cameo.

All these details help us to a fuller appreciation of the character of the master potter. Some later writers have shown a tendency to decry his works; yet from the "trials and experiments" we learn that Wedgwood was gifted with that perseverance which, if it is not true genius, often attains results infinitely superior to the sparkling efforts of the man who has no lasting power. Hence, from the initial stages of any particular "body," or, similarly, any particular colour, it is quite possible to trace the proof of his skill, his unlimited tenacity, and his final success so thoroughly deserved.

HERACLES IN THE GARDEN OF THE HESPERIDES.

Many of the colours and effects produced are very charming; in some instances they are known as "chance" colours—"chance" from the fact that the uncontrollable vagaries of the fire played a very important part in the ultimate beauty of the product, though in its early stages temporary defects may have been found. But Wedgwood laboured on until he had succeeded in securing the exact ingredients for both paste and colour; until he was able to produce the cameos so consistently that the gold and silversmiths, the steel-workers and the cabinet-makers of the latter part of the eighteenth century all found the advantages of using the fine cameos of Wedgwood, in conjunction with their own artistic designs.

Mr. J. A. Austin, whom Mr. C. Wedgwood was good enough to send to see me with regard to this information, was also able to give some interesting details relating to the impressed marks on the earthenware. The three-letter marks were first used in 1846. The first two letters of the three-letter mark were for use of the workman, and were always subject to change, and the third letter always signifies the year. The alphabet for the third letter has been used twice since the letter A marked 1846.

The ten years that have elapsed since 1897 bring us to the letter " J." Associated with this J a new mark for the cycle has been adopted. As we have seen, two cycles have passed, and the third cycle is now in progress. In 1907 and 1908, the first mark is a figure " 3," for the cycle, the second is a letter indicating the workman, and the third letter indicates the year. For 1910 the fourth letter is M which is the thirteenth letter in the third cycle of marks.

Since the formation of the Museum in the Etruria Works many distinguished visitors and collectors from all parts of the world have visited it. Of these, many were purchasers of modern specimens of Wedgwood, which are now in their possession, and of which they are none the less proud because similar pieces are shown in the museum. We want to rouse national enthusiasm for purely British art.

On the next page we show sketches of four fine plaques, two of which are given in our illustrations at the end of the book.

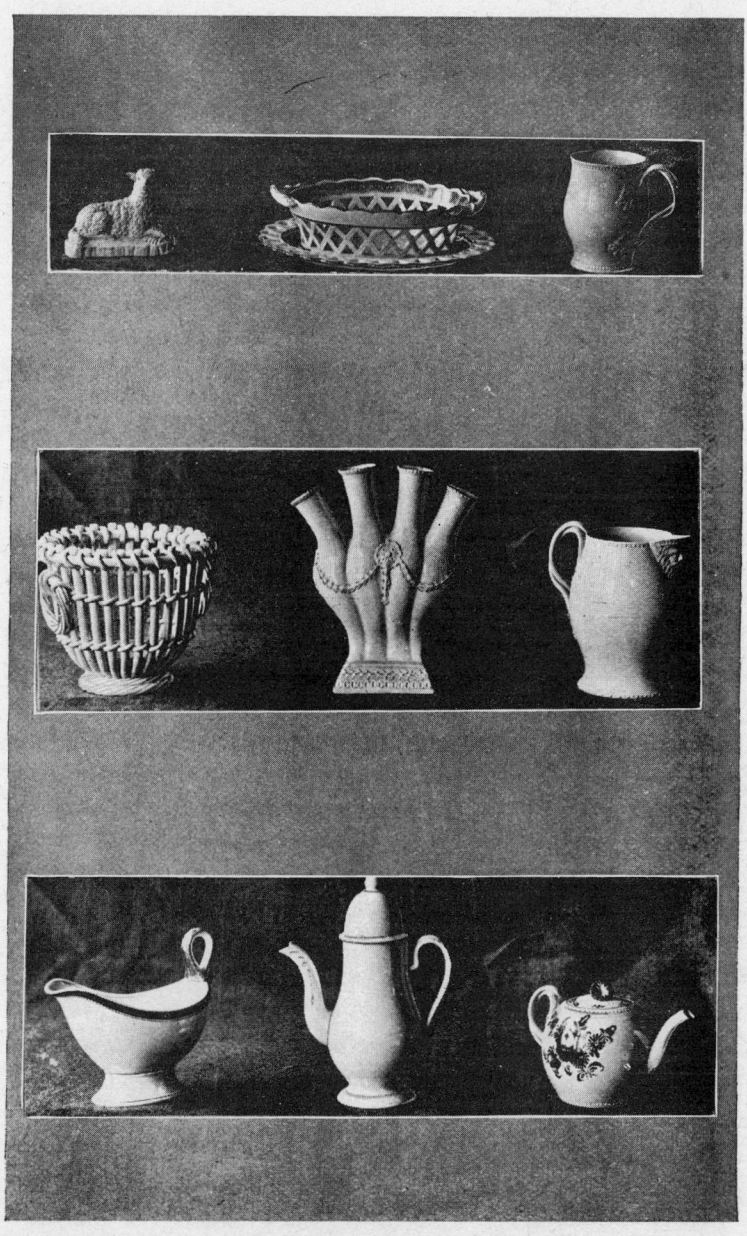

LEEDS WARE.
From Mr. A. M. Broadley's Collection.

A SENATOR.

AN APOTHEOSIS.

ENDYMION.

DIANA.

CHAPTER XXII

WEDGWOOD AND HIS RIVALS

The Rivals of Wedgwood or his Imitators, Which ?

NATURALLY the success of the great potter stirred up his contemporaries in the district to try to produce the same kind of ware. Chief among the imitators were John Turner, W. Adams, Henry Palmer, I. Neale. Whilst not proposing to deal at any great length with these, it is necessary to know who imitated Wedgwood so well that frequently, if it were not for the absence of marks, the specimens might be accepted as true Wedgwood ware.

John Turner

John Turner worked at Stoke as a potter up to 1756, removed to Lane End 1762, and died in 1786. He was a clever potter, apart and aside from his imitative work, and amongst his productions were fine jugs in stoneware and beautiful jasper ware in blue and white, which got very close indeed to the standard of Wedgwood. But there are differences. The body is different—being much nearer being true porcelain than Wedgwood ware. It showed a remarkably fine grain. Next, the colour was different: instead of being pure blue it was usually too purple or too green. Turner made very good statuettes or figures in black basaltes, and busts also in the same material, some of these being of very fine quality. A few are found marked " TURNER " or " TURNER & CO.," impressed or stamped in the paste. The second mark indicates the period when Abbott joined the firm, which was then described as

WEDGWOOD AND HIS RIVALS 187

Turner & Abbott; and later Turner's sons John and William were associated with him, and the business continued till 1803. Turner's cream ware and cane-coloured stoneware were very good in modelling and decoration; the necks and

JOHN WILKES. STAFFORDSHIRE, BURSLEM, C. 1765.

BENJAMIN FRANKLIN. STAFFORDSHIRE, R. WOOD, JUN.

handles of the jugs may be recognised by being coated with chocolate-coloured glaze, and sometimes they are found mounted in silver for ordinary use, showing that they had a distinction of their own apart from any imitation of

Wedgwood. Turner's busts were not confined to black basaltes, but may be found in cream colour, on black plinths. These are not imitations at all. With regard to the paste or body used by Turner, this had Cornish clay in

WESLEY. STAFFORDSHIRE, 1790.   WHITFIELD. STAFFORDSHIRE, 1790.

its composition, which accounts for the fine texture of the jasper ware.

William Adams

William Adams was a pupil and friend of Wedgwood. He had a factory at Tunstall, and, in addition to the ordinary ware made by all the potters, he manufactured jasper ware, beginning it in 1787. He died in 1805. Several generations of

Adamses, and several branches of the family from the middle of the seventeenth century till the present time, have been potters at Stoke-upon-Trent, Cobridge, and Burslem. The advertisement date claimed for the origin of the works at Tunstall is 1657. There were three William Adamses, of whom the Tunstall one was the chief imitator of Wedgwood. His productions included jasper ware, cream-coloured ware, and china glazed ware. In 1786 the firm was William Adams & Co. By comparison, here again, Adams only falls very slightly below Wedgwood in some of his jasper

DEEP BLUE PRINTED PLATE, 1820 PERIOD.

ware, but the Tunstall products were usually unmarked, and Wedgwood is almost invariably marked. The value of fine Adams ware is shown by the following:—A plaque of "Diana resting with her Dogs after the Chase" fetched under the hammer £171. The marks are W. ADAMS; W.A.; W.A. & S.

We received a very interesting letter from Messrs. William Adams & Co., Greenfield and Greengates Potteries, Tunstall, Staffordshire, as a result of our note on William Adams, the old Staffordshire potter. In the booklet which was kindly forwarded to us, the following information is given, which may be of interest to our readers, and we acknowledge with thanks the privilege of using the illustrations of this chapter.

One of the oldest names in the Staffordshire Potteries is that of Adams. No fewer than twelve persons having the name of William Adams have been occupied in producing Staffordshire pottery. The early history of the present firm shows that, in 1617, a William Adams was a potter, and his father Nycolas Adams, who flourished in the reign of "Good Queen Bess," and was buried in the church of Burslem in 1568, owned both a pottery and a colliery. The most noted potters of this family were William Adams, of Greengates, 1745-1805, the famous Staffordshire potter and founder of the Greengates Potteries, Tunstall; and his cousin, William Adams, of Stoke-upon-Trent and Tunstall, 1772-1829.

AN 18TH-CENTURY BLUE-AND-WHITE JASPER CUP, WITH SHEFFIELD-PLATE RIM. DR. SIDEBOTHAM COLLECTION.

The present head of the firm, William Adams, is ninth in direct descent from the eminent old master potter. In 1657, John Adams built and founded the Brick House Potteries, which, a little more than a hundred years later, were let to the famous Josiah Wedgwood for some ten years, when the heir of the Adams family was a minor. The old William Adams made jasper ware having a blue ground with classical figures in relief, and an unglazed or matt surface. He also made fine stoneware, black basaltes, blue painted and printed ware, and was, as we have seen, not alone a formidable rival of Josiah Wedgwood, but of John Turner, another good potter of the eighteenth century. The original Adams jasper ware ceased to be made when the son of William Adams died, in 1820, but during the last twenty years it has been revived by the family. The ware is made at the original factory and produced on the lines of the original recipes and from many of the finely carved models which have been preserved.

Chaffers, in his " Marks and Monograms on Pottery and Porcelain," could scarcely have given higher praise than he

BUSINESS CARD OF THE FAMOUS STAFFORDSHIRE POTTER, USED FROM 1780 TO ABOUT 1810.

does to the beauty and quality of the early productions of Adams; and other writers, such as Professor Church, Litchfield, and Rathbone, speak very highly of them. The biography of W. Adams was written in 1904 by W. Turner, F.S.S. It gives a descriptive criticism of the works of Adams, which were ranged under various headings, such as transfer-printed ware, enamel cream ware, Burslem Greengates fine stoneware, plaques, vases, medallions, etc., in jasper ware. The original Adams jasper ware was made at the time when Wedgwood was producing his jasper ware, hence the query at the head of our present chapter, " Rivals or imitators, Which ? "

The Adams pieces in public collections such as the

British, Victoria and Albert, and English provincial museums, including Tunstall, compare very favourably with any made at about the close of the eighteenth century, when the Staf-

VASE, 9½ IN., BLUE AND WHITE JASPER UPON POLISHED EGYPTIAN BLACK (BASALTES) BASE. FRITTON COLLECTION. 1790 PERIOD.

A VASE MADE IN THE FAMOUS ADAMS BLUE JASPER, WITH CLASSIC FIGURES IN WHITE RELIEF (LUNA).

fordshire potters reached the very apex of their fame and produced such results as gave them a world-wide reputation. It is said that Adams and Turner were both very

192 a

BOTT'S SHAKESPEARE.   QUEEN CHARLOTTE.
LARGE STAFFORDSHIRE BUSTS.

WEDGWOOD AND HIS RIVALS

careful not to use the designs of other potters, so at the time when they made jasper ware they were supplied with designs from casts from Italian models, and from prints published in England; hence, although it may happen that a few of the designs were similar, most of them were quite different. Adams himself was a clever modeller, and amongst his artists was a Swiss, whose works, dating from 1785, attained great popularity. Many of the original Adams specimens command, as we have shown, specially high prices. The present firm are making every effort to maintain the high reputation which the old potters' work attained in early days. We amend our marks.

List of the more important marks used by the ADAMS firm, Tunstall, Stoke-upon-Trent, since 1770.

Adams & Co.	For Cream ware. Plain and Enamelled, 1770-90.
ADAMS & Co.	Earlier mark used for the Solid Jaspers, 1780 to probably as late as 1790.
ADAMS	Mark used for Printed ware, Fine Stoneware and Jaspers, both surface colour, and Solid Jasper, 1787 to about 1810.
W. ADAMS & Co.	Jaspers, very occasionally.

The above marks are not now employed.

Henry Palmer

Henry Palmer, of Church Works, Hanley, was working as a potter about 1760, and he made jasper ware in imitation of Wedgwood, cream-coloured ware, and a sort of red china, made from fine red clay, which was turned on the lathe and required no glaze. Palmer deliberately set himself to reproduce Wedgwood's productions, for as soon as the new models of "Wedgwood & Bentley" arrived in London they were purchased and sent to Hanley to be copied. It ought to be known that neither the red engined china nor the black basaltes ware were Wedgwood's inventions. He improved the black basaltes in 1762, but it had been known for many years previously, and pieces were continually

COLOURED EARTHENWARE, SIR ISAAC NEWTON. STAFFORDSHIRE, BURSLEM, C. 1780. RALPH WOOD, ENAMEL COLOURS.

HANDEL. STAFFORDSHIRE. RALPH WOOD, JUN.

produced by many potters. Wedgwood acknowledged to Bentley that Palmer's work was very good with regard to the body, shape, and composition; and, he added, "we must proceed, or they will tread on our heels." Palmer and his London partner, Neale, set out next to copy the Etruscan painted vases, which were mostly in basaltes. The painting was done in encaustic colours and then fired. Trying to avoid trouble, the body only was made in Staffordshire, and the painting was done in London. An injunction followed on behalf of the Etruria firm, which was compromised by the acquisition by Palmer of certain rights from

COLOURED EARTHENWARE. TOWN CRIER, BELL AND NOTICE. STAFFORDSHIRE, 1780.   GEOFFREY CHAUCER. RALPH WOOD, JUN. ENAMEL COLOURS.

Wedgwood. Palmer's marks were H. PALMER, or the same in a circle. NEALE AND PALMER marked the period of partnership, which was dissolved in 1766, when Palmer got into difficulties, and from that time to 1777 Neale carried on the factory alone, and with his own mark, I. NEALE, HANLEY, or in a circle. In 1777 Robert Wilson joined the firm, which changed its name and its mark to Neale

& Co. The chief products of this firm were blue and white jasper ware, just like Wedgwood, and green and gold wares. One of their specialities was the manufacture of figures and Toby jugs, of which they sold a great number. A beautiful set of figures of "The Seasons," coloured and gilt, may be seen in Lady Charlotte Schreiber's Collection in the South Kensington Museum.

The Woods, of Burslem.

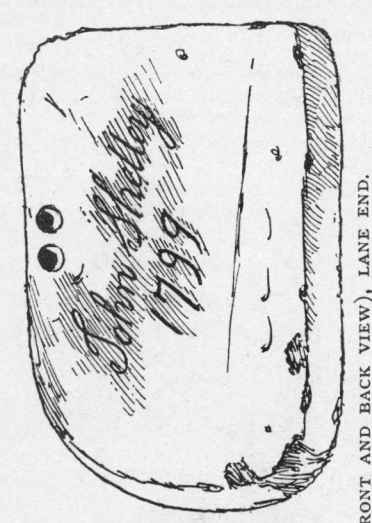

AN OLD STAFFORDSHIRE PLAQUE (FRONT AND BACK VIEW), LANE END.

There is some misconception with regard to this family and the work they did. The father of Ralph and Aaron Wood was Ralph Wood, of Burslem, a miller. Ralph Wood the potter was born in 1716, and died in 1772; he was two years older than his brother, Aaron Wood, also a potter, who was born in 1718 and died in 1783. Ralph Wood, jun., also a potter, was born in 1748 and died in 1797. Enoch Wood, also a potter, was the youngest son of Aaron. He was born in 1759 and died in 1840. So you see there were two potters named Ralph Wood, and the two brothers and the two cousins were engaged in the potteries at Burslem. The Woods were the first to mark specimen productions at their works, but the marking was

WEDGWOOD AND HIS RIVALS

not methodical; some pieces were marked, but by far the larger number of pieces had no mark, and can only be identified by comparison.

R. WOOD.—The mark R. WOOD is generally conceded as the distinguishing mark of the father, whose productions resembled those of Whieldon so closely that we may safely assume that many of the best figures in glaze colours ascribed to Whieldon were really the work of this Wood.

Ra. Wood; Ra. WOOD, BURSLEM.—These two marks with Ra. WOOD are assigned to Ralph Wood, junior. The pieces so marked include some of the finest specimens of old Staffordshire pottery, which for sharpness of modelling,

STAFFORDSHIRE FIGURE. GLAZE COLOURS. RALPH WOOD, SEN.

softness of colouring and glaze, stand in the first class. The coloured glaze was at first applied with a brush, and it is not uncommon to see small portions of the surface without any coloured glaze; the brushwork had not been properly applied. This fault(?) and another which may often be distinguished in the best Whieldon and Wood figures—that is, the running of the glazes into one another—were remedied later, when the son adopted enamel colouring for figures, busts, etc. Not alone was greater accuracy obtained in the effects of the colouring, but a greater range of colours was secured. The Willett Collection in the Brighton Museum gives many instances of these figures, which have generally a very quiet tone. They have been reproduced in France, Germany, and the Potteries with colours so strong and modelling so poor, so lacking in character and sharpness, such a contrast to the highly finished and fine work of the genuine Wood period, as to be comparatively valueless. A few figures, such as "A Pair of Haymakers," 7½ in. high; "Charity," 8 in. high; and "Old Age," are marked R. WOOD. Others, such as "The Vicar and Moses," "The

STAFFORDSHIRE FIGURES.   RALPH WOOD.

Parson and Clerk," "Beckford," "Sir Isaac Newton," "Milton," are marked Ra. WOOD, or Ra. WOOD, BURSLEM.

Aaron Wood was apprenticed to Dr. Thos. Wedgwood in 1731, and he worked for him for five years after his apprenticeship was completed at a wage of 5s. per week; then for seven years he hired himself out to John Mitchell, of Burslem, and after that he started for himself as a potter about 1750. On his death, in 1783, his youngest son, Enoch Wood, took over the pottery. He was a good potter and a skilful modeller. Some of his busts attained a very great popularity, such as that of "John Wesley," which he modelled from life, in 1781. Wesley's religious work had made great headway in Staffordshire, and in connection with it he was a frequent visitor to Enoch Wood, who was not only a potter and modeller, but one of the first collectors of old English pottery, and especially of old Staffordshire. It seems a great pity that when his collection was broken up, in 1835, the nation did not acquire it as a whole, for 182 of the finest pieces went to the Dresden Museum, and although there are some fine specimens in the London museums, the loss sustained by the breaking up of the collection is irreparable.

The specimens marked ENOCH WOOD, or E. WOOD, are excellent in every way, and go far to prove what a skilful artist this Wood was. The large bust of "Shakspeare" was modelled by him, though Bott & Co. produced one almost identical. Other fine specimens are "St. Sebastian," the bust of "Wesley," before referred to, showing an oval tablet at the back bearing the inscription:

VICAR AND MOSES.   RALPH WOOD.

THE REV. JOHN WESLEY, M.A., aged 87; and two later busts of "Wesley" and "Whitfield," with circular tablets at the back and suitable inscriptions: "THE REV. JOHN WESLEY, M.A., died March 2nd, 1791, aged 88. ENOCH WOOD, SCULP., BURSLEM." "THE REV. GEORGE WHITFIELD, died September 30th, 1770, aged 56. ENOCH WOOD, BURSLEM." In 1790, a partner named

J. Caldwell was taken into the firm, and the business was carried on, till 1818, in their joint names, and the mark used was WOOD & CALDWELL.

Good specimens of the "Woods" figures are worth from £5 upwards. The presence of the mark increases the value

THE PARSON AND THE CLERK.
STAFFORDSHIRE.

STAFFORDSHIRE FIGURE.
RALPH WOOD.

about a hundred per cent. Exceptionally rare and fine pieces, however, cannot be judged by this standard. Recently as much as £30 was given for a Toby jug, but it was of the best quality; and the large figure of Milton, 15½ in. high, is not dear at £15. Again we may note that for fine genuine pieces prices have a strong upward tendency, which is not affected by thousands of spurious figures, Toby jugs, etc. To identify the *soft glazes—greens, greys, blues, yellows*—of Whieldon, Wood, and the other old potters, to recognise the glaring attempts to make modern productions look old, is not difficult if you know! The glaze colours are the most valuable.

The Spodes

For many of these notes concerning the early history of Spode at Stoke-upon-Trent we are indebted to the kindness of the proprietors of Copeland China Works, Stoke-upon-Trent. The manufactory was founded by Josiah Spode, the first

STONE CHINA, SPODE.

of that name. There were three Josiah Spodes, each of whom in turn became the proprietor of the pottery. The founder, born in the year 1733, was apprenticed to the firm of Thos. Whieldon, at Fenton, where he had as fellow-apprentices Josiah Wedgwood, W. Greatbach, and other distinguished potters of that period. His remuneration was very small, for in 1749, April 9, Whieldon's account-book reads as follows:—" Hired Siah Spode to give him from this time to Martelmas next 2s. 3d. or 2s. 6d., if he deserves it. The second year 2s. 9d., and the third year 3s. 3d., paid full earnest." This hiring was per week.

After leaving Whieldon's works at Fenton he commenced

to manufacture on his own account in 1754. His ware attained very considerable merit and was mainly cream ware, blue painted, blue printed, old willow pattern, black printed, black Egyptian, etc. He also produced jasper ware, though the marked specimens of this are rare. In the year 1754 the second Josiah Spode was born, who, in due time, acquired the rudiments of potting at his father's small manufactory—which, however, was extended by the acquisition of the pottery at Stoke, previously carried on by Messrs. Banks and Turner. Josiah Spode's name occurs

JUG.   FINE STONEWARE.   SPODE.

amongst the eighty potters who are named in the list of manufacturers of pottery ware in Staffordshire, in 1786, where he is mentioned as one of the six potters at Stoke. Many of the specimens of early Spode are unmarked. The elder Spode died in August, 1797, and his son Josiah, who had previously been taken into partnership by his father, had gained business experience by being sent to London to assist at the London warehouse, which was at that time under the management of William Copeland, a native of Stoke, who had at first travelled with productions of the Stoke works, and when trade became so good as to

WEDGWOOD AND HIS RIVALS

warrant the establishment of a London warehouse, Copeland took charge of it.

At this period the London merchants and shippers were supplied with china from Worcester, Derby, and Caughley, and with earthenware from the Staffordshire and other potteries. Still Spode's trade continued to increase, and the headquarters were removed from Fore Street, Cripplegate, London, to Portugal Street, Lincoln's Inn Fields.

On the death of his father, in 1797, Spode returned to Stoke, leaving his partner Copeland in charge of the London business. He now gave all his attention to the manufacture of his ware, and engaged many good modellers and artists. Henry Daniell, his enameller, introduced, in 1802, the method of ornamenting porcelain in raised and burnished gold, but Spode himself introduced transfer printing on his earthenware. The application of the prints to the ware, and the beautiful light tint of blue in which the pattern was produced, gave results which are to-day much prized by collectors.

In the year 1805 he made a fine opaque porcelain, which enjoyed wide popularity on the Continent as well as in England, as did the beautiful earthenware which, under the general name of "Ironstone China," had such a large sale.

Spode commenced to make porcelain before this. In 1800 he invented a paste, in which bone and felspar figured largely. Perhaps the style of decoration, in which reds, yellows, and dark cobalt-blues predominate, after the style of the old Japanese patterns, are the most popular of the reproductions from the original patterns, which have been widely imitated.

It is interesting to note that the second Josiah Spode made a fortune in his business. Before he died, in July 1827, he had done much to elevate the character of the ware produced at the Potteries, and his earthenware may be said to rival the productions of the best early china manufacturers. W. Copeland, his partner, predeceased him, in 1826, and his son, William Taylor Copeland, who was Lord Mayor of London 1835-6, bought the entire business as a going concern from the executors of the third Josiah Spode in 1833, and ten years later his principal traveller,

Thomas Garrett, became a partner, and from that date till 1847 the title of the firm was Copeland and Garrett. Then the partnership was dissolved, and the business was carried on under the title of W. T. Copeland, late Spode. Twenty years later Alderman Copeland took his four sons into the firm, and now the title of " W. T. Copeland and Sons " was adopted. At the present time the best artists are at work producing very beautiful china.

SPODE PASTILLE BURNER.

TRADE MARKS USED BY THE FIRM.

We give on the opposite page the various marks which have been used on the ware produced by the firm from Spode's days to 1847.

The last illustration shows a vase with a perforated cover or a pastille burner, mounted on a stand formed by three dolphins on a triangular base. The body is red with black ornaments in relief, in the Wedgwood style. The mark impressed is SPODE.

SPODE This was sometimes stamped in the clay, and at others printed at back in the colour of the pattern. On china, it was usually done with the pencil by the decorator.

SPODE
Felspar Porcelain

These were printed on the china when felspar was introduced.

 or

These were the stamps used upon the celebrated Ironstone China.

These were all printed on the ware.

SPODE, SON
& COPELAND   or SPODE & COPELAND, both impressed and printed.

The following marks were used during the Copeland & Garrett partnership from 1833 to 1847:

COPELAND
& GARRETT

C & G
with the name of
the pattern.

CHAPTER XXIII

LUSTRE WARE

METALLIC lustre was an interesting material much used in the early nineteenth century for decorative purposes, and long ago it was a striking feature in old majolica and in Hispano-Moresco ware. The lustres were also termed " iridescent colours," " reflets métalliques," " colori cangianti," and " madreperla." These were properly the names for the effects produced by the various metallic pigments used for the decoration of the surface of the ware, in the same way that the ordinary colours were used, but having a metal as their base. The metal was held in such a state of extreme subdivision that when it was applied it produced a film of exceeding thinness, and successive films were painted when necessary one over the other, so that the colours were reflected according to the relative depth of the films, thus producing very beautiful effects, some of which, however, may be due to atmospheric action.

Modern chemists and manufacturers have failed to discover the marvellous lustre of the fine old majolica ware, of which the two chief colours were the celebrated crimson or ruby lustre, which died out early in the sixteenth century, and the very beautiful gold or yellow lustre, which was also more ancient than the copper, and its decline was coincident with the close of the sixteenth century. The best English imitation of the old lustre ware has been the recent work produced by William de Morgan, who since 1870, and still later and better after 1888, at Fulham, has done much to popularise this kind of ware, imitating not alone the ancient Hispano-Moresco, but also the old Persian lustre ware.

LUSTRE WARE

The earliest English product which had lustre in its decoration was made by Richard Frank at Brislington, near Bristol, about 1770. This was copper lustre.

Silver lustre ware, made for domestic use, was produced in large quantities at the Staffordshire potteries, Robert Wilson, who succeeded Neale and Palmer, taking the lead in this direction; and his brother David, also of Hanley, was no less successful. Pink lustre was not alone made by Wedgwood, whose silver lustre is amongst the best of

MAJOLICA WARE PLATEAU. PORTRAIT OF PIETRO PERUGINO, 1515-20 A.D.

the lustre productions, but also by the Sunderland and Newcastle factories, in such abundance that it is not uncommon for some collectors to ascribe most of this pink lustre to Dixon & Co., Sunderland, and to the other Sunderland manufacturers, named later. The dispute which has arisen as to the inventor of lustre ware leaves it a question as to whether John Hancock, of Hanley, or John Booth, of Well Street, had the best right to the honour. Amongst the early makers were J. Gardner, who is said to have introduced decoration in the form of silver lustre at Woolfe's

Works, Stoke, and afterwards at Spode's pottery; Horobin, of Tunstall and Lane End; and Aynsley, of Lane End. Dr. S. Shaw ascribes the early lustre to J. Hancock, J. Gardner, and W. Hennys. They seem to have been employed by

SUNDERLAND LUSTRE. A PERFECT SET SOLD FOR £25.

other potters, as sometimes marked pieces are found with names, such as "Lakin & Poole," "Spode," "Wood & Caldwell," and "Davenport," of Longport.

We have noted the several metallic lustres, of which the rarest is gold or yellow, which contains a small quantity of

STAFFORDSHIRE. QUAINT CUPIDS.
From Miss Edith Feilden's Collection.

gold in a film so fine that the actual colour of the metal is preserved; silver and steel lustre, both derived from the actual presence of platinum; and copper and pink, which are produced by the reducing action of the fire in the kiln upon the metal. Lustre is used either on a plain surface or on an embossed surface with other ground colours, such as brown, green, and blue, or even with painted decoration. Of course, its simplest form is where it is applied as a whole

MAJOLICA LUSTRE-WARE VASE, BY MAESTRO GIORGIO.   GOLD AND RUBY LUSTRE, C. 1518 A.D.

surface-colouring to the piece. This is sometimes called solid lustre, but, whether in copper, bronze, or silver, this whole-lustre class is the least interesting; it is simply using the lustre *as a wash or glaze* in the ordinary way, and its beauty depends upon the quality of the paste and the shape of the piece. Lustre is also used *as a paint*, and applied with the brush on the white, blue, or green surface below the glaze, generally in a decoration of curves or leaves, or again as a framework to the white reserves. The best pieces are the figures. Where stroke is laid upon stroke the intensity of the colour is increased. The most interesting, and, indeed, valuable of our English lustres is known as *resist* lustre.

A simple explanation of *resist* lustre will be, no doubt, helpful to many who have often heard and used the term without knowing how or why the name was derived. Let us discuss the process of decorating *resist* lustre ware, but first look at a piece where the silver lustre reveals a pattern in white, which is often very delicate, and where the white glaze and paste are contrasted with the silver lustre which forms at one and the same time the ground and the ornament. Now, in the process of carrying out this ornament, the parts to be reserved in white were first painted over with a solution usually of treacle or glycerine, through which a thin coating of lustre could not penetrate. When this was dried the whole surface was covered with the lustre wash, and again left to dry. The solution used for the reserves, being treacle or glycerine, was soluble in water and the lustre applied to the pottery resisted the action of water—that is, it did not dissolve—so that when the piece was plunged in water the solution, being dissolved, left those parts white to which it had been applied; all the rest was covered with the lustre, which had the power to *resist* the action of the water. Hence the name, which, by the way, is generally asso-

WEDGWOOD PLATINUM LUSTRE. DECORATED BY SCRAPING OFF THE PLATINUM BEFORE FIRING.

ciated with silver lustre, though pink lustre is similarly treated.

Many of the finest pieces of English *resist* lustre were first transfer-printed in blue or other colours *under the glaze*,

SILVER RESIST LUSTRE JUG, OF FINE QUALITY, PROBABLY LEEDS.

and the transfer pattern was blocked out by being painted over with the treacle or glycerine solution as before described. Then the silver lustre was applied by the same process as for simple *resist* lustre, with the result that the pattern printed under the glaze was visible in the reserves or panels of the *resist* lustre work. The brilliancy of the lustre colour depends largely upon whether the lustre is applied to a light or to a dark clay body. The film of lustre is so thin as to allow the colour of the underlying clay to have a great modifying effect on the brilliancy of the lustre itself. Another modification is seen in pieces where lustre has been applied as a paint, each stroke of lustre pigment, painted over a previous one, making a considerable difference in the shade and intensity of the colour. Several tints of bronze and pink will be found on the familiar Sunderland lustre jugs, for instance, with the view of the bridge over the Wear on the one side, first transfer-printed and then coloured in enamels; usually on the other side is a motto, or verse, similar to that given in the frog mug in our chapter on "Jugs and Mugs." The one before me gives the verse:—

"Forget Me Not.
"The sailor tost in stormy seas,
 Though far his bark may roam,
Still hears a voice in every breeze
 That wakens thoughts of home.
He thinks upon his distant friends,
 His wife, his humble cot;
And from his inmost heart ascends
 The prayer, Forget me not."

These jugs show how the reserves, left white, are often decorated with transfer prints, which are somewhat curious, because they are printed and burnt in *over the glaze*, and then further coloured with enamels, more or less rudely painted, in green and yellow and blue, also *over the glaze*. Where raised ornament is used, two tints of lustre are frequently found upon it, the ground tint being pinkish, and the raised ornament of a bronze colour; but seemingly the whole pattern has been coloured with the pink tint first, and, after drying, a further bronze lustre has been added, so as to distinguish the raised ornament, usually conventional grapes and vine-leaves, which is a style of decoration largely used for *resist* lustre too. Other raised ornament makes crude attempts to produce scenes in proper colours. A well-known pattern showing one cupid leading

LUSTRE WARE

a lion, on which another cupid is mounted, whilst a third follows, is an illustration of this. Green enamel is used for the grass; green, yellow, and brown for the foliage; brown for the trunks of the trees, the lion's mane, tail, and paws; whilst the cupids and the body and head of the lion are in flesh-colour. The wings of the cupids are enamelled in green. The whole result on a band of a curious blue shade, with a moulded bronze lustre band at the top and a bronze lustre stand and base, is a fair illustration of the lustre ware used about a hundred years ago for cottage decoration.

Amongst the productions in earthenware, and even in the finer work in china, it is questionable whether England produced anything much better than the silver *resist* lustre, especially that which has been described as having the reserves filled with a blue transfer-printed pattern under the glaze.

SILVER LUSTRE. FINELY MODELLED SOLDIER ON HORSEBACK.

When the reserves were painted out by the solution, to which we have before referred, sufficient white was left surrounding the whole of the subject, landscapes, birds, animals, etc., to give much brilliancy and decorative effect, not alone to the central panel, but also to other reserves similarly transfer-printed and decorated with roses and leaves, with the convolvulus and with birds in separate small reserves on the rim. This effect may be noticed in the jug given as an illustration, the whole outline round the bird showing very clearly.

The commonest application of silver *resist* is used on a white or ivory ground, but occasionally interesting and valuable specimens with canary, turquoise, blue, and pink

SILVER RESIST LUSTRE JUGS.

or apricot ground are met with. These coloured grounds are as rare as are the coloured Whieldon and Leeds ware. With regard to various articles made, jugs and mugs are far more common than any of the other forms. Cups and

BRONZE LUSTRE JUG.

saucers are more common than whole tea services, as we should expect with the lapse of time. Tobacco jars, two-handled cups, and goblets are seldom seen, and vases are

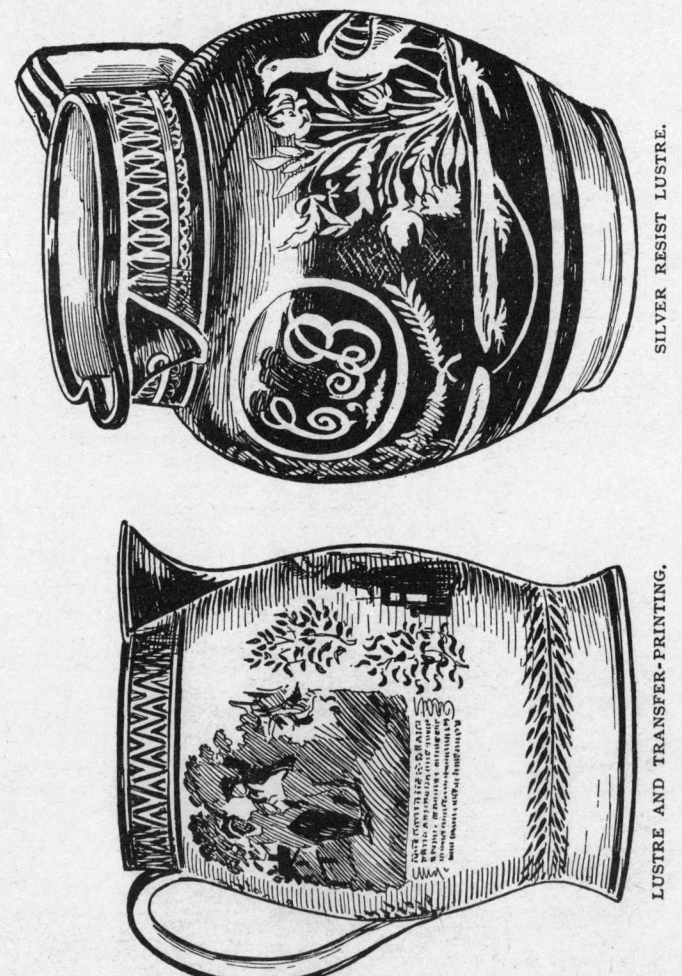

SILVER RESIST LUSTRE.

LUSTRE AND TRANSFER-PRINTING.

scarce. The commonest pattern is the conventional vine-leaf and grapes. Bird decoration, especially exotic birds, is often on the best specimens. Hunting scenes, animals of various kinds, conventional leaf decoration, ships, Chinese,

216 a

STAFFORDSHIRE GROUPS.

STAFFORDSHIRE.
From Miss Feilden's Collection.

LUSTRE WARE

figures and scenery, armorial bearings and masks on jugs, all come within the category of *resist* lustre.

The *dated* pieces do not seem to be earlier than the beginning of the nineteenth century; the dates 1812, 1813, and 1814 are the most frequent, though about twenty years had elapsed since the invention of the process. We have already noted the Sunderland pink lustre on jugs, etc. Amongst the manufacturers of these were Dixon, Austin, & Co., Philips & Co., J. Philips, Dixon, Philips & Co., and Dawson at Sunderland; Sewell & Donkin, Fell and Sheriff Hill Pottery at Newcastle. The rarest pieces from these factories are those decorated with a pink lustre ship in full sail, and slabs for hanging on the wall, with metallic lustre frames decorated with transfer-printed ships.

CHAPTER XXIV

LEEDS WARE

SOMEWHERE about the year 1760 two brothers named Green founded the Leeds Pottery Works at Hunslet. After a few years they took a partner, in 1775, and the firm became "Humble, Green & Co." In 1781 or 1783 W. Hartley joined the business, with a corresponding change in its title to "Hartley, Greens & Co." The active period seems to have been from this time to 1791, though the best period was from 1775 to 1781. The early products

CREAM-WARE LEEDS TEAPOT. NOTE THE LIGHTER SHADE ON HANDLE, SPOUT, ETC. PAINTED FLOWERS.

differed little from the usual earthenware produced at all the potteries. They included a glossy black, and black basaltes, not made in imitation of Wedgwood, for in this he was not an inventor; he improved black basaltes, so that a special quality became all his own, although he had worthy rivals. Again, Wedgwood did not invent cream ware; he evolved from it his Queen's ware, it is true; but here again he had rivals, and amongst the most formidable of them was the Leeds Pottery, which produced an excellent cream ware just at the time when the salt glaze was displaced by the soft lead glaze. This lead-glazing process spread rapidly, and the Leeds glaze was of excellent quality—a rich creamy glaze, which showed a greenish or bluish green tint where it ran thick. The body or paste was cream-coloured too, being a composition in which clays from Cornwall and Poole were mixed with pipe-clay and ground flint. The usual forms of decoration were employed on the Leeds cream ware. Allusion has been made to the lustre decoration, which was very fine indeed, but the other means of decoration were no less well applied, especially the enamel colouring painted in green, blue, red, yellow, etc., which, although it was not finely painted, was very soft and quiet in tone. The transfer-printing was good; in fact, it can scarcely be distinguished from Wedgwood. This is what would be expected when we know that both early Wedgwood ware and Leeds ware were sent to

LEEDS CREAM-WARE BUST OF AIR. $6\frac{1}{2}$ INS. HIGH.

Liverpool to be transfer-printed. Later, in 1791, Leeds had extensive printing plant in its own factories. The Leeds ware of fine quality with gilt decoration is rare.

There is a special style of decoration, however, which reached considerable excellence at Leeds. We might well say that in pierced work this factory was pre-eminent. The clay was stamped with a geometrical design more or less complicated, but always very sharp and accurate. The open work was produced by the removal of the clay, either by means of the stamp itself or by hand. The basket work, too, was a feature of this factory. The twigs were made by hand, cleverly adjusted, and decorated by twisted, braided, or plaited strips, also made and applied by hand. This style was so well carried out as to give quite a distinction to the product of the factory, in which also we find gadrooned, fluted, and moulded patterns of considerable delicacy. Dessert services, as shown in the illustration of a plate, were often decorated by pierced borders combined with transfer-printing.

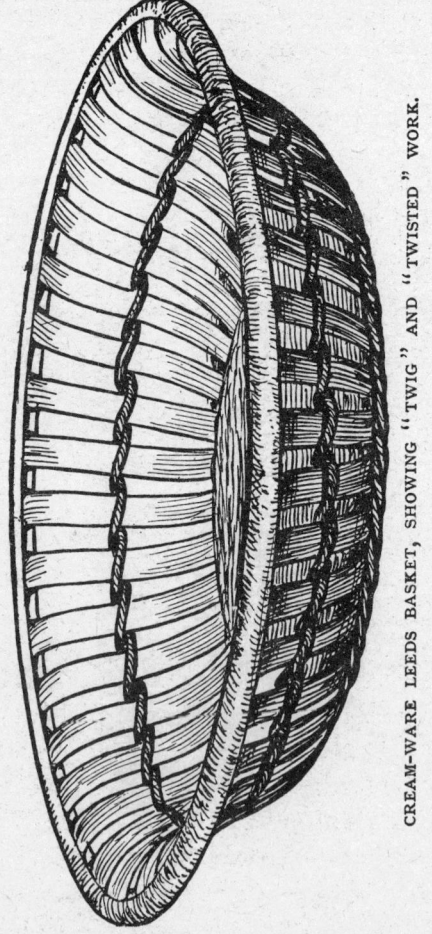

CREAM-WARE LEEDS BASKET, SHOWING "TWIG" AND "TWISTED" WORK.

In comparing Leeds ware with that of other factories we must remember that it was particularly light and, as a rule, elegant in shape. Its cream colour causes it often to

LEEDS WARE

be mistaken for salt-glaze ware, but the difference between the salt glaze and the lead glaze should be easily determined: the lead glaze is transparent, the salt glaze is not, and the latter never appears to run thick in the way that lead glaze does. It must not be imagined that even the fine pieces of the perforated ware have a great value. Unless they are marked the value is small in the absence of surface decoration. The chief points to be borne in mind are the creaminess of the colour, the glaze, and the weight. Then transfer-

DESSERT PLATE WITH PIERCED BORDER AND TRANSFER-PRINTED DECORATION.

printing increases the value, though this is a mechanical process, and that which may be produced by a machine never attains to the artistic or, indeed, to the monetary value of hand painting. So we find that Leeds ware with flowers, etc., painted, is most sought for. This is exactly what has been remarked on salt glaze: when painted it is valuable. The double-twisted handles of mugs, jugs, etc., and the fine moulding on the borders, are also distinctive of Leeds.

Old Leeds ware is very admirable. Its clear, rich cream-colour, combined with good potting, enabled it to compete successfully with the Queen's ware of Wedgwood. Particular attention should be paid by the collector to the glaze, which is extremely good, owing perhaps to the somewhat unusual use of arsenic, which, however, was so harmful to the potters that they were disabled in three or four years. The chestnut basket given in the illustration is an example of elaborate open pierced work; the handles are double-twisted and terminated in flowers. It is claimed by some that the open work was punched or pierced by hand, and, if so, the skill of the workman must have been extremely great—unless, as is more likely, he simply removed the clay that had been separated by the process of stamping. Such a piece as this chestnut basket would be marked in the catalogue of 1794 at 8s. 6d., wholesale. The twig-work was, as we have noted, made of strips of clay, either long or short, simply plain, or twisted into any shape required. Wedgwood produced similar twig-pieces, which were imitated at the Don Pottery, at Castleford, and in many Staffordshire potworks. Basket-work, combined with perforated and embossed patterns, became a speciality at Leeds. The process was as follows: The plate or dish was formed in the mould in such a way that the pattern stood out in relief above the part which was to be treated by incision. It was the relief work that was cut out by hand and removed, so as to leave the open basket-work pattern.

A testimony to the enterprise of the Leeds Pottery, also

CREAM LEEDS WARE CHESTNUT BASKET, WITH ELABORATE PIERCED PATTERN. TWISTED HANDLES, TERMINATING IN FLOWERS.

to its vast business, is to be found in the numerous catalogues or books of designs, printed in English, French, and German. Not only with these countries was a large trade carried on, but also with Holland, Spain, and Russia. In the 1783 catalogue the French list had the following title :—

"Desseins de divers Articles de Poteries de la Reine en couleur de Crême, Fabriqués à la Poterie de Hartley, Greens and Company, à Leeds, avec une Quantité d'autres Articles ; les mêmes émaillés, imprimés ou ornés d'Or à chaque Patron, aussi avec des Armes, des Chiffres, des Paisages, etc., etc., Leeds, 1783." This catalogue is rare: has any one of our readers ever seen one ? Or even more to the point, is any reader the happy possessor of a copy of one of these most interesting old pattern books ?

Amongst the illustrations in the catalogue are the following : — Terrines (tureens), with spoons and stands ; dishes, in the form of various shells ; table plates and dishes, compotiers, pierced dessert dishes with openwork rims, pierced single and double salts, jugs and mugs, covered and uncovered ; butter tubs and stands, water bottles and basins, ice pails, strawberry dishes and stands, large casters

TWO FIVE-FINGERED FLOWER VASES OR QUINTAL FLOWER HORNS. ONE WITH THREE FINGERS.

for salt, mustard and pepper, oil and vinegar stands, candlesticks in a variety of patterns, ewers and basins, fruit baskets and stands of elegant basket, twig, and open-work, chestnut baskets and stands, jars for potpourri, sweetmeat cups, baskets and stands, inkstands, tea ware, teapots, coffee-pots, milk jugs, tea canisters, slop basins, sugar bowls or basins and covers, cups and saucers of various patterns, and a multitude of other articles. One hundred and fifty-two general articles are described in the 1783 catalogue. In a later one, published in 1794, there was a Spanish list; in the 1814 edition 221 articles are described; the whole of the plates had " Leeds Pottery " impressed on them. Besides this ware, forty-eight patterns of tea, coffee, and chocolate services are included.

In the middle of the eighteenth century a tramway was laid down from the colliery at Middleton to the town of Leeds, which passed through the pot works. This happened in 1758, and may be noted, in passing, as a testimony to the early foundation of the " Leeds Potteries." They must have existed before that date. We note shortly that various changes occurred in the proprietary. " Hartley, Greens & Co." became " Greens, Hartley & Co.," and then, in 1825, Mr. Samuel Wainwright had the predominant interest, and " Samuel Wainwright and Company " infused new spirit into the enterprise until 1832, when Wainwright died, and " The Leeds Pottery Company " appointed Stephen Chappell as the sole manager until 1840. In that year he became sole proprietor, and his brother James joined him as partner. In 1847, bankruptcy overtook the firm of " Stephen and James Chappell," and for the next three years Richard Britton was manager for the creditors. Samuel Warburton purchased the works, and as " Warburton and Britton " the concern was carried on until 1863, in which year Warburton died and Britton became the owner. He took into partnership his sons in 1872, and the firm was known as R. Britton & Sons.

As showing the extent of the works, the turnover for 1791 was no less than £51,500, and we find that the copper plates used for producing the transfer-printing were valued

224 a

STAFFORDSHIRE. WALTON.
From Miss Edith Feilden's Collection.

STAFFORDSHIRE SILVER LUSTRE.

LEEDS WARE

at £204. They were engraved with various patterns, such as willow and other Nankin designs, borders and groups of flowers, landscapes, and ruins. In combination with the transfer-printing, fine resist lustre ware was made, and this, like the Leeds gold and silver lustre, is rare. There is a contrast between the black basaltes of Wedgwood and the black ware of Leeds, in that the latter has a decided bluish tint, combined with an extremely hard compact body. About a hundred patterns and sizes of teapots alone were produced in basaltes up to the year 1813. The old marks given are forged continually. We have seen very fine figures and services stamped with the LEEDS POTTERY marks which have puzzled those who really ought to know better. The genuine old Leeds is, we repeat, both creamy in colour and light in weight.

CHAPTER XXV

SWANSEA POTTERY

A SMALL pottery was in existence in Swansea shortly after 1764, which became known as "The Cambrian Pottery" when G. Haynes occupied it about twenty years later; the date for his occupation, usually accepted, being 1780. In 1800, the works underwent very extensive alterations, and were remodelled after the plan of the Wedgwood works opened at Etruria in 1769. Commodious rooms, suitable furnaces, and baking kilns were built for the manufacture of the various kinds of earthenware and china by a process which was kept secret. The earliest ware, though called porcelain, was really an "ironstone ware"—an opaque china—something after the style of "Mason's."

Haynes was joined by L. W. Dillwyn, and the firm became "HAYNES, DILLWYN & CO., CAMBRIAN POTTERIES, SWANSEA." This is used but rarely as a mark. Owing to the friction between the partners, Haynes retired in 1802. A lawsuit followed, at the close of which Dillwyn chuckled over the fact that he had "saddled Haynes with about £1,200 costs." Dillwyn was very enterprising, and further experiments led to an improvement in the body of the opaque porcelain, although it was not until 1814 that translucent porcelain was made. The earliest Swansea was decorated by W. W. Young, whose beautiful paintings of shells, fruit, birds, feathers, butterflies, and insects are quite remarkable. His flowers are not so good, as by comparison with Billingsley and Pollard they are stiff and formal.

L. W. Dillwyn retired in 1813, the year before the manufacture of the translucent porcelain, and made way for his son, L. L. Dillwyn, under whose management Swansea porcelain reached a high standard of excellence. Swansea porcelain and Billingsley's paintings have been dealt with in " The A B C of Collecting Old China," so that we only mention them to pass on to the further consideration of the earthenware. This was nearly all decorated at the works, and many well-known artists besides Billingsley and Young were employed. Amongst these were Pollard

SWANSEA POTTERY. MARBLED BLUE, MARKED "CAMBRIAN POTTERY,"
IN BROWN.

and Morris, two of Billingsley's pupils, who closely imitated their master. Baxter's " cupids " are well known: this was Thomas Baxter—not G. Baxter of " Baxter Print " fame—he excelled in landscape and figure subjects. Thomas Pardoe was a distinguished flower painter, who had an especial affection for the passion flower. Beddow painted landscapes, and the chief painter of birds was Colclough.

It is well to note that the earthenware was painted as well

228   OLD POTTERY

as the china. Services may be found painted by Young with sprays of flowers and foliage, whilst Pollard's paintings of fruit and foliage subjects, such as the wild strawberry, are just charming. As seen in our illustration, Swansea

SOME RARE EXAMPLES OF WELSH POTTERY.

did not confine itself to any particular form of decoration. Imitations of Wedgwood were produced, such as black basaltes, and white cameo decoration on a black ground, in addition to a rather remarkable Etruscan ware, which

SWANSEA POTTERY

may be easily mistaken for Italian ware, especially those pieces which have no impressed Italian name. Lustre ware has already been noted. The main product was the ordinary ware, either cream, white with a bluish glaze, or buff with unglazed figures in relief. Many of the so-called Staffordshire figures were made at Swansea, but they were, as a general rule, unmarked. It is said that they may be identified by a chocolate or orange line which runs round the pedestal.

After Billingsley left Swansea, in 1817, the manufactory ceased to be successful, and the next year Dillwyn dissolved partnership with the two Bevingtons, who had evidently taken a large part in the management, for we find some pieces marked "*Dillwyn Etruscan Ware*, BEVINGTON & CO., SWANSEA," and others as shown below.

The works ceased in 1820, and the business was removed to Coalport. The marks may be found, impressed, painted, stencilled, or transfer-printed, in red or other colours, and sometimes even written in gold.

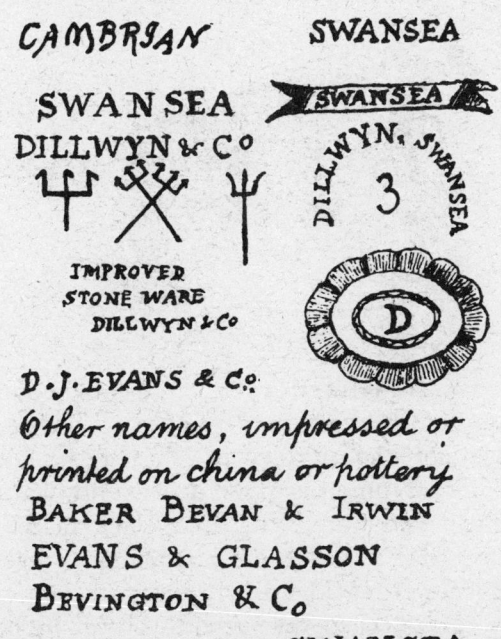

CHAPTER XXVI

JACKFIELD POTTERY

IN Shropshire, the Jackfield Pottery commenced early in the seventeenth century, the earliest dated piece being 1634; but it was at the beginning of the eighteenth century that this pottery, and those at Caughley and Broseley, displayed more activity. Little is known of their early products, although John Thursfield at Jackfield made salt glaze and the ordinary tableware—white stoneware. He withdrew afterwards to Benthall, and his son, Maurice Thursfield, carried on the Jackfield works from 1751 to about

WHAT IS IT?

1772. A few years later, in 1780, Rose made china here for a short time, before removing to Coalport, where he became the purchaser of the pottery of Turner, his old master: the mark after the union is given at the end of this chapter.

The Jackfield red ware, with fine black lustre glaze, was distinctive, so that it has been customary to ascribe nearly all of such pieces to Jackfield, without sufficient proof. The black lustre glaze was very good—being highly vitrified and glazed—and the decoration of scrolls and flowers in relief is well known. Locally, these black articles were called "black decanters." There is no doubt that the black-glaze ware of Whieldon was copied in Staffordshire and at Jackfield too. Some of this Jackfield pottery was finely incised and coloured in conventional patterns. We have dealt with this factory next after Swansea, because it

A JACKFIELD JUG.

was also removed to Coalport, on the other side of the river Severn, from Caughley, where commodious premises had been erected by Rose.

Black ware was produced at Benthall by John Thursfield when he retired from Jackfield. The clay, of very fine quality, was drawn from a pit quite close to the kilns. It is said that the secret of the black glaze was only known to Thursfield, and that it died with him there. This is not at all probable, because of the amount of this black ware

OLD POTTERY

which is still in existence. The black jugs and tea ware were decorated with raised ornament, usually vine-leaves and grapes. Just as the rose was the top for the cover of the Worcester china, so a bird was generally the top of the black pieces—not for black pieces alone, but for salt-glazed ware made in Shropshire and in Staffordshire, in imitation of the Whieldon ware, which had a similar bird. The raised decoration, the shape of the handles and spouts, and the claw feet are common to the black glaze family, which was often gilded or coloured in oils, and even japanned.

Mr. Peter Stephan, son of Stephan the modeller of Coalport, had a small pottery here, where he made encaustic tiles and earthenware, painted with fine blue arabesque patterns. His signed pieces are rare. In the absence of marks, identification is very difficult, and must remain a matter of opinion.

The curves indicate Coalport Salop. The initials show Caughley, Swansea, Nantgarw.

Stephan

CHAPTER XXVII

VOYEZ AND HIS WORK

J. VOYEZ, a Frenchman, was a very clever modeller—" the best in London"—who was employed by Wedgwood. He served his time with a silversmith, was employed several years at the china works, had been two or three years carving in wood and marble for Mr. Adams, the famous architect, and worked with equal facility in wax, wood, or stone. Wedgwood was very unwilling to lose his services, for he felt that his rivals were in need of some person to instruct them, and he knew that Voyez could do this more effectively than all the potters in the country put together. However, Voyez eventually modelled for Palmer of Hanley, and others, some of whose products he signed; there are several marked specimens in the London museums. Voyez's signature appears on the relief of a Palmer bust in the British Museum. The piece illustrated, known as the "Fair Hebe" jug, modelled in high relief, is his most popular, as it is his most common work. Whether he designed this when he was working for himself, or during his partnership with Hales at Cobridge, is not known. Examples of his work are found dated 1788, and the probabilities are he made them at first when he was employed as a modeller, and later when he himself was a pottery owner. A catalogue of his products was issued in 1773, in which he stated that he was a sculptor, and a member of the Royal Society of Arts of Great Britain. The articles he made were on sale at his house at Cobridge, near Newcastle, in Staffordshire.

He manufactured a fine black porcelain, having nearly the same properties as the basaltes, and used this for intaglios

OLD POTTERY

and cameos, and in cameo or intaglio produced equally good designs of Marcus Aurelius, of a man making a vase, and hundreds of other subjects, chiefly from antique gems. An

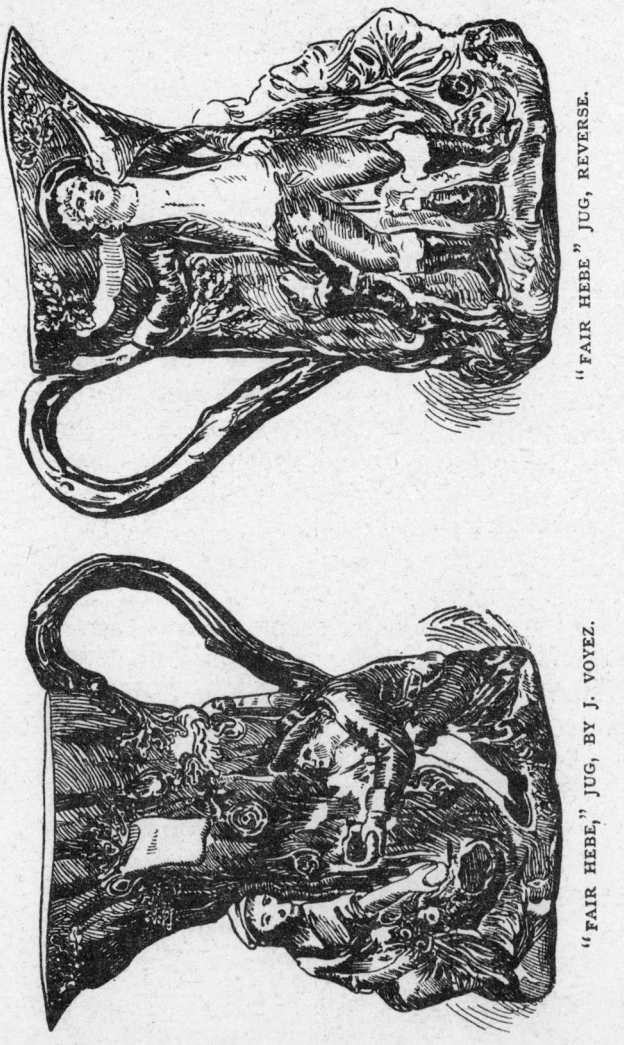

"FAIR HEBE" JUG, REVERSE.

"FAIR HEBE," JUG, BY J. VOYEZ.

interesting note is given as to the prices at which these were sold; unset at 1s. each, or neatly set in gilt metal from 2s. 6d. to 3s. 6d. each. He also made excellent vases

STAFFORDSHIRE FIGURES. SEE MARK NEXT PAGE.

and tablets for chimneypieces in various sizes; and other pieces were plaques with three grooms drinking, with a cask serving as a table, eleven inches high; a triple match-holder; vases with a tree stem with an owl perched upon it, with a boy and girl, lamb, and dog at base. The shape, colouring, and absence of glaze are peculiar features of Voyez's work. In these they resembled early Wedgwood, and the products of the elder Ralph Wood.

The two seated figures are old Staffordshire, but, like some other figures which have been submitted to us, they are puzzling as far as the maker is concerned. The mark on the base of one is given. Perhaps some one of our readers can trace the name of Owen, Burslem, Staffordshire. If so, we shall be pleased to have any information that can be given. So far we can find no trace of Owen as a potter. It is easy to conclude that they were made for, and not by, Owen. The figure of Diana is Staffordshire. The modelling is very good.

NAME SCRATCHED IN THE PASTE UNDER BASE.

Joseph Owen
Burslem
Staffordshire
sc

VOYEZ
1788

J. VOYEZ

CHAPTER XXVIII

YARMOUTH POTTERY

THE plate given as an illustration is a specimen of those pieces marked "Absolon, Yarmouth." It has two rings of a very vivid, yet not unpleasing, green under the glaze, and it is porcelain. A lady brought it to me, and said it was one of six. The rough sketch and mark were sketched whilst she kindly waited. The painting is exceedingly crude on the plate itself, but the mark is a facsimile of that given. There are many collectors who would gladly buy such a specimen, but it was not for sale.

The information which is available regarding this Absolon, of Yarmouth, and his works is very limited. Possibly some day the difficulty about Yarmouth Pottery and its products may be settled on lines similar to those which once and for all disposed of the tons upon tons of old and modern china which masqueraded under the title of old "Lowestoft." It has been stated that neither china nor pottery were made at Yarmouth, but we do know that Absolon had a kiln, called by the expressive name of "The Ovens," where pottery and china were decorated with designs of flowers and views, either painted by Absolon or his men. We know, too, that white ware was procurable from Turner, and it is said that some of the pieces signed by Absolon are stamped "Turner." This is the more remarkable because it is questioned whether Turner ever did stamp his ware for this purpose. Various factories—Caughley, Coalport, Leeds, Staffordshire, and the Wigan Pottery—sent out white ware, which was decorated elsewhere. With regard to Caughley and Coalport, we do know that large quantities were sent from these factories in white to be painted in London.

The site of Absolon's kiln is still known as " The Ovens," and some day excavations there may help to decide what Absolon really did make. Many years since, in 1867, the products of Bow were exposed to collectors, by excavations made for Messrs. Bell & Black's match factory; so, in our next chapter, we shall show how Nottingham stoneware

Absolon Yarm^o
N° 25

was identified from discoveries made there. The solution of the Yarmouth problem on similar lines ought to be comparatively easy. Perhaps these remarks may reach the eyes of some one who holds authenticated historical records of Yarmouth; at present we have the story—the usual one—of " the decorating potters." Nearly all the authorities say that white ware was imported and decorated with flowers and landscapes in the local ovens: how, then, can we account for the impressed arrow which is found accompanying Absolon's name, and which, no doubt, is the mark of the

YARMOUTH POTTERY

maker ? Now, this arrow has not been ascribed as an impressed mark to any earthenware factory. The ware manufactured was mainly that for the table, dishes and plates with brown or gilt rims, and with green bands.

Sometimes a flower was painted on the plate, and its name written in red or brown at the back. On this point Professor Church says, "There is a strong resemblance between the plates and dishes decorated by Absolon and those made and painted at Swansea," but the painting on the piece given is very crude, and resembles much more the early decoration of English delft in style. The local records would settle the relative importance of the works; the old rate books, for example, would show the annual value for rating purposes of "The Ovens." Two early plates of coarse paste were described by Marryat as being in his collection; they had blue borders, and bore the inscription :—

QUINTON	QUINTON
BENJAMIN	MARY
YARMOUTH	YARMOUTH
1752.	1752.

Of course, they may have been made at the neighbouring town of Lowestoft, which can point to dated examples of pottery from 1752 to 1760; but from 1762 to 1789 dated examples of Lowestoft are all china, and it seems futile to say that at the same period, that is, the latter half of the eighteenth century, the Yarmouth Pottery would only undertake the work that could be done by an enamelling kiln.

There are two other considerations which should be borne in mind : the mill for grinding the material for the Lowestoft works was at Gunton Dene, and this was not far from Yarmouth, again, the great distance from the other potteries, which were said to supply Absolon with the white ware, taken in conjunction with the great expense of carriage by horses, seems to make it improbable that the white ware was brought either from Leeds, from Staffordshire, or from Shropshire. Hence we are driven to the conclusion that the truth about the Yarmouth works will never be found out unless the site of the old works is excavated, as has been done elsewhere; then the question of porcelain or pottery and its decoration will be settled by actual observation.

It is said that some ware similar to Wedgwood's Queen's ware was made here, and also that lustre ware was produced, and figures after the Staffordshire style, having the impressed mark—the arrow. Here is a field for the investigator. At present no collector is satisfied with what he does not know about Yarmouth. Other marks on Yarmouth are

Absolon Yarm⁰

The arrow impressed

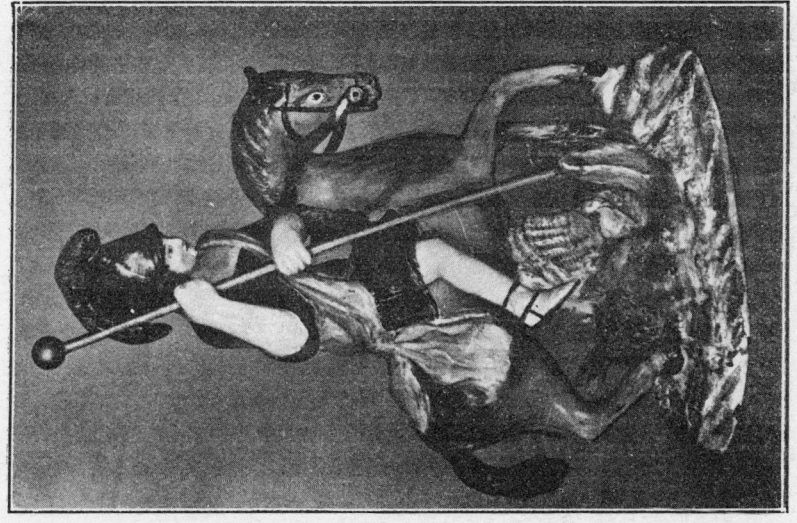
STAFFORDSHIRE. ST. GEORGE AND THE DRAGON.

STAFFORDSHIRE. THE DEPARTURE INTO EGYPT.
From Miss Edith Feilden's Collection.

CHAPTER XXIX

NOTTINGHAM POTTERY—STONEWARE

IN the historical account of Nottingham, written by Dr. Deering in 1751, mention is made that coals, lead, timber, corn, and *Potters' ware* were sent down the river. More than one hundred years earlier, in 1641, only one potter's name appears in the list of trades of the town, but in a similar list, dated 1739, two are mentioned. Still later, in 1757, in the "Annals of Nottinghamshire," a statement was made that Mr. Morley "was a manufacturer of brown earthenware carrying on his works in the lower part of Beck Street, and by the business he amassed a very considerable fortune." The making of pots and pans, etc., of Nottingham ceased about a hundred years ago. Little was known of the products except that they were mainly stoneware mugs for the use of public-houses. In this connection it is curious to know that the old Morley Pottery was situated in Mug-House Yard, Mug-House Lane, Beck Street. Many of these old mugs have figures of men, animals, and houses, etc., in stamped relief, but a more interesting feature was the names and inscriptions that were scratched on the ware before firing, and not the names of the makers, but those of the persons for whom the ware was made. We give an example:—

John Smith Junr of Basford near Nottingham. 1712.

The name of John Smith here given has been found on other pieces as John Shaw.

Referring to our last chapter, we spoke about the difficulty of identifying the Yarmouth products, because there had been no excavation on the site of the old works. Now, at Nottingham, the exact ware made from the earliest times has been rendered familiar by the discoveries resulting from

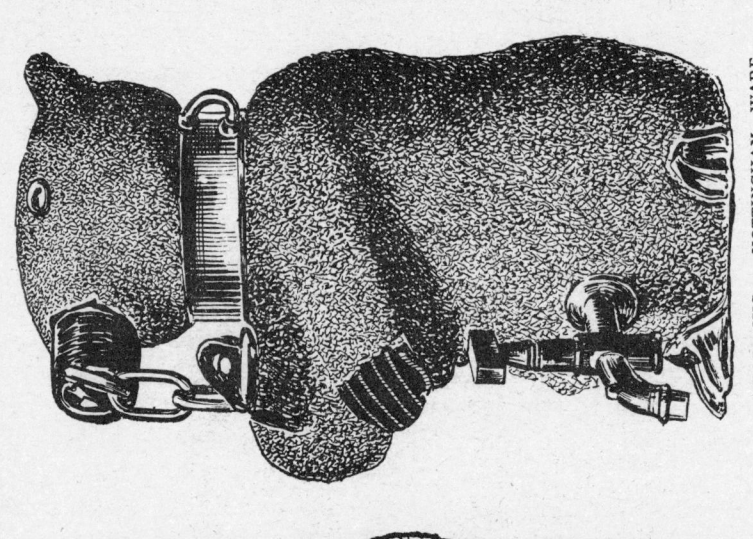

BEAR JUG. NOTTINGHAM WARE. COMPARE WITH THE OTHER JUG, WHICH IS STAFFORDSHIRE.

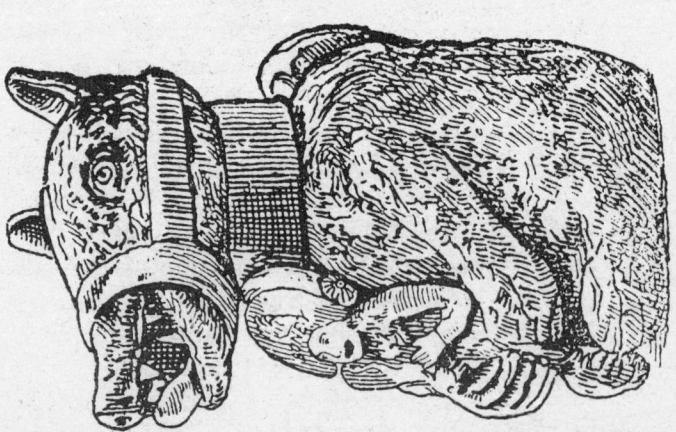

JUG. EARTHENWARE, IN THE FORM OF A RUSSIAN BEAR HUGGING NAPOLEON; "BONEY" STAMPED ON HIS PLUMED HAT. H. 7¾ IN.

excavations during building operations in 1815, 1874, and 1879. The sites of a number of kilns were investigated, and not alone were complete pieces found, but many wasters and broken fragments. These showed that from a very early period there had been extensive works at Nottingham, where

NOTTINGHAM POTTERY—STONEWARE

a coarse unglazed earthenware was produced—the common pottery—as well as a reddish body partly covered with a green glaze, as noted in our earlier chapters, or, again, a reddish body covered with a thick brownish glaze. The latter part of the seventeenth century saw the production of the excellent brown salt-glaze earthenware. Many pieces of this earthenware are of such fine quality that they denote the existence of a well-equipped factory, a factory indeed that could produce superior ware highly finished. It is to this period that we must ascribe many of the pieces with ornamentation in relief having scratched inscriptions, which should

BEAR JUGS, NOTTINGHAM AND STAFFORDSHIRE.

be compared with the brown Fulham mugs, having a relief portrait of Queen Anne between two Beef-eaters, and impressed decorations of dogs and a horse, whilst round the base are words and inscription such as this, incised:—

"On Banse downs a horse wee found
Thatt led uss all a smoaking round."
William Marsh, 1729.

The hare hunt was also a favourite subject; so was the stag hunt. Nottingham ware was very hard and durable, and was covered with a light brown lustrous glaze. Amongst the illustrations that we give are a jug in earthenware, with the tap attached, in which the head was used as a mug, and the curious example of a Staffordshire jug relating to Napoleon and his defeat at Moscow, for comparison.

"Sitting bear" jugs were, like the Nottingham mugs and puzzle jugs previously described, the ordinary drinking vessels in inns and beerhouses late in the seventeenth and during the next century. They were made in the other potteries, but the bright brown Nottingham stoneware products were quite popular, varying in tone from a red to an orange brown with a lustrous glaze; the pieces were marked by good potting and generally by graceful shapes. The blackish brown stoneware jugs may be ascribed to Chesterfield or to Brampton, and the white stoneware pieces to Staffordshire. It will be noted that whilst the surface of the salt-glaze is not absolutely smooth, these brown bears are sometimes quite smooth, but many examples are covered on the head and body with tiny fragments of clay. The Nottingham stoneware was largely manufactured by the Morley family, who made a great success of the business, which, after the decease of Charles Morley, a sheriff of Notts in 1737, was unsuccessful, and only dragged out a feeble existence till early in the nineteenth century. The last note on Nottingham stoneware should be carefully marked. Posset-pots, large and small mugs, globular jugs, puzzle-jugs, two-handled cups, punch-bowls, and tiles were among the objects made in addition to the "bear jugs." The decoration consisted of incised ornament—bands and concentric rings, conventional floral designs, birds, and flowers. The scratched inscriptions were often dated, the last date being 1805. The Museum at South Kensington has several specimens dated and inscribed, with a motto,

Old England for Ever, 1750,

with a name,

Edw. Stark, 1727,

or with a factory mark,

Made at Nottingham ye 17th Day of August A.D. 1771.

CHAPTER XXX

QUAINT JUGS AND DRINKING-CUPS

AMONGST the early potters right back to the Anglo-Saxons, curious old pitchers were made—very rough and unfinished from our point of view, but still most interesting and rare. The Norman potter produced many quaint specimens, some of which have been given as illustrations in our earlier chapters, figures of mounted knights on horseback in that early green glazed ware which specially marks the thirteenth and fourteenth centuries. Even so early, Toby jugs appear—at least, jugs shaped as men in costume, with the head modelled on the top. These again had the old green glaze; so, too, had the early puzzle jugs, which were comparatively common in the Tudor period. The cream-slip ware followed, and the fuddling-cups in buff ware, both preceding the advent of the decorated slip ware of the Toft school. It appears, however, that the cups and jugs shaped in the form of bears, dogs' heads, foxes' heads, etc., had their origin about the time when Whieldon and Astbury forsook the red and black ware of Elers in favour of a more homely style, though for quaintness and beauty Whieldon ware, in its finest specimens of agate, tortoiseshell, mottled, cauliflower, and pineapple patterns, suffers nothing by comparison with the embossed or stamped patterns of the turned ware of Elers.

The old Astbury bear-shaped jugs are not now easily found, but they are very quaint. The bear's head formed the cup from which the liquor poured from the jug was drunk. These old bears are very rough on the surface, because they were covered with tiny bits of clay which were stuck on whilst the piece was wet. At the same time the head, claws, teeth, etc., were modelled, not moulded, as at a later period. The glaze was usually brown, though some of the bears are found to be made of a dark brown clay decorated on the edges with white.

VARIOUS DRINKING-CUPS IN STAFFORDSHIRE POTTERY—WHIELDON AND ELERS WARE—AND IN ROCKINGHAM AND DERBY CHINA. FROM THE COLLECTION OF MR. E. NORMAN, BURNLEY.

The early Toby jugs with the soft blue, green, yellow, and brown glazes are described in a succeeding chapter. We need only add that quite a number of small jugs of this class were made by Ralph Salt of Hanley. Still, these were much later than the Whieldon period, as Salt's factory does not appear to have commenced before 1820. His small jugs varied from $3\frac{1}{2}$ to $4\frac{1}{2}$ inches in height. Going back to the " Woods," we find they made fine Toby jugs, but they also manufactured many curious cups with satyr-head masks, and handles imitating a piece of crab stick or cane. Here we find soft green, brown, and gray glazes. Many of these cups were shaped as foxes' heads, dogs' heads, bears' heads, etc., and jugs of the same period were modelled in the form of the head of a Bacchante. Turner, too, followed the lead of the other potters. However, he varied the process somewhat, for some satyr-head mask cups have been found in black basaltes, marked TURNER.

Amongst the products of the Leeds Pottery, and of

QUAINT JUGS AND DRINKING-CUPS

Chesterfield, and generally of Staffordshire, may be found these drinking-cups, in the shape of a hand and of various animals, such as the dog, fox, bear, and deer. Some of the small ones are traced to Liverpool, the rarest of these being a fox's head, coloured yellow. No doubt many of our readers are familiar with the Nottingham jug, a sitting bear, resembling that which has just been mentioned as Astbury ware, and having, like it, a roughened surface.

In another class altogether we have the stoneware spirit bottles. Chesterfield's many pot works produced a hard brown ware as well as a stoneware from clays obtained either

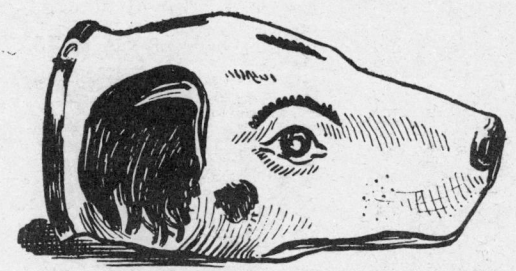

MODERN DOG'S HEAD DRINKING-CUP. THE EARS ARE NOT IN RELIEF, AND ARE ONLY TO BE DISTINGUISHED FROM THE HEAD BY THE DARKER COLOUR; THE MODELLING IS BAD.

from the East Moor in Derbyshire, or from Brampton, a few miles away, where ordinary brown pottery having a close hard body, was also largely made. At Lambeth, Messrs. Doulton & Watts years ago carried on a most extensive trade at their old-established pottery, where stoneware was specialised. Their stoneware spirit bottles were shaped as busts or figures of noted politicians. Prominent among these, at various factories, are the figures of Wellington, or of Daniel O'Connell; the latter bore a scroll on which was written "Irish Reform Cordial," and the name of the maker is given as "Denbigh and Codnor Park, Bournes Potteries, Derbyshire." William IV. is another figure, having an inscription "William IV. Reform Cordial," and the maker's mark, "Lambeth Potteries, Doulton & Watts, High Street, Lambeth." The Lambeth "Nelson" jug has the "Doulton & Watts" mark, so well known to collectors, and it may be noted that the pigtail forms the handle. Sir Robert Peel appears in this series, the jugs being inscribed with his name, and the

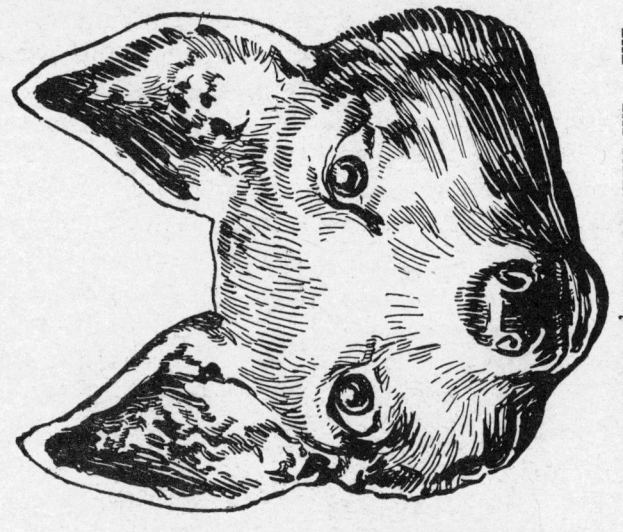

THE GENUINE FOX'S HEAD DRINKING-CUP. THE COLOURING IS GOOD, AND THE MODELLING IS FAR FINER THAN THE MODERN COPIES.

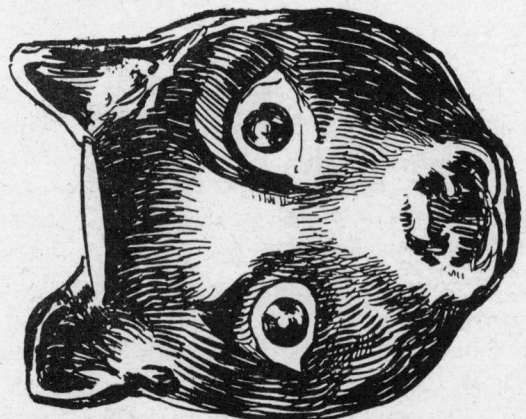

MODERN FOX'S HEAD DRINKING-CUP. MODELLING AND COLOURING ARE VERY POOR.

scroll, which he is holding, reads "Bread for the Millions." Not alone was earthenware used for the purpose of making these curious jugs and cups, but china as well. Hence we have rhytons or drinking-cups formed as heads of deer, dogs,

EARLY VICTORIAN SHEEP, LAMBS AND DOGS. STAFFORDSHIRE.
From Miss Edith Feilden's Collection.

or foxes, made at Rockingham and at Derby. These factories also made jugs formed as masks. They are worth about £1 to £5 each, according to size and quality.

We give the prices of specimens sold in a recent sale:—

> "A rare Swansea Etruscan Drinking Cup formed as a horse's head," £2.
> "A rare Staffordshire Pottery Goblet formed as a fox, goose, and dog," 30s.
> "An old Staffordshire Pottery Drinking Cup formed as a pointer's head," impressed mark "Neale & Co," £2 15s.

As a rule, in auctions, such pieces are included with others in one lot, as, "A group of bear and dog, 10½ in. high, and jug and cover formed as a bear and dog, 12½ in. high," sold for 9½ gns. "A bust of the Duke of Wellington, 13 in. high; a mug and cover formed as the head of same; and bust of Charlotte Corday," 11½ in. high, 7½ gns. Certainly to this class belong jugs modelled with rustic figures in relief by Voyez, three of which, 8½ and 10¼ in. high, were sold recently for 21 gns. (see priced catalogue in the Appendix).

JOSEPH THOMPSON, HARTSHORNE POTTERY, DERBY. FORMERLY THOMPSON WAS PROPRIETOR OF THE "WOODEN BOX" POTTERY, DERBYSHIRE.

OLD POTTERY

Frog mugs were made largely at Sunderland, where Messrs. Brunton and Company, afterwards Moore & Co., carried on an extensive business. The frog was modelled and placed inside the mug, so that when the contents were about half consumed the frog appeared. An inscription is frequently found transfer-printed on the outside. The illus-

FROG MUG.   SUNDERLAND WARE.   MISS EDITH FEILDEN'S COLLECTION.

tration is a rare Sunderland mug, dated 1793, "The opening of the bridge over the Wear." The black frog with pink mouth and transfer-printed flowers is quite uncommon. Thanks are due to Miss Edith Feilden for permission to use this illustration from her valuable and interesting collection. The most curious specimen that has come under our notice was a double-handled loving-cup, having inside two frogs climbing up the sides and a lizard at the bottom. It must not be assumed that all of these frog mugs were made at Sunderland; many were made at Leeds, and in the Staffordshire potteries.

CHAPTER XXXI

THE WILLOW PATTERN

WITH the five illustrations we give of the willow pattern, the story of the plate may not be amiss. It is a Chinese story. Though English plates and dishes in earthenware are very common, English porcelain plates and dishes with the same pattern, transfer-printed, are comparatively rare, and old Chinese plates and dishes are very scarce. So English earthenware plates and dishes are cheap; though old, they will only sell for about 3s. per plate and 10s. per dish. The English porcelain plates and dishes are worth three or four times as much, and old Chinese ones are worth much more than this. Now for the plate! Looking down upon the scene, we notice just one corner of the mandarin's house peeping out behind on the right. Then in front there is a pretty pagoda-shaped pavilion, over which an orange tree in full fruit spreads its branches, whilst to the right is the peach tree in bloom. The peach tree, in the land where flowers, plants, trees, and animals were symbols, is itself an emblem both of marriage and longevity. In such a scene, was it a wonder Li-chi, the mandarin's daughter, and Chang, the grandee's secretary, should learn to love each other? Drayton, the poet, knew human nature:—

> "Each little bird, this tide
> Doth choose her loved peer,
> Which constantly abide
> In wedlock all the year,
> As nature is their guide:
> So may we too be true
> This year, nor change for new
> As turtles coupled were."

THE WILLOW PATTERN

so he wrote in England's golden age. What did Li-chi care if her lover were poor or if his home were only the island cottage shown on the top of the view? True, her father was obdurate; nay, more, he was cruel. The lovers fled; they escaped to the home of Chang, after having remained concealed for a time in the gardener's cottage over the bridge. You

can see the three of them—Li-chi, Chang, and the gardener—crossing the bridge, near which the willow is growing by the waterside. But, though for the moment a respite came, it was all too short. The passage across the water—note the boat with Chang at the oar—had been negotiated in safety, and he had welcomed her to share his lot. Never was anger greater than that of Li-chi's father. How he found out where his daughter had gone will never be told! Possibly a rival, who naturally hated Chang, had seen him with the

gardener, and then had hurried to tell the mandarin, as soon as news of the elopement had become known. The rest was easy—perhaps not for the gardener. There was

THE WILLOW PATTERN 255

the bastinado, and the truth might have been divulged under treatment by it. Be that as it may, the mandarin, breathing threatenings and slaughter, found out the lovers' retreat, and was about to beat them to death with a whip when the gods took pity on them and changed them into turtle-doves. "There, too, the dovecot stood, with its meek and innocent inmates murmuring ever of love."

The willow pattern is so called because of the willow, in the foreground, which began to shed its leaves just about the season when the elopement took place.

Differences will be noticed between the details of the number of oranges, the number of catkins on the willow, the blossoms of the peach, the arrangement of the fence, etc. The first and foremost blue-printed willow-pattern English china plates, etc., were made at Caughley by T. Turner, and later at Coalport, and are known in the trade as the "Broseley pattern." It was most popular. Early examples with the Caughley, C mark, or the Salopian, S mark, are rare, especially cups without handles, ribbed and finished exactly like the Chinese originals. Most of the potters have made the willow pattern, but comparatively few applied it to porcelain. So when the collector gets a marked piece of earthenware the value is increased by about 25 per cent. over the prices given above. These prices are the actual prices at which willow-pattern plates and dishes can be sold.

CHAPTER XXXII

TOBY JUGS

WE have had the privilege of seeing hundreds of these in Mr. Turner's collection; and apart from their quaintness, we were struck with their fitness in his scheme of room decoration. Fine specimens are always saleable. These Toby Fill-pot, Fillpot, or Philpot jugs were the homely, highly valued treasures of the farmers and farm-hands, which were used, as their name implies, more for filling the smaller vessels with liquor than as drinking-pots themselves. They were made mostly in Staffordshire. The earliest belonged to the Whieldon or Tortoiseshell school, having the beautiful soft markings and glaze which were associated with the works at Little Fenton and Fenton Low. Whieldon began his work about 1740, and first produced knife-hafts, snuff-boxes, toys, and chimney ornaments, in white as well as tortoiseshell, and Toby jugs, representing a figure seated with jug, pipe, and barrel. In 1754 Wedgwood and Harrison became Whieldon's partners. Harrison soon retired, but Wedgwood continued in the firm till 1759. Here, in 1754, he produced his famous green glaze, but more, he learnt the business that was to make him famous. The question as to whether Wedgwood made any large number of Toby jugs or other pieces of coloured and glazed earthenware has not yet been solved. Most Wedgwood ware is marked; very few specimens of Old Staffordshire have any mark, only now and then is a Toby jug definitely attached to a factory as being made, say, by Ralph Wood the elder, or the younger; by Whieldon, Aaron Wood, J. Neale & Co., R. Garner, Lakin and Poole, Enoch Wood, Wood & Caldwell, John Turner,

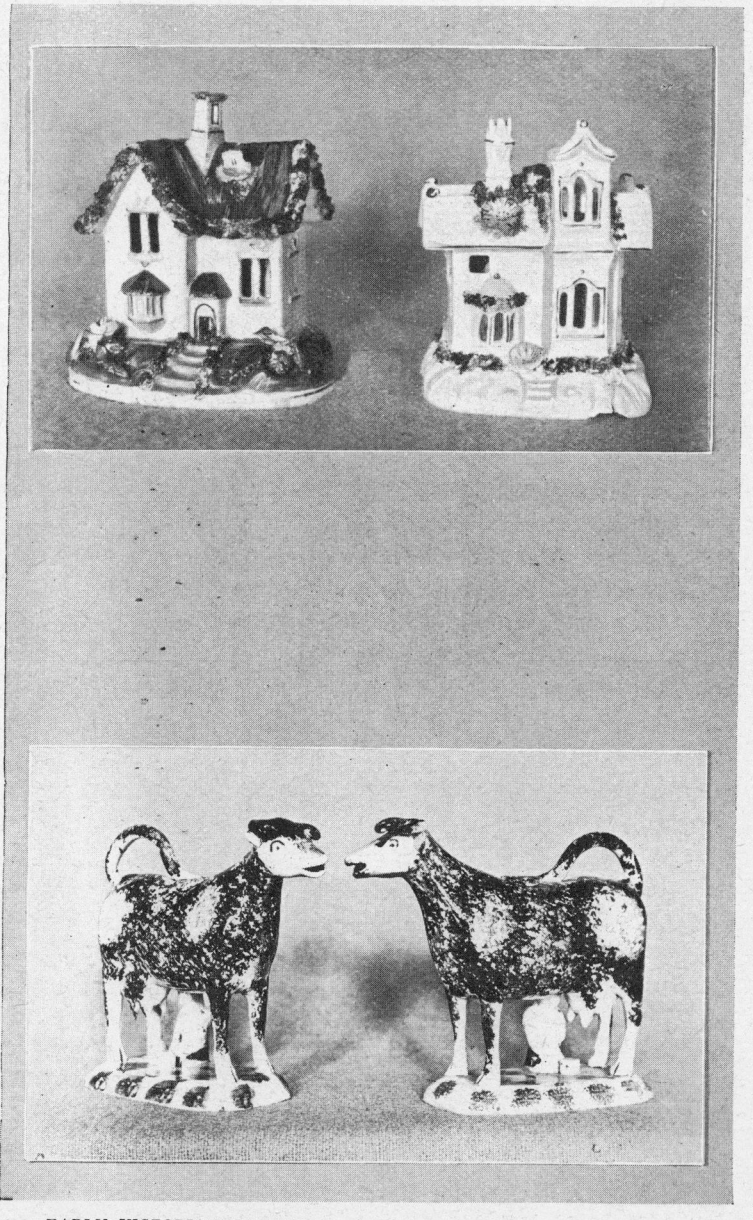

EARLY VICTORIAN COTTAGES.   COWS AS MILK-JUGS.
GREENISH CREAM BODY MOTTLED BLACK AND SPLASHED PINK.
From Miss Edith Feilden's Collection.

Turner & Co., R. Wilson, R. Salt, J. Walton, W. Adams, B. Plant, Bott & Co., J. Lockett, I. Dale, Davenport, Barker, Edge & Grocott, Barker, Sutton, and Till, or Bentley of Swansea. Not one jug illustrated here is marked; the general name, "Staffordshire," is given to

them all, and the price varies according to the modelling, the decoration, and the rarity of the piece. There are many on the market, the majority, unfortunately, being "*wrong ones*"; but these reproductions and forgeries are comparatively easy to detect. The softness of the colour in the old specimens, to say nothing of the marks of ordinary wear, is due to atmospheric action, and sudden dirt cannot imitate this. Still more interesting, though not yet widely known, is the test of the colour. In many of the finest Toby jugs, as also in the figures, notably those made by the Ralph Woods, father and son, the colour glazing was applied with a brush, so that *some parts have no glaze*. Then the modern pieces have a weaker, poorer modelling altogether. Since there are but few examples marked, collectors are advised to avoid strong colouring in favour of a soft, quiet harmony. Ralph

Wood the younger was the first to use *enamel* colours in order to secure a greater range of colour and to overcome one of the greatest difficulties of the early potters—the running of one colour into another.

The Toby Fillpot jug was, at first, in the form of an old man holding a jug with one hand whilst in his other hand was a pipe. Variations in the sitting or standing postures were common. Now, any figure of a man in jug form is a Toby. The first illustration does not show the mass of blue, soft in tone, in the coat of the man who holds a brown jug in his left hand and a pipe in the other. This was sold for £3 10s. The figure, on page 260, has a white coat with a few streaks of blue, and holds a similar jug and pipe, height the same as the first, 10 in. This is worth £4 10s. In the first group, the three figures have a mauve or puce coat, yellow coat, and blue coat from left to the right; their height is 11¼ in., 9 in. and 10¾ in., and the values in the same order are £4 10s., £1 10s., £4 15s. The group below, is again three Toby jugs; mauve, dark brown, light red, are the colours of the coats,

the height 10 in., 9¼ in., 9½ in., prices £3 10s., £4 10s., £3. The whole of the last three figures have yellow breeches, white stockings and black shoes. By the way, was the term Toby derived from Sterne's "Tristram Shandy," where the lovable old "Uncle Toby" is the inimitable hero of so many of his own stories? It would be quite easy to imagine him as the soul of a convivial party, immortalised in a concrete form. We note in the consideration of the specimens that one jug represents a sailor seated on his sea-chest. Like the others described, it is of coloured Staffordshire earthenware, and was made about 1770. Its height is 12 in., and the following inscription is incised :—

> "Hollo, Brother Briton,   Hard Dollars by me
> Whoever Thou be.   And drink a health
> Sit down on   To all sealors Bold."
> That chest of

The "Toby Fillpot," page 261 is also coloured Staffordshire

earthenware. The opposite figure, 11½ in. high, is seated, and holds a jug with the right hand on his knee, whilst in the left hand he raises the glass. The date of its manufacture is about 1760. We have seen the jug and pipe, the jug and glass, which sometimes have the addition of a barrel with or without

TOBY JUGS

a dog. There are other forms, such as "John Bull" seated, white earthenware coloured, and a man with a glass seated on a barrel, which are old. Modern Staffordshire jugs do not profess to be anything else. "Mr. Punch" seated, coloured earthenware, and the bust of "Father Christmas," coloured earthenware, are samples which may be bought for a few shillings. The last Toby is a type of the Rockingham ware

of Greens, Bingley & Co., of whom Green had been a partner with Hartley in the Leeds Pottery under the title of Hartley, Greens & Co. At this Swinton Moor Works a beautiful brown glaze, so well known upon the Cadogan teapots, acquired a great reputation. The figure, one of a pair, "The Snufftakers," was also made, and similar figures are still produced, at the Swadlincote Potteries in Derbyshire, both in Rockingham ware, in all brown glaze, and in coloured earthenware.

OLD POTTERY

It is necessary to insist that ordinary Old Staffordshire will never be valuable in the sense that Worcester and Chelsea are, but, on the other hand, the finest Old English Pottery, a genuine English product, without the foreign influence which is so evident in our old china, has already attained a high level of value, which will rise yet higher as the years pass away.

ROCKINGHAM "SNUFF-TAKER."

CHAPTER XXXIII

A SHORT ACCOUNT OF OTHER ENGLISH POTTERIES

OLD pottery is often marked in impressed letters with the potter's name. More frequently the pattern name of the ware is transfer-printed, with or without the name or initials of the potter, as in the well-known Minton Pottery, " Amherst, Japan."

ABBEY, RICHARD, 1790–6, Liverpool.—He was an engraver, and, in partnership with Mr. Graham, founded a pottery on the south bank of the Mersey and made Liverpool-printed ware. In 1796, the works were acquired by Messrs. Worthington and Co., who, in rival to " Etruria," named his pottery " Herculaneum." At least one example of Abbey's engraving has been found on Liverpool mugs. The transfer bears the name *R. Abbey, sculp.*

AYNSLEY, JOHN, *c.* 1780 to *c.* 1802, Lane End.—This name is sometimes wrongly given as Ansley, L. Aynsley manufactured the ordinary services decorated with plain or coloured transfers ; in the latter the coloured enamels were somewhat coarsely painted. He seems to have made a speciality of the mugs with moral sayings which were presented to good boys and girls when they left school. Silver lustre was also made. When his pieces were signed, the mark was *John Aynsley, Lane End.* Two firms of the name are producing pottery at Longton (Lane End), John Aynsley & Sons being the successors of the founder of the works.

BADDELEY, R. and J., *c.* 1750, Shelton.—This firm produced Queen's ware of a high class both as to potting and decoration. About 1780, transfer printing was adopted.

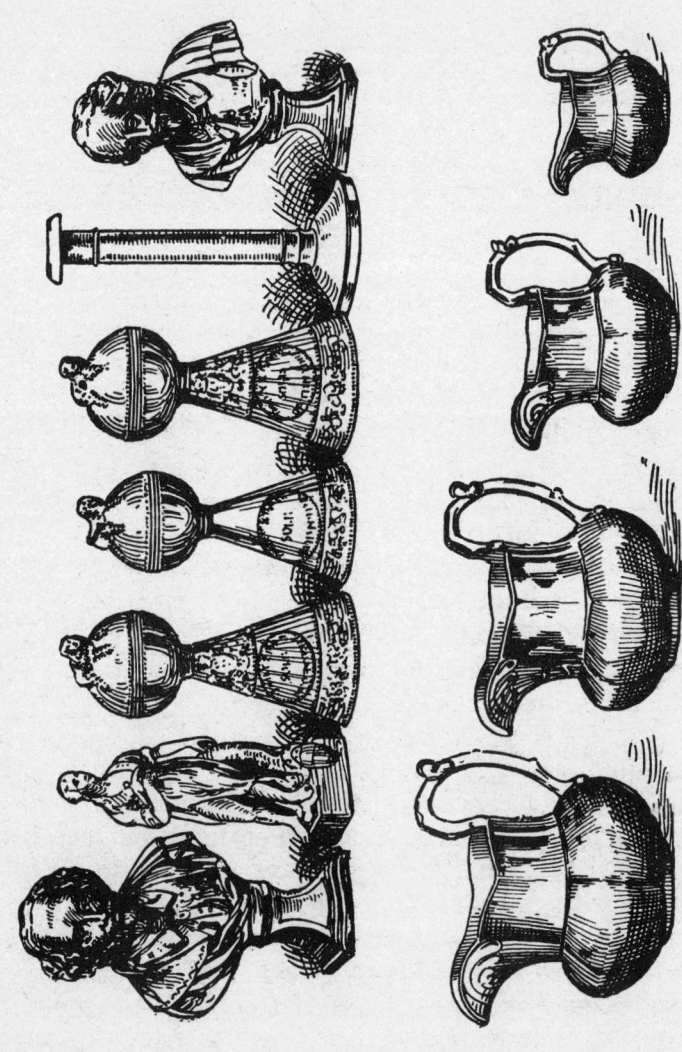

SILVER LUSTRE. BAILEY AND BATKIN. FROM MR. E. NORMAN'S COLLECTION.

From 1780–1806, after R. Baddeley had retired, *John and Edward Baddeley* were the proprietors, and probably the mark J. E. B. belongs to this period. Then, in 1806, the Baddeleys were succeeded by *Hicks and Meigh*, who, from 1820 to 1836, extended their firm into *Hicks, Meigh, and Johnson*, and produced china and pottery of good quality. The works, acquired by *Ridgway, Morley, Wear, and Co.*, adopted R. M. W. and Co. as a mark. Then Ridgway left in 1845, leaving *F. Morley and Co.* G. L. Ashworth joined as a partner in 1850 or 1851, just after the purchase of the patent for ironstone china and all the moulds, etc., of Mason, of Fenton, formerly called Lane Delph. The present firm is Geo. L. Ashworth and Bros., of Hanley.

BADDELEY, WILLIAM, early nineteenth century, *c.* 1802 to *c.* 1822, Hanley.—This W. Baddeley was a brother of the J. and E. Baddeley, of Shelton. He made the ordinary Staffordshire

STAFFORDSHIRE, LANE END, C. 1813.

ware, cream and black, and from the situation of his works and his desire to be distinguished from his brothers, he marked his products EASTWOOD, which is found impressed on vases, matchboxes, etc., for some of which he used a yellow clay with blue raised figures and foliage. He was a Wedgwood copyist.

BAGSTER AND PHILIPS, 1820 to 1828, Hanley.—These potters were the successors of the Wilsons. Robert Wilson had been a partner of Neale, who was noted as a rival of Wedgwood when the firm was Palmer and Neale. So that Bagster and Philips were intermediary between the old firm of Wilson and the new firm of Ridgway. At first, when it became one of the six Ridgway works, in 1830, *W. Ridgway, Son and Co.* were the proprietors; later, the title varied, with "Ridgway" always prominent. Bagster and Philips made stoneware, lustre ware, and general earthenware.

BAILEY AND BATKIN, early nineteenth century, Lane End.—This was the only firm which took out a patent for lustre pottery. They excelled in silver lustre—whole lustre without reserves. In the illustration on page 264, which is from the collection of Mr. E. Norman, of Burnley, are shown three of the old pieces used for advertisement, and these have an inscription in an oval, BAILEY AND BATKIN, SOLE PATENTEES. William Bailey's name occurs in the list of potters for 1802 as a "gilder of earthenware."

BARKER, S., 1834, Don Pottery, Doncaster.—It was in this year that Barker, who owned the Old Pottery at Mexborough, bought the Don Pottery, which had been founded by John Green, who came from the Leeds Pottery in 1790 or thereabout. Green made a varied selection of earthenware goods, services for dinner, tea, and dessert, vases, baskets with pierced work, mainly after the Leeds style and pattern, some of it very cheap ware with transfer-printed and coloured decoration. The mark used was either "DON POTTERY" or "GREEN," on cream-coloured and fine earthenware;

OTHER ENGLISH POTTERIES

Barker continued to make pottery in the same style, but later he altered his mark to S. B. and S., which, however, was not constant till quite late. The earlier pieces had "Barker" with the lion and garter, sometimes with the name above; the flag was inscribed "Don," and "Pottery" below. Another mark was an eagle arising out of a ducal coronet. S. B. and S. refers to Samuel Barker and Son.

BELL, WILLIAM, 1820–40, Belle Vue Pottery, Hull.—The mark given is that of a factory which, during the period of its existence, produced vast quantities of domestic earthenware, cream-coloured. It was either painted in a comparatively poor style, or transfer-printed with the usual subjects —landscapes, flowers, etc.—in blue or in brown. The expenses of the factory reached in 1837 nearly £1,500, exclusive of rent, materials, etc.

LEEDS, 1780.

In the list of men employed whose wages are arranged under the nature of their work, we find that printing, biscuit painting, and enamel painting are considerable items. Bell's earthenware was largely exported to Germany.

BIRCH, EDMUND JOHN, c. 1800, Hanley.—Pieces marked E. I. B. or "Birch" were by this maker, whose productions included black Egyptian ware in imitation of Wedgwood. The present firm is, I believe, J. Dimmock and Co., Albion Works, Hanley.

BOOTH, ENOCH, c. 1750, Tunstall.—The manufacture of early pottery was very much improved by Enoch Booth's introduction of the *fluid glaze*. But he also modified the body of the earthenware by carefully refining and mixing the local clays with others brought from Cornwall, Devon, and Dorset, and adding certain proportions of whitelead and flint. His mark, "ENOCH BOOTH," is rare. His son-in-

268 OLD POTTERY

law, Antony Keeling, was a man of considerable enterprise. Not content with simply carrying on Booth's business, to which he succeeded, he was one of the little group who, in 1777, manufactured porcelain under Champion's patent for Bristol china. Hollins, Warburton, and Clowes were his partners in this work, which was carried on in his premises until he retired, when it was removed to New Hall, under the control of Hollins, Warburton, and Co. Reference is made to him, in 1786, as "Antony Keeling, manufacturer of Queen's ware in general, blue painted and enamelled, Egyptian black, etc." In 1802, two potteries were at work for the

STAFFORDSHIRE, LANE END, C. 1813.

STAFFORDSHIRE LUSTRE, LANE END, 1820.

Keelings, whose mark was "A. & E. KEELING." Some of the best of their ware is richly gilt and painted in bright colours with Oriental landscape and figures.

BOOTH AND CO., *c.* 1839, Hanley.—These potters produced red ware—a kind of terra-cotta, decorated with medallions, wreaths, etc., in relief, sometimes in black and at others the whole of the body and ornament were in red. The mark was the name, address, and date, in a border—"Published by G. R. Booth and Co., Hanley, Staffordshire, May 29, 1859."

BOURNE, E. and J., *c.* 1840, Denby Pottery, near Derby.—The early products of this factory were imitations of Wedgwood's black Egyptian and Etruscan wares, marked with

"E. BOURNE," or "Belper and Denby, Bourne's Potteries, Derbyshire."

BROMLEY, WM., *c.* 1800, Brampton.—Brampton ware was hard brown pottery with a reddish brown glaze in ordinary jugs, tobacco-jars, puzzle jugs, Toby jugs, etc. Quite early in the nineteenth century a cream-coloured earthenware was produced and decorated with transfer prints.

BROWNE, *c.* 1751, Caughley.—From the small beginnings of this pottery arose the operations of Thomas Turner, who came here from the Worcester factory, and produced the

ARMS OF THE UNITED STATES IN CENTRE.
STAFFORDSHIRE, DATED 1802.

NAPOLEON AS FIRST CONSUL.
COLOURED STAFFORDSHIRE.
BURSLEM, 1802.

celebrated Caughley porcelain, notably the "willow pattern," and the "blue dragon pattern" which have remained public favourites for so many years.

BURTON, S. and J., 1843, Hanley.—The pottery originally belonging to Edward Keeling, whose name is in the 1786 list, was taken over by the Burtons from James Keeling, successor to Edward. James Keeling took out a patent in 1796 for a leadless glaze, to be used on cream-coloured ware. Also in conjunction with V. Close, another Hanley potter, he took out another patent for improvements in kilns and ovens. The productions of this firm were notable with regard to the transfer prints of views in the East—Turkey, Persia, and India; a celebrated dinner service reproduced the illustrations from Buckingham's "Travels in Mesopotamia."

BUTLER, EDWARD, 1757, Swinton.—This potter succeeded Twigg, who established a factory on the Marquis of Rockingham's estate, hence the ware was known as "Rockingham ware." The mark TWIGGS has been found on a dish decorated with the "North-West view of the Earthenware Manufactory at Swinton, near Rotherham, in Yorkshire; established in the year 1745."

CHETHAM AND WOOLLEY, c. 1795, Lane End.—This firm,

BULL BAITING.   COLOURED STAFFORDSHIRE.

at about the date given, introduced a ware without glaze, having a *dry* body of fine grain, presumably non-absorbent, a body which was unaffected by change of temperature. Other attempts made to produce pearl ware were generally failures; nothing approached it in delicate whiteness amongst the earthenwares. It was marked "PEARL WARE," and specimen figures in this uncommon material have been found stamped "*Chetham and Woolley, Lane End*, 1798." Notable amongst these is a life-sized bust, inscribed "Admiral Lord Viscount Duncan, who defeated the Dutch fleet, commanded by Admiral De Winter, off the coast of Holland, on Wednesday, the 11th of October, 1797." This

OTHER ENGLISH POTTERIES

was formerly in the Litchfield Collection. There must be many pieces of this pearl ware still in existence unrecognised because it is unmarked. It was not stoneware, but fine-grained earthenware, bearing the same relation to white pottery that jasper does to the coloured. The present Pearl Pottery Company use P P in a diamond as a mark.

CHILD, SMITH, c. 1763, Tunstall.—This was not an important pottery. Queen's ware, "warranted Staffordshire," was made and the mark CHILD impressed. Sometimes the rims of plates in this cream-coloured ware were decorated with an embossed pattern. Later the business was acquired by J. H. Clive, whose ornamental engraving introduced to the transfer-printing a new and successful feature. In 1823, Joseph Heath and Co. were the proprietors.

CLEMENTSON, JOSEPH, 1855, Shelton.—The present firm, Clementson Bros., Phœnix Works, Hanley, are the successors of Joseph Clementson, who, in 1855, purchased the Bell Works, where W. Edwards, early in the eighteenth century, made domestic pottery with fine enamel colourings. About 1790, Job and George Ridgway were the proprietors. Job set up the new Cauldon Pottery, and left George, who retired some time previous to 1824 in favour of his nephews, John and William, who were Job's sons. We shall deal with the Ridgways later. Clementson made cream-colour ware, granite ware, etc., and supplied the American market largely. He died in 1871.

CLEWS, J. and R., 1814, Cobridge.—This pottery was noted for cream-coloured ware, and though for a few years china was made, it was owing to the earthenware and its success that they were able to retire about 1836. A year later, we find James Clews, with the aid of American capital, starting a factory in the United States called "The Indiana Pottery Company" at first, and changing its name later to the "Lewis Pottery Company." The venture was not a success, and Clews lost his money.

CLOSE AND CO., *c.* 1850, Stoke.—This pottery manufactured cream ware and white ware decorated with transfer-printing for the most part, though some of it was painted. One of the three W. Adams had a large business here before his death in 1829. He was not *the* W. Adams, but a distant relative. The firm seems to have continued as W. Adams and Sons until they were succeeded by Close and Co., whose mark was " CLOSE AND CO., LATE W. Adams and Sons, Stoke-upon-Trent."

DALE, I., 1830 ? Burslem.—This potter made Staffordshire figures, such as " Water," a figure of a girl with a creel in the left hand, and carrying two fishes in her right hand, which is holding up her skirt, fish at her feet, and the usual Staffordshire tree at her back. The impressed mark is

I. DALE,
BURSLEM.

Dale's Bust of Wesley is stamped I. DALE, BURSLEM, and impressed on the back is

THE REV. JOHN WESLEY
M.A.
BORN AT EPWORTH
JUNE 17th 1705
DIED MAR. 2nd
1791
AGED 88.

DANIEL, HENRY, 1826, Shelton.—Daniel was an enameller from Spode's, and began to make fine china at Stoke. At the date given above he manufactured stone china at Skelton. Shaw says that, in addition to the ordinary enamelling, he adopted grounds of different colours and used gilding both burnished and embossed. The firm became " H. and R. Daniel," which was the mark. The ware rightly won a good name for the excellence of shapes, patterns, and decoration.

DANIEL, RALPH, *c.* 1743, Cobridge.—This Ralph Daniel succeeded his father, who bore the same name, and whose establishment existed in Hot Lane or Cobridge before 1710. He conferred immense benefit upon the Potteries by intro-

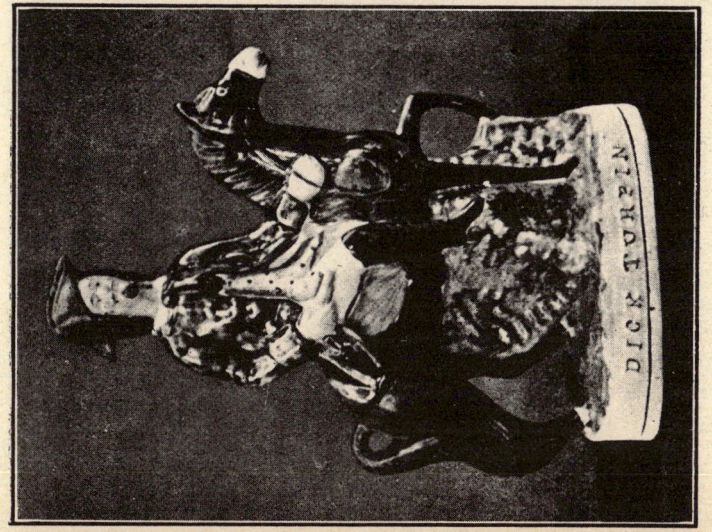

ORDINARY COTTAGE STAFFORDSHIRE. LATE PERIOD.
From Miss Edith Feilden's Collection.

OTHER ENGLISH POTTERIES

ducing moulds of plaster of Paris from France. These moulds were soon widely adopted, because of the ease with which they could be made and used. There were other

DOULTON WARE.

potters named Daniel—John, Richard, Robert, Thomas, Timothy, and Walter, several of whom appear in the Burslem list for 1786. Those pieces which came from Cobridge may have the mark R. DANIEL.

DAVENPORT, J., 1793, Longport. Brindley's earthenware made at this factory from 1773 cannot now be distinguished. When, twenty years later, J. Davenport acquired possession of the works, he at first continued to make the ordinary pottery, blue-printed, white and cream, resembling the products of Herculaneum, varied in pattern and of good quality. Later, porcelain was manufactured, and its richness contrasted with the earthenware, which had but the usual features of good ware. The mark is an anchor with or without " Davenport " or " Longport."

DAWSON, early eighteenth century, Sunderland.—Pink metallic lustre, with transfer-printed figures, was produced at this pottery, of which little is known, save that it was

POTTERY PROCESSES. TERRA-COTTA PANEL BY G. TINWORTH, THE MOST FAMOUS MODELLER OF MODERN TIMES.

engaged in making pottery and earthenware services early in the eighteenth century. In 1857 Thomas Dawson and Co. was the title of the firm, which does not now appear in the list of manufacturers.

DIXON, AUSTIN, AND Co., early eighteenth century, Sunderland.—Like other Sunderland factories, ordinary ware was made at this pottery with the pink metallic lustre decoration and transfer printing so usual on jugs, bowls, mugs, and dishes. Some figures were made and marked " DIXON, AUSTIN, AND CO., SUNDERLAND." Many pieces, notably the flat dishes with a ship of war and a verse, were marked " DIXON & CO., Sunderland Pottery."

DOULTON AND WATTS, 1815, Lambeth.—We hope that one day we may have an opportunity of doing full justice

OTHER ENGLISH POTTERIES 275

to the great modern manufacturers, Messrs. Doulton & Co., who have very kindly sent the following information which concerns the early history of their famous works. "Originally established in 1815, on a very small scale, the works remained for many years devoted to the manufacture of ordinary stoneware for household, chemical, and sanitary purposes. No attention had been paid to the production of art wares; and salt-glazing, as applied to decorative pottery, had practically died out in England, until its revival by this firm." In fact, in the 1867 Paris Exhibition "a few vases and jugs only were produced of good form, well

thrown and turned, with bands of blue and brown for decoration." Which brings us to Doulton's marvellous modern ware, and we must stop. We give the present marks, and a few others, with an important note which should be remembered. All marks where "England" is added to the name or the pattern are not earlier than 1891, when the place of origin had to be fixed on all goods imported into the United States in order to comply with "The McKinley Tariff Act"—'(American Customs Regulations).''

The marks impressed at the foot of all pieces are now as shown above.

Among the stamps formerly used have been the following :—

DUNDERDALE, DAVID, c. 1790, Castleford.—This potter

made the finer kinds of pottery at his works, a few miles from Leeds. He paid especial attention to cream ware and black basaltes, but he produced in addition a distinctive ware known

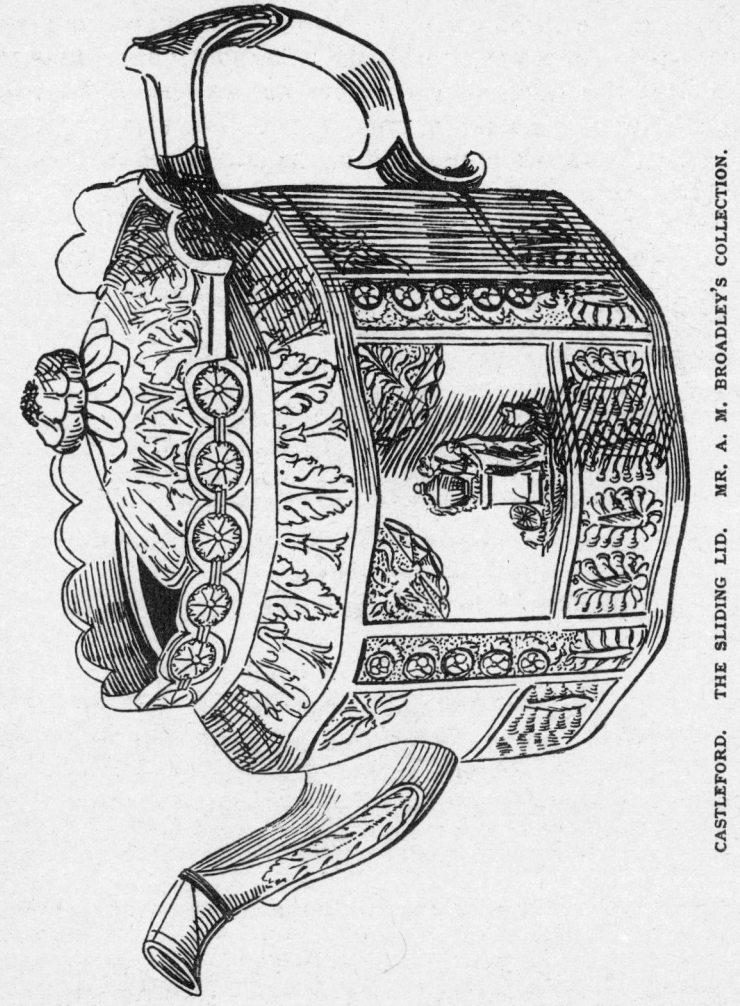

CASTLEFORD. THE SLIDING LID. MR. A. M. BROADLEY'S COLLECTION.

as "Castleford" to all collectors, and distinguishable at a glance when once learnt. It is difficult to describe, but here is an attempt to teach from the illustration given. The paste is like Parian ware with a smear of glaze; really it is a cream stoneware. The edgings are blue or brown—the typical Castleford colours—and the general shape and ornament are quite good. The medallions are classical, very similar to the Flaxman designs for Wedgwood, who seems to have been the inspiration for the black basaltes, and the white wares both decorated with raised figures or flowers, as well as the knobs of the covers for tea- and coffee-pots modelled with a classical figure of a woman seated. Some of Dunderdale's lids were most ingenious devices to prevent slipping. One had a hinged arrangement, a hole in the material of the hinge, through which a thin rod of metal passed, which was fixed to the rim on both sides. Another lid ran in a groove, and could be removed where the groove

CASTLEFORD TEAPOT.

ended, about half-way across the mouth of the pot. A third had a groove and a stop, so that the lid was not removable, but slid back over the handle. The name "DUNDERDALE" is sometimes found impressed as a mark. Later, Plowes was taken into partnership, when the firm became D. DUNDERDALE & CO., the impressed mark being generally D. D. & CO., CASTLEFORD POTTERY. In 1820 the pottery was closed.

FELL & Co., *c.* 1820, Newcastle-on-Tyne.—The names FELL; FELL & CO.; T. FELL & CO.; F. and CO. are found impressed or printed on cream ware, bronze lustre ware, and common earthenware, sometimes with an impressed anchor, or with the arms of Newcastle in transfer and the name below the shield on a label. This was one of the many factories which produced the ordinary willow pattern.

FERRYBRIDGE, 1804, Knottingley, 1792.—This latter pottery, afterwards merged into Ferrybridge founded by Tomlinson, is worth noting, because in 1796 Ralph Wedgwood, a relative of Josiah, became a partner in the firm, and the articles produced were poor imitations of the real Wedgwood in jasper and other wares. The mark has often been confused with the Etruria marks, but there is a difference. This firm used "WEDGWOOD & CO." (Note " & CO.") Again, this last mark must be distinguished from that used by W. Smith, of Stockton-on-Tees, who stamped "WEDGEWOOD" (as spelt) upon his ware until he was stopped by an injunction in 1848. Coloured earthenware figures were made at Ferrybridge, such as "Two Cupids struggling for a heart." A few examples are marked "Ferrybridge."

GLASS, JOSEPH, c. 1670, Hanley.—About this period Thomas Toft and his school were producing those curious coarse buff-ware dishes decorated with coloured slip. Glass may take his place in this school, for his dishes and tygs are decorated in the same style, and his name is painted round the pieces in brown slip.

GOULDING, WILLIAM, 1760, Isleworth.—This was a factory for both porcelain and pottery. It was founded by Joseph Shore, who came from the Worcester works. William Goulding was his son-in-law, and Goulding's father was Shore's chief painter. Leaving out of consideration the porcelain, which was just like Worcester, we note that the earthenware was of a strong close texture and streaked with yellow and brown glaze. Some few pieces have been found marked with William Goulding's name and dated. The factory was moved to Hounslow about 1825, but it failed, and was closed a short time after.

HACKWOOD AND SONS, 1842, New Hall, Skelton.—The old New Hall stock of china was sold when the manufacture ceased in 1825. Then after a few years W. Ratcliffe started a pottery, which Hackwood and Sons took over at the date given above. The name was used as an impressed mark. Then the elder Hackwood died in 1849, and "*Hackwood*" became the mark, still impressed. A later mark, "C. & H.,"

OTHER ENGLISH POTTERIES

showed that Cockson and Harding were the proprietors in 1862. The early ware was cream-coloured, some of it being well painted; but the later products, in blue and brown glazed earthenware with relief ornament in white, come into the modern period.

HARLEY, T., c. 1805, Lane End.—The usual transfer-printed earthenware, Queen's ware, and black basaltes were made at this Longton pottery. But some curious old jugs, painted with caricatures of Napoleon, have been found marked "*T. Harley, Lane End*," and some of the pottery is stamped "HARLEY."

HEATH, J. and C., 1750, Cock Pit Hill, Derby.—The early pottery, many pieces of which are dated, was of a different character to that made by the Heaths. It resembled the coarse earthenware coated with a dark chocolate-coloured glaze which was common from 1600 to 1680. The earliest date on a specimen of this Derby pottery is 1643. The Heaths —John and Christopher— made enamelled cream ware, plain cream tea-table ware, white, stone, and brown ware, etc., from 1750 to 1780, when the whole stock-in-trade of the extensive factory was sold without reserve.

AN UNUSUAL SET OF JUGS, MARKED "HERCULANEUM." IN MR. S. FAIR'S POSSESSION.

HERCULANEUM POTTERY, 1790, Liverpool.—The early factory that merged into *Herculaneum* was founded by Abbey at the date given; then, in 1796, Messrs. Worthington, Hurable, and Holland—Worthington and Company—took the works over and gave them the name of "Herculaneum." They made Queen's ware and blue-printed china, and commenced to manufacture china in 1800. The earthenware services for dinner and dessert were often painted with roses and rosebuds on a maroon or other coloured border. Under various proprietors the company continued till 1833, when the works were sold. They were let to Thomas Case in partnership with John Mort, a potter, who carried them on till 1836, and by Mort and Simpson for five years longer. The site is now occupied by the Herculaneum Dock. The early mark was "Herculaneum" printed in blue, as given.

A Liver

Sometimes, however, the name was stamped. The bird—the liver—the arms of the town, was used by Case, Mort and Company about 1833-6.

HOLLINS, RICHARD, 1750, Hanley.—The early ware was the ordinary Staffordshire. Richard Hollins, died 1780, was the father of Samuel, of Shelton, and his other sons, T. and J., who succeeded the father in the Hanley Works, afterwards admitted their brother Richard into the firm, which remained T. J. and R. Hollins till 1820. Their best work is to be found in the careful imitation of Wedgwood's jasper ware, some of which was highly finished in blue cameo decoration on a white ground, and had the mark impressed "T. and J. Hollins." They also made the ordinary Staffordshire ware, which never has any considerable value, being simply transfer-printed.

HOLLINS, SAMUEL, 1774, Shelton.—Amongst the partners in the New Hall works at Shelton were S. Hollins and Peter

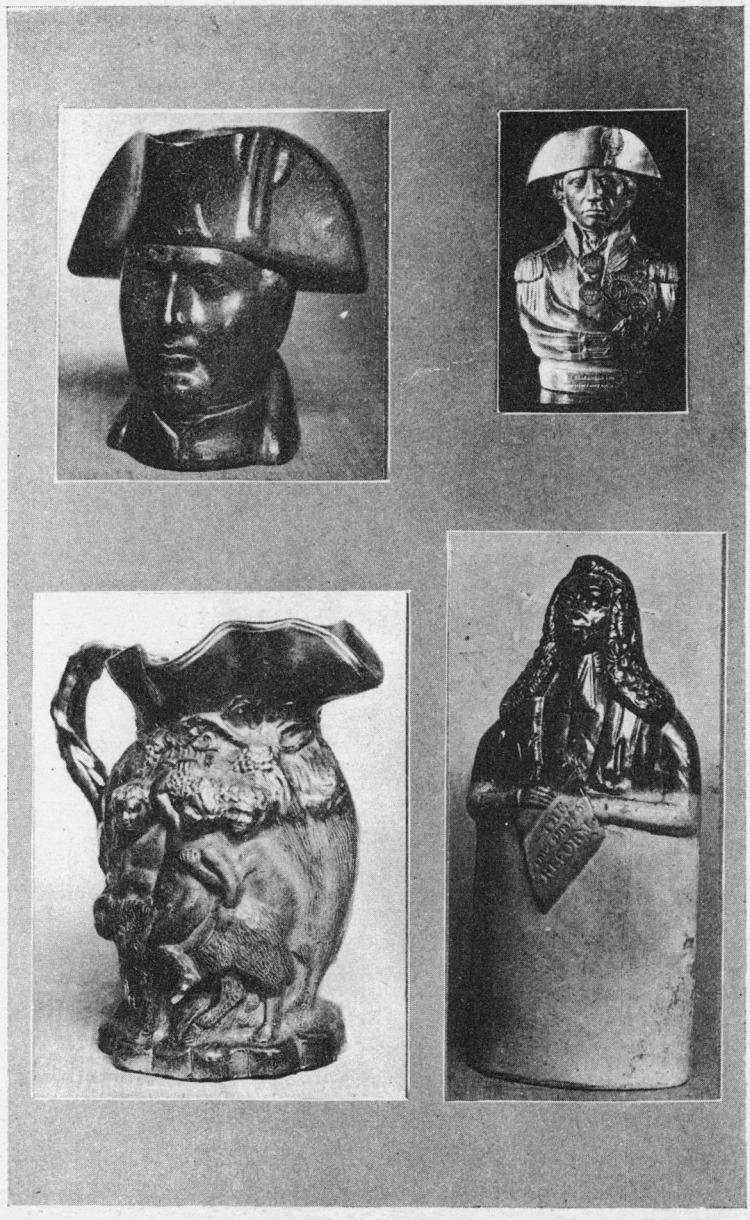

NAPOLEON AND NELSON JUGS. BACCHANALIAN JUG AND REFORM SPIRIT FLASK. DOULTON WARE.
From Mr. A. M. Broadley's Collection.

Warburton. Some of the finest black busts of Shakespeare and Mercury, and tea and coffee services, were made by Warburton probably when he was in partnership with Hollins. We find that the latter produced fine red ware in his own factory at Shelton during the same time, as well as black basaltes. And further he made coloured grounds such as maroon and sage green. The general style of ornament was embossed hunting scenes or flowers. The mark impressed was "S. HOLLINS."

KEELING, J., 1796, Hanley.—Here we have another instance of potters who, under the name of *Keeling, Toft and Co.*, made black basaltes and ordinary dinner services with views. The stamped mark of the name of the firm is sometimes found. From 1806 to 1824 Keeling's name appears as a partner, but in the next six years Toft and May were the proprietors. The works are not now in existence.

STAFFORDSHIRE. SHELTON, 1797.

LAKIN AND POOLE, 1770, Hanley.—The chief products of this pottery were cream-coloured ware and black basaltes. Some of the latter were decorated with raised groups and other ornament, in very good imitation of Wedgwood; but, as we have shown, the black ware was made by a great many factories, and the so-called classical style was for some time in fashion, though now black ware is most difficult to sell at anything like a good price. The mark used was the impressed "LAKIN & POOLE," whilst on the printed earthenware another impressed mark, "Lakin & Poole," may be found, or a similar mark printed. Classical ruins and English landscapes furnished the printed patterns in blue.

Some pieces are well decorated with painted birds and landscapes, and these are of more value. In fact, all painted earthenware is increasing in value, and so, too, are those specimens which have the printed English landscapes named. The firm made figures, of which the chief group is

the "Assassination of Marat," by Charlotte Cordé (Corday), given as an illustration.

In dealing with Staffordshire figures, it will be useful to the reader to have some idea of the prices paid for good but not fine old examples. Those given below are from a sale of old English pottery which was the property of a well-known collector. The auction took place in May 1908.

A Ralph Wood Toby jug, representing an old man seated holding a jug on his knee with left hand, with his right holding a cup of ale, **sold for £6 6s.**

OTHER ENGLISH POTTERIES 283

Another similar, but the right hand placed upon the jug, realised £6 15s.

A Ralph Wood group, representing the vicar asleep in the reading desk and the clerk praying earnestly in the pew below, pew broken, stamped inscription, " The Vicar and Moses," fetched £15.

A Ralph Wood group of a shepherd and shepherdess, seated upon rustic bases, with dog, lamb and goat under (he is playing a flute and the shepherdess holds a crook, her head resting in her right hand) cost the buyer £12.

A Ralph Wood group, representing St. George and the Dragon, made £14.

(The above pieces bore the Whieldon type of colouring—yellow, green, brown, manganese-purple, also a brown-black and blue.)

A large jug, on one side a man hugging a bag of gold, inscribed by side, " The Miser " ; on reverse a man representing " The Spendthrift " ; in the centre a portrait in relief of Shakespeare, inscribed "Shakespeare, The Poet," decorated in translucent colours, was very cheap at £3 5s.

LINTHORPE POTTERY, c. 1880, modern, Middlesbrough-on-Tees.—The following information regarding the Linthorpe pottery, now extinct, has been most kindly communicated by Mr. Henry Tooth, of the Bretby Art Pottery, Woodville, near Burton-on-Trent :—

One of the choicest, and assuredly most notable, of new art centres is that of Linthorpe, near Middlesbrough-on-Tees, to whose productions we desire to direct brief attention. The works were, we believe, formerly simply a brick-yard, known as the " Sun Brick Works," but they were placed on a seam of such remarkably good and fine clay as to induce their energetic owner, Mr. Harrison, to feel a confident hope that it was capable of considerable art development. Applying to Dr. Dresser, a series of experiments was at once commenced, and the necessary means taken to convert the works into a manufactory of ornamental pottery. Dr. Dresser undertook the important post of art-director to the new works, and the whole concern was wisely placed under the management of Mr. Henry Tooth, to whom the world is indebted for bringing the productions of these now famous works to their present high state of perfection. Mr. Tooth, it is worth recording, was not a practical potter when he undertook the task of managing and carrying on this manufactory, but he was a man of great capacity, of remarkable aptitude in the mastering of all the necessary details, of great energy, and endowed with natural good taste and artistic feeling. He set about his task in a spirit and with a determination that ensured success, and we have it from

himself that until he saw those that emanated from his own hands
he had never seen any one of the processes of pot-making carried on.
" I may just say," are his own words, " that I never saw a pot made
until I undertook the management of this venture, and that during
what we may call the experimental period I ' made, burned, and
finished the ware entirely myself.' We have now about eighty hands
employed, and purpose setting on more when we get our new buildings
completed." The productions of the Linthorpe Pottery, so far as
we have an opportunity of seeing them, are remarkable for the originality, the boldness in many instances, of the designs; the strength
and quality of the body, and the faultless beauty of the glaze. Some
of the examples are eminently beautiful, and all have a stamp of
originality about them that is very striking, and at once lifts them
to a level peculiarly their own. The body, which is simply an ordinary
red brick clay, but of far more than average fineness, is much closer,
harder, and more compact than the bodies usually used for majolica,
and is capable of delicate and careful manipulation; and the glaze
is clear, firm, hard, and of more than usual brilliancy. The colours
used and the styles of decoration adopted are thoroughly good, and
the manipulative processes seem in all cases to have been carefully
carried out. We do not on the present occasion purpose to speak
of any one of the designs in particular, or of any of the surface colourings, for the variety is so great that it is unnecessary to do so.—*Reli-
quary Journal and Review*, July 1880.

Another account :—

The establishment of a fresh industry in any place with a probability
of success is always a subject for congratulation, but when a district
like that in the immediate neighbourhood of Middlesbrough, in which
the collapse of the iron trade has had such a disastrous and ruinous
effect, has the prospect of a new application of its great mineral wealth
opened up, the matter becomes doubly interesting, as it may later
on become proportionately valuable. A clay found at Linthorpe,
near Middlesbrough, hitherto exclusively confined to brick-making,
has recently been utilised for the production of a new species of art
pottery, decorated and undecorated. The body is of a rich red,
thrown into forms more or less elegant, and sometimes original;
they are also decorated with incised ornaments, all worked by hand,
then coloured with glazes and tinted with oxides, producing rich
mottled and semi-translucent enamelled effects, very suggestive
of some of the best methods of the Japanese. In fact, occasionally
there is an affectation of the eccentricities of Japanese art, which,
however, is not absolutely out of place in a decorative aspect. Dr.
Dresser suggested the experiment of founding a pottery at Linthorpe
to Mr. John Harrison, of Darlington. The hint was acted upon,

the establishment being placed under the direction of Mr. Tooth, who, when he commenced the organisation of the new branch of manufacture, appears to have had the singular qualification of knowing nothing about potter's art; nevertheless he has been successful in the production of a large variety of pleasing articles. The idea is to produce a ware which shall be both highly artistic and within reach of the general public, and the object is certainly attained.—*Art Journal*, February 7, 1880.

The wares of Linthorpe will be valuable as time goes on. The collector should now secure fine specimens which present all the variety and mingled riches of hue which are found in old Chinese variegated and single-glaze ware, "sang de bœuf," apple green, turquoise-blue, low-toned reds, mottled olives, browns, and yellows, varieties, in fact, too numerous to mention. Then, again, the Linthorpe incised and perforated wares are really artistic; so, too, are the shapes. Many are quite quaint, and others are highly graceful and beautiful, being derived from classical and foreign sources, or from original designs. It seems a pity that these works should have been closed; but the same fate has overtaken a number of other potteries. The outlook is rather disquieting from the collector's point of view. The only encouragement is to be found in the fine products made by the leading manufacturers of the present day, and, indeed, by some whose works are not large.

LOCKETT, J., *c.* 1786, Burslem.—Reference has previously been made to the manufacturers' list of potters, dated 1786. In that list Timothy and John Lockett are mentioned as *white stone* potters. The white stoneware was salt glaze, then commonly made. Lockett's stonewares were decorated in relief with the vine-leaves and grapes so well known in the Whieldon productions. The difficulty with the collector is to find the make of unmarked pieces. When the impressed mark—" J. LOCKETT "—is found either on the white stone or chocolate-coloured ware, it may properly be ascribed to Burslem. Later, in 1802, Lane End appears to have become the home of the pottery. The firm was then J. and G. Lockett, and in 1829 J. Lockett and Sons.

LOWESBY POTTERY, *c.* 1835, Sir Francis Fowke.—The

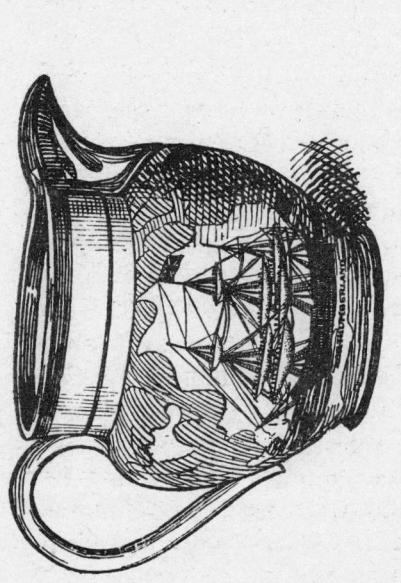

"NORTHUMBERLAND" (47 GUNS) JUG. SUNDERLAND. BACK VIEW OF "NORTHUMBERLAND" JUG.
FROM MISS E. FEILDEN'S COLLECTION.

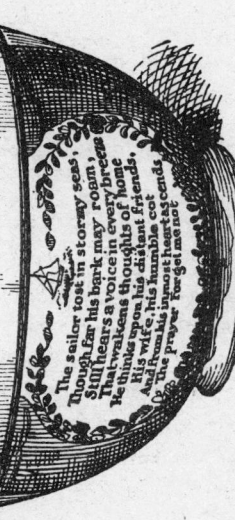

THE SAILOR'S FAREWELL. SUNDERLAND. THE SAILOR'S FAREWELL. BACK VIEW.
FROM MISS E. FEILDEN'S COLLECTION.

marks given are to be found on red terra-cotta ware made in imitation of Wedgwood and decorated with relief ornament in black. The works stopped long ago.

MAYER, ELIJAH, c. 1770, Hanley.—Several potters named Mayer appear in the Staffordshire records, but E. Mayer was a formidable competitor to all the potters in the district, his output being greater than almost any other. The usual cream-coloured ware and black basaltes common to the contemporaries of Wedgwood were only a part of his work. Brown line ware; drab, terra-cotta, unglazed, with coloured festoons in relief; and services that might be termed Nelson services, were mostly marked " E. Mayer," impressed. The naval engagements of the Nile and Trafalgar furnished patriotic material for decoration. Nelson, Britannia, Fame, the Pyramids, crocodiles, and a monument all appealed to the national spirit. E. Mayer took his son into partnership, and the mark was altered to " E. Mayer & Son." Joseph Mayer took over the works at his father's death, and they were closed in 1830. Some pieces have the mark " *Joseph Mayer & Co.*"

MAYER AND NEWBOLD, c. 1820, Lane End.—The early owners of this pottery, the Johnsons, made that early salt-glaze ware which was known as *crouch ware*, but salt glaze was seldom marked. Now and then some cursive letters are found, or an enamelled mark such as a cross, evidently a workman's mark, purely a caprice. The Johnsons, T. and J., were succeeded by Mayer and Newbold, whose mark was " May^r & $Newb^d$," or " M. & N." They produced large quantities of china.

MEIGH, JOB, 1770, Hanley.—At the Old Hall, Job Meigh and his son, aided later by Charles Meigh, his grandson, produced many varieties of earthenware, blue-printed, white,

QUEEN CAROLINE MUG. "ROCKET" ENGINE JUG, LIVERPOOL AND MANCHESTER RAILWAY.
From Miss Edith Feilden's Collection.

stone-ware, jet ware and Parian. The body was of good quality, often decorated with relief work, plain, silvered, or gilt. The mark MEIGH was used, and also "Indian Stone China" in a circle, "Opaque Porcelain," "Enamel Porcelain," and "Stone China Indian," with "O. H. E. C. L." (Old Hall Earthenware Company, Limited). The last mark was adopted in 1861, ten years after medals were granted to C. Meigh at the Great Exhibition. The inscription at the base relative to the Society of Arts medal will be familiar to collectors.

MIDDLESBROUGH POTTERY, c. 1831.—These were the first works established in Middlesbrough. From 1831 to 1844 the title of the firm was "The Middlesbrough Pottery Company," which was changed from 1844-52 to "The Middlesbrough Earthenware Company," then to "Messrs. Isaac Wilson and Company." The ordinary wares in opaque china and pottery were produced, and enamelled flower-pots, bread-trays, as well as lustre. The printed patterns were indicated in conjunction with the printed initials of the firm. Thus scenes, "Nunthorpe," "Trent," or flowers, "Convolvulus," were used with "M.P. & Co.," "I.W. & Co." The other marks given were usually impressed.

The anchor and London used at Middlesboro'. 1848.

MINTON, 1790, Stoke-upon-Trent.—Thomas Minton and Joseph Poulson entered into partnership when these famous works were founded. Poulson had been Spode's manager. This firm began with the manufacture of earthenware, and until 1798 made nothing else. The chief employment was blue transfer printing, imitating Nankin blue and white. Thomas Minton had been apprenticed to an engraver, and his skill had much to do with the development of this ornament. In 1817 Thomas and Herbert were admitted into partnership with their father, the firm being "Thomas Minton and Sons," but, in 1821, Thomas studied for the Church, and

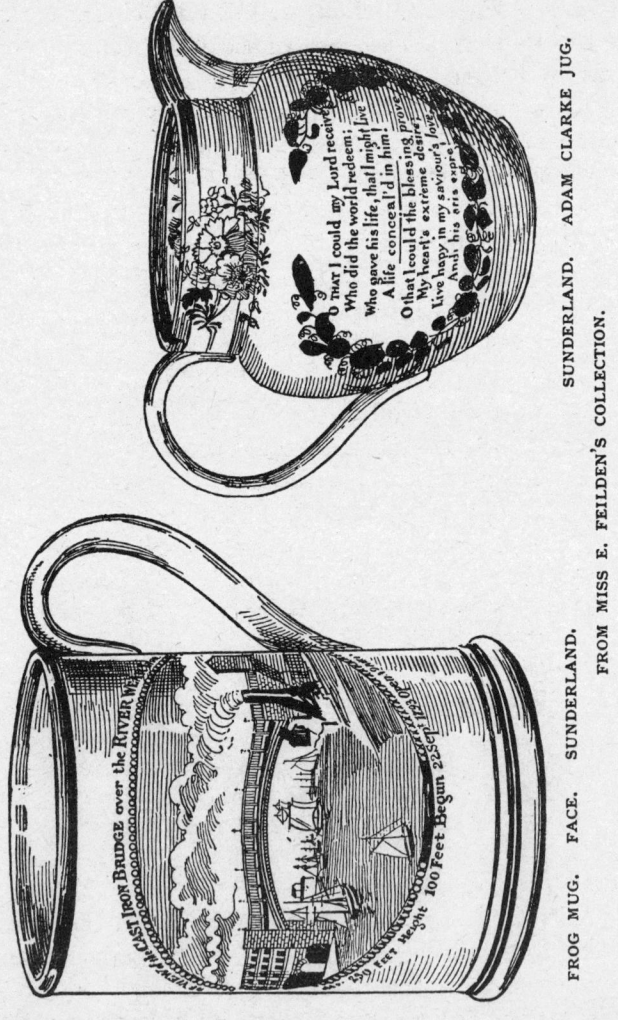

SUNDERLAND. ADAM CLARKE JUG.

FROG MUG. FACE. SUNDERLAND.

FROM MISS E. FEILDEN'S COLLECTION.

became curate at Chesterfield in 1825. About this time great improvements in the body and glaze were notable. The white was clearer, and in the glaze, lead was largely displaced by borax. Thomas Minton died in 1836, and his son Herbert admitted John Boyle to partnership, but after five years the latter left to join Josiah Wedgwood and Sons. The mark used during this period was "M and B," or "Minton and Boyle," with the date, on "stone china," "semi-china," "felspar china," or "opaque china." These intermediary stages between pottery and porcelain were, at this period, improved still more, and in 1845 a rather common, but more or less puzzling mark appears, the explanation of which may be of service. "B.B." "New Stone." The B.B. indicates Best Body, and refers to the paste or body used in the manufacture. Another mark dating from about 1823 appears, so our experience shows, to create much interest. We give it here :—

The collector will note that before 1798 the wares made were earthenware—white, cream-coloured, and blue printed. In that year semi-transparent china was manufactured until 1811, when it was given up, and for ten years earthenware only was made.

The copy by Mintons' of the St. Porchaire or Henri Deux candlestick in the Museum at South Kensington is far removed from the thick and clumsy imitations, which should not for a moment deceive the collector. Mintons' is a very fine reproduction, showing the true *renaissance* style of François I. and Henri II. See page 293.

Parian Ware.—In 1821 the manufacture of semi-transparent china was resumed, and shortly after porcelain was commenced, which maintains to the present day the highest excellence. Whether we consider the glaze or paste, we find both faultless. The decoration is rich, clear, and artistic, and the potting leaves nothing to be desired. Who introduced

MINTON FIGURES.

Parian—Minton, or Copeland? The jury of the 1851 Exhibition could not decide, so settled it thus. Whichever party may have actually been first in publicly producing articles in this material, both were contemporaneously working with success towards the same result. Parian was introduced to these works at Stoke-upon-Trent in 1842, and was largely manufactured. Curiously, it has never quite received the pubic recognition which it deserves.

OTHER ENGLISH POTTERIES

Majolica Ware.—Eight years later Majolica entered upon its pre-eminent career as an art production, and Mintons' Majolica brought increased reputation to the firm, owing to its purity of design and colour, its sharpness in detail, and excellence of glaze. Useful and decorative articles were made in immense variety. In 1851 two other reproductions were commenced—Della Robbia and Palissy wares. The same year saw the "Great Exhibition," where the firm received the highest recognition for its meritorious work, and since then honours have been showered upon it on each occasion when the products have been exhibited. Mintons' have displayed an intelligent interest in securing the finest artists, experts, and designers.

"ST. PORCHAIRE" OR "HENRI DEUX" CANDLESTICK.

Expert Workers.—When the works at Derby closed down in 1825 the skilled workmen were engaged at Mintons'. When Samuel Bourne, the enamel painter, pupil of Wood and Caldwell, had revealed his talents and shown his industry, Mintons', in 1828, was

OLD POTTERY

the field for his services, where he maintained his high reputation till 1848. John Simpson was chief enameller from 1837 to 1847. M. Arnoux, the expert from Toulouse, was employed as a superintendent; M. Emile Jeannest as a sculptor, to whom in 1854 succeeded another Frenchman, M. Carrier de Belleuse, whose skill as a sculptor led to his

MINTON VASES.

appointment later at Sèvres. M. Protât, the sculptor of some of the stone statues at the India Office, succeeded him.

Solon's Pâte-sur-Pâte.—That eminent artist M. Solon-Milès, the master in *pâte-sur-pâte*, belonged to the modern period—is, in fact, of our own time, yet no notice of Mintons' would be complete that did not recognise his marvellous treatment of liquid clay instead of enamel colour—a method which he has made entirely his own, and in which he stands alone, unrivalled. Centuries before Solon's time the Chinese used that decoration, chiefly on a celadon ground. Solon's specimens are very effective on a similar ground, though he used others, such as green, grey, and chocolate. He signed his works "Solon" or "Milès," or in monogram M.L.S. interlaced; the L. Solon being another form of his name. For prices see Appendix.

Marks on Minton.—Attention is specially called to the fact that as a mark "MINTON," stamped or impressed in the body of the ware, was not used till 1861, so that it is modern; and here we must leave the interesting story of Mintons', not without hope of resuming it as opportunity permits. The "M" mark—two examples given—is painted on the ware in blue, usually on fine porcelain, though the M occurs alone on some specimens. The ermine spot, in gold or colours, is also a late mark in occasional use. In the other marks "MINTON" is printed on a globe or circle, and under a crown.

EWER AND STAND. MINTON.

MOORE & CO., 1789, Southwick, near Sunderland.—Reference has been made previously to Sunderland lustre. The Southwick works were established by Brunton and Company, who were succeeded in 1803 by "MOORE & CO.," which name with "SOUTHWICK" is used on jugs, mugs, bowls, etc., having pink metallic lustre decorations. Miss Edith Feilden's kindness enables us to show some typical specimens, including the frog mug, said to be made to commemorate the building and opening of these potteries. The transfer decoration is on a creamy white ground, like Liverpool and Leeds ware. Dawson, Dixon, Fell, Phillips, Sewell, and Donkin are names which appear on similar ware —pink metallic lustre made either at Sunderland or New-

MINTON MAJOLICA.

castle. Amongst other transfers are Nelson's victories, ships of war, sailors' songs, and other popular subjects. The willow-pattern plate was also made at this factory, and may be found occasionally with the name.

MOSELEY, c. 1819, Burslem.—The Churchyard Works—the school where Josiah Wedgwood served his apprenticeship to his brother—belonged to the family from 1700 or earlier; his grandfather occupied them in 1710. They remained with the Wedgwoods till 1795, when they were sold to Thomas Green. In 1811, a manufacturer named Johnson bought them, to sell them a few years later to Moseley. He made, amongst the other common ware, black basaltes or Egyptian ware, with fluted bodies and classical figures, some of which are impressed with his name "MOSELEY."

NEALE, J., 1776, Hanley.—In the chapter on Wedgwood and his rivals, we saw that Neale was the partner of Palmer, a most unscrupulous copyist of Wedgwood's wares. This was before 1776. Two years later Neale took Robert Wilson as partner, and "Neale & Wilson" was adopted as the mark, which was sometimes used on cream-coloured earthenware, enamelled in colours. Amongst this class of products were Toby Fillpots—the Toby ale jugs which have been before described. The other mark, showing that other partners had been added to the firm, is found about 1790. "Neale & Co." is inscribed or impressed on very good Staffordshire figures, on blue and white jasper, and black basaltes, as well as cream-coloured ware. Recently an old Stafford pottery drinking-cup, formed as a pointer's head, impressed "Neale and Company," rare, was sold by auction for £2 15s. We give the marks of Palmer, Neale, and Wilson.

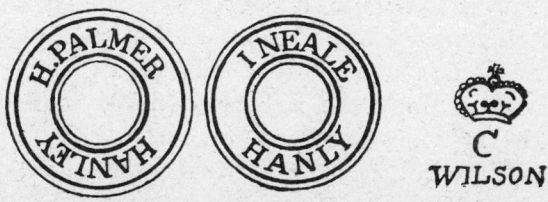

PALMER, H. C., 1760, Hanley.—John Palmer, the father of H. Palmer, was a potter, too, and according to Dr. Shaw, the employment of Devonshire pipeclay supplied the chalk-body ware made by Chatterly and Palmer, of Hanley; and, further, he is credited with having introduced salt and litharge in the glaze. H. Palmer may be classified with Neale as an unblushing pirate. He seems to have used his wife, or perhaps it would be better to say that Mrs. Palmer herself laid plans, for securing Wedgwood pieces as soon as they were put on sale. Hanley employed Voyez as his modeller in 1769, and it may have been through Voyez's knowledge that Palmer's imitations were so fine. (See previous chapter on "Imitators of Wedgwood.")

COCK FIGHTING. STAFFORDSHIRE, C. 1790.

PHILLIPS & Co., c. 1810, Sunderland.—This firm used the mark "PHILLIPS & CO," with Sunderland and a date or "Sunderland Pottery," and produced the usual cream ware and lustre so common to the district. The works were called the Garrison Pottery, and must be distinguished from the Hylton Pottery, near Sunderland. This was established in 1780, and a view is sometimes found on jugs, etc., of the Hylton Pot Works, marked "J. PHILLIPS, Hylton Pottery." Pink lustre was also made here. There was another Phillips, of Longport, who manufactured cream ware, and was one of those who used the well-known willow pattern.

PIERCE, W., & Co., c. 1800, Benthall.—We have said something about John Thursfield and the Jackfield ware. He went to Benthall on leaving Jackfield, and with him carried the secret of the black glaze. When he died his secret died with him, and though his son of the same name, with his partner, W. Pierce, continued "The Mug House" factory,

A PAIR OF SMALL GROTESQUE FIGURES OF MEN. STAFFORDSHIRE, COPIED FROM DERBY. VERY UNCOMMON.

it was only till 1813. Some pieces have *W. Pierce and Co.* as a mark.

PLANT, B., c. 1780, Lane End.—Amongst other Staffordshire ware, this potter made figures. Some of his lions are inscribed "Benjamin Plant, Lane End," others "B. Plant, Lane End." Jugs in the form of lions, etc., were also produced at his factory. Lustre-ware lions and jugs marked are quite uncommon, and the collector of old English pottery will be fortunate if he finds one marked by this maker.

POOLE, R., *c.* 1790, Burslem.—The firm of Lakin and Poole carried on an extensive trade towards the end of the eighteenth century. The mark used on the billhead was a garter and star surrounding a vase, on which was an inscription, "Manufacturers of Staffordshire earthenware." On the garter another inscription stated "Burnished gold got up as in London." Blue painted table services, services enamelled with arms, crests, cyphers, etc., were advertised, but soon the word *painted* was altered to *printed* in the billheads, and the products of the factory were limited to transfer-printed and coloured earthenware. In 1795, the firm altered its title by the admission of another partner to *Poole, Lakin, and Shrigley*. Next year another alteration took place by the withdrawal of Lakin, the firm being "Poole and Shrigley." The goods manufactured were in great variety of cream ware, blue-printed fawn-colour, black and other wares, and figures in great variety and of excellent character in modelling, printing, and decoration. The mark of the firm was "LAKIN AND POOLE," impressed, though on some pieces the name LAKIN and on others POOLE only is found.

EARL HOWE. COLOURED EARTHENWARE. STAFFORDSHIRE, 1794.

REED, J., 1839, Mexborough.—This Reed was the successor of Messrs. Reed and Taylor, also of the Ferrybridge Works. The first products of the "Rock Pottery," as it was named, owing to the workrooms having been built close up to the rocks, which indeed formed the back wall of the factory, were brown and yellow wares of the ordinary type. Native clays only were used, and dishes, jugs, etc., for household use, garden and root pots, and pitchers, were the objects chiefly made. J. Reed's father introduced the manufacture of the finer kinds of earthenware with such success that the premises were enlarged several times. In 1873 Messrs. S. Woolf and Company, the owners of the "Australian Pottery" at Ferrybridge, became the owners, and entered into full competition with the Staffordshire houses. The mark used occasionally at the Mexborough Pottery was the name of the proprietor, in large capitals, REED. It should be noted that vases in imitation of Oriental were a speciality of this firm.

STAFFORDSHIRE. BURSLEM, C. 1790.

The Bell Works.—RIDGWAY, J. and G., 1790, Shelton. The Bell Works in the early eighteenth century produced a variety of earthenware with the lead glaze under the direction of W. Edwards, a clever potter and chemist, who made very fine enamel colours. He died in 1753, and it was not until about 1790 that Job and George Ridgway acquired the control of the factory. Job had been a pupil of Josiah Wedgwood, and worked here with his elder brother till 1813, when he left to build the Cauldon Works, so that George carried on the Bell Works alone. When he retired, just before 1824, the sons of Job—John and William Ridgway—succeeded him, though they worked together for six years only, as John left to carry on by himself the business at the Cauldon Works. William was a man of considerable enterprise, and occupied eventually five other potteries, the names of which are worth recording. George and Thomas Taylor's china works merged into W. Ridgway and Son. So were the factories of Elijah Mayer, Palmer and R. Wilson, and Toft and May, whilst Baddeley's was taken over, in 1836, by W. Ridgway, Morley, Wear and Company. The marks of the Bell Works are impressed or printed with "W. R. & CO.," with various designs, such as an anchor, a harp, etc., often in a very intricate pattern.

The Cauldon Works.—Job Ridgway lived only for a year after he had built these works; his sons and partners, John and William, continued to work together till 1830, both here and at the Bell Works, as before noted. The arrangement that was then made left John in possession of the Cauldon

Works, from which he retired in 1858. Amongst the varied productions of the Ridgways were services painted with flowers, willow pattern and other transfer-printed earthenware, and generally the varied porcelain and earthenware of the well-known Staffordshire type. John Ridgway obtained several patents "for improvements in the moulds," "for improvements in apparatus and machinery, and improving and preparing bats of porcelain and earthenware, and shaping them into articles"; "for improvements in the manufacture of paste boxes and similar articles in china, etc."; "for improvements in the method of ornamenting china, etc., by applying the art of electrotype." In 1858, when John Ridgway retired, the works at Cauldon Place, Stoke-upon-Trent, were acquired by T. C. Brown-Westhead, Moore, and Company. The mark "Ridgway and Sons" represents the Job Ridgway and Sons period. The J. W. R. is the John and William partnership, then John alone uses I. or J. Ridgway. The last mark, with the crown, was used in 1850, when the potter was patronised by royalty.

SALT, R., AND SON, 1812, Hanley.—Amongst the makers of figures and groups this pottery takes a somewhat prominent place. Not alone were the ordinary Staffordshire figures made, but SALT is occasionally found as a mark on lustre figures—not, however, as often as MAYER, to whom we have referred. The variety of English figures in pottery is immense. There are figures in decorated slip ware, early agate, salt-glaze, lustre, Whieldon, Leeds, Liverpool, Salopian, Staffordshire, Swansea, Nottingham, Sunderland, Chesterfield,

STAFFORDSHIRE FIGURES.   NOT WALTON, BUT SALT.

and Rockingham, besides the early and late Lambeth. Now Ralph Salt made figures just as Walton did; a pair—ram and sheep—might quite easily be mistaken for Walton, but they are marked SALT. Salt was an enameller and manufacturer of *porcelain* tablets. His son Charles succeeded to the business in 1846, having previously been a partner of his father, whose death occurred at that date. In 1864 Charles died, and the works ceased. His specialty was Parian, and in this ware he produced a good bust of Wesley.

SCOTT BROTHERS AND CO., 1788, Sunderland.—Antony Scott carried on the Newbottle Pottery, which was established in 1755, and moved to the Southwick Pottery in 1788. His family succeeded him in the business, and pieces of the usual Sunderland ware were marked *Scott Brothers & Co.* during their control of the works. Later, in 1837, the firm became Antony Scott and Sons.

SEWELL AND DONKIN, 1780, Newcastle-upon-Tyne.—The products of the Newcastle factories cannot be distinguished from Sunderland ware in the absence of marks. Queen's ware and pink lustre and imitations of Wedgwood were made at St. Antony's, near Newcastle, by the firm, whose marks were SEWELL & DONKIN, SEWELL ST.

LIVERPOOL PUNCH-BOWL.

ANTONY'S, SEWELL & CO., SEWELL. Some pierced baskets, etc., in the Leeds style, have been found with these marks, and others in the same style only whiter than Leeds with "Newcastle" as a mark with stamped numbers underneath.

SHAW, ALDERMAN THOMAS, *c.* 1710, Liverpool.—Enamelled and painted earthenware, usually called Liverpool delft, was made here early in the eighteenth century (see chapter on Liverpool delft). Mugs with dates and punch-bowls, such as that shown as an illustration, were amongst the best productions. The punch-bowl was made for presenta-

304 a

SUNDERLAND LUSTRE WARE (THE MUG HAS A FROG INSIDE).
From Miss Edith Feilden's Collection.

tion to Captain Metcalf by the owners of his vessel in 1753.

SHERIFF HILL POTTERY, Newcastle-upon-Tyne.—This name is found as a mark upon pieces made by Lewins and Patterson, but the works seem only to have been in operation a short time.

SHORE, J., 1760, Isleworth.—Earthenware and pottery were manufactured here on quite a small scale. In 1787 porcelain was no longer made. Twelve years later, a red ware resembling Samian was produced and marked " S & C." Shore was succeeded by W. Goulding (see Goulding).

SHORTHOSE, J., 1783, Hanley.—This name is found on imitations of Wedgwood in black basaltes ware, on pierced cream-ware baskets, dishes, and stands, and the later marks—SHORTHOSE & HEATH, SHORTHOSE & CO.—on similar ware, as well as upon vases, etc., decorated with transfer-printing. The works became extinct in 1823 or thereabouts.

SMITH, W., 1810, Stockton-on-Tees.—In the early part of last century Queen's ware and imitations of Wedgwood were made here. The ware was marked STOCKTON POTTERY, or W. S. & CO. Some of it, however—and here we venture to draw the particular attention of our readers—was stamped WEDGEWOOD, a colourable copy of WEDGWOOD. An injunction applied for by the Wedgwoods of Etruria was granted in 1848 to stop this practice.

STEEL, DANIEL, 1802, Burslem.—There were several potters named Steel in the various lists of potters. Moses Steel, in 1715, made the cloudy ware then prevalent; Thomas Steel, in 1750, made moulded ware. In 1821 Daniel is described as a jasper and ornamental earthenware maker, and his name occurs—STEEL, BURSLEM—on ware like Wedgwood, and on medallions having white cameo subjects on a blue ground, again like Wedgwood. The factory was closed in 1824.

STEVENSON AND DALE, c. 1800, Cobridge.—The firm became Ralph Stevenson in 1815. The ordinary earthenware, cream-coloured, with raised borders, or decorated with transfer-printing, was made. The mark was "Stevenson, warranted Staffordshire," in a circle, surrounding a crown or a ship, with Stevenson impressed or printed.

TAYLOR, R. MINTON, 1875, Fenton.—He was a nephew of Herbert Minton, and formerly managed the tile department of Mintons', in which firm he was a partner. His factory must be distinguished from that at Stoke, which was purchased by Mr. Campbell in 1875, when he retired from Minton, Hollins and Company. The encaustic and majolica tiles and slabs

STAFFORDSHIRE TOBY TEAPOT. A VERY UNUSUAL SPECIMEN. THE PROPERTY OF MR. S. H. EGLINGTON.

WALTON FIGURE.

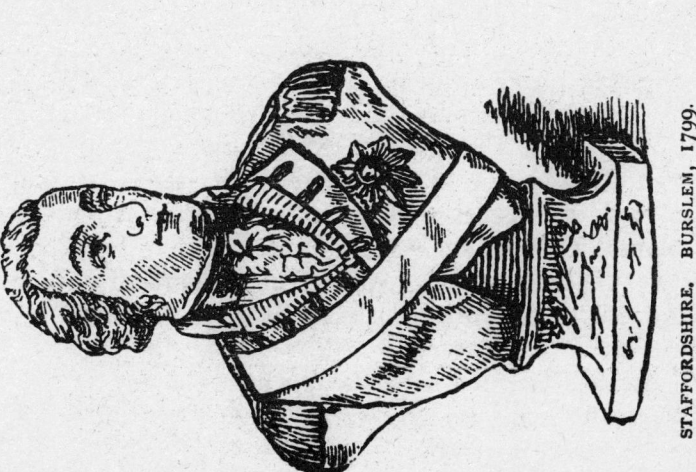

STAFFORDSHIRE. BURSLEM, 1799.

made by the firm of "R. Minton, Taylor and Company" are very fine, but they are modern. A mark frequently found is FENTON STONE WORKS. There were quite a number of Taylors engaged in the potter's art. Thomas Taylor appears in the list of Burslem potters in 1750. In 1788, Ring, of Bristol, took one Taylor into partnership, when the firm became "Ring and Taylor." John Taylor, of Burslem, and George Taylor, of Hanley, are mentioned in the list of 1802. Taylor, Harrison and Company were the owners of the Castleford Pottery prior to 1854; Taylor and Pope appear amongst the Shelton potters in 1786; Thomas Taylor, as a maker of moulded ware, about 1715; and, lastly, W. Taylor, Son and Company took the Hanley works of Joseph Mayer and Company in 1830.

WAGSTAFFE, Vauxhall and Mortlake.—The old Vauxhall Pottery was by the side of the Thames, close to Vauxhall Bridge. Near the end of the seventeenth century teapots were made here "as good as any came from abroad." On the death of Wagstaffe, about 1803, John Wisker, his nephew, succeeded him, and in 1833 patented "certain improvements in apparatus for grinding covers and stoppers for jars, bottles, etc." Later, from 1835 to 1865, Alfred Singer owned the works, which have since been demolished and built over. One wonders whether much of the Lambeth delft was made at "Foxhall" when we read: "We viewed the pottery and various apartments. Was most pleased with that where they were painting divers colours, which yet appear more beautiful and of different colours when baked." This was written by Thoresby in 1714. Did the factory really begin in the reign of Charles II.? The Mortlake Pottery is supposed to be much later. It was not in existence until towards the middle of the eighteenth century, and though near the end of that period Wagstaffe took over the works, leaving them to John Wisker at his death, we only learn that delft and stoneware were the chief products. There is in the Museum at South Kensington a fine bowl, which was presented by Alfred Singer. It is of Mortlake enamelled earthenware, blue and white.

The blue painting in scrolls, medallions, masks, flowers, and birds is well done. Similar painting is seen on a framed panel of twelve tiles of Mortlake delft of the same period. These specimens were removed from the pottery in 1820, in which year the business was transferred by Wisker to Princes Street, Lambeth, being finally closed there in 1846.

WALTON, J., 1790–1839, Burslem.—Walton ware is familiar to all collectors of old Staffordshire. Early in the nineteenth century he produced toys, then the coloured figures of the shepherd and shepherdess, Falstaff, and a number of animals. Some of these are of large size, and though they have not nearly the merit of the Wood school, they are quaint and interesting. The modelling is rather coarse, it is true, and the colouring often crude, but in their day they had a considerable sale. Perhaps amongst the best may be mentioned the set of the four Evangelists holding books and having emblems at their feet. The name WALTON is found impressed or printed on a scroll.

WARBURTON, J., c. 1800, Hot Lane.—This John Warburton made cream-coloured ware at one of the most important potteries of that day. Mrs. Warburton carried on the works at his death, and effected much improvement in the ware by the adoption of Enoch Booth's fluid glaze. We know that Wedgwood sent his Queen's ware to Liverpool to be printed, but it is not so generally known that he sent it out to be painted and enamelled. Mrs. Warburton did much of this kind of work for Wedgwood until he set up departments in his own pottery for both printing and painting. We have already noticed Warburton as one of the partners who took over Champion's patent when he sold it in 1777 to the Staffordshire China Company. This was Jacob Warburton, son of John, who succeeded his mother, and carried on the business till 1826. The name WARBURTON impressed is sometimes found upon pieces of distinct merit. Warburton, like Taylor, was a common name amongst the potters.

WHITE, WM. J., c. 1760, Fulham.—Before John Dwight, the celebrated Fulham potter, died in 1703, and left his daughter Margaret in partnership with Thomas Warland, he anticipated such a failure as took place in 1746, when they became bankrupt. So he buried before his death all the models, tools, and moulds connected with the ornamental branch of the business—the classical figures. When, later, Margaret Dwight married William White, the old pottery was once more put into working order. In fact, White took out a patent in 1762 for " A new manufacture of crucibles for melting metals and salts, etc., called by the name of white crucibles or melting pottes, made of British materials, and never before made in England or elsewhere, and which I have lately set up in Fulham." Though the date 1760 is given as the probable date when White reopened the Fulham Pottery, pieces marked W. J. White are much later. This name and the date " 1800 " have been found scratched on stoneware, beer pots, and punch or flip cans with decorations of raised borders and raised figures or scenes from the hunting field. Often the spout is a moulded head. Another mark, " Fulham Pottery," is sometimes found stamped on jars, pots, jugs, etc. Specimens may be seen in the museums.

WILNECOTE WARE, 1862.—Mr. George Skey purchased a coal-mine at Wilnecote, near Tamworth, and on sinking shafts he discovered fire-clay and other clays suitable for pottery purposes. Workrooms were fitted with machinery, competent workmen were employed, and, in 1862, the factory was opened. As regards workmanship and material both were good, and the works grew so that in 1864 a limited liability company, the "Wilnecote Company, Limited," was formed with a capital of £60,000. Later this was altered to " George Skey and Co., Limited." The goods produced are of fine and durable quality—fountains, vases, tazzas, flower-vases, and every kind of terra-cotta for architectural design. As the colour is a light cream, and as the body is very fine, the relief patterns are exceedingly sharp and beautiful. The mark usually used is GEORGE SKEY, WILNECOTE WORKS, NR. TAMWORTH, in an oval, impressed. Of course, this ware is modern.

WINCANTON POTTERY, *c.* 1720, Ireson.—Our two illustra-

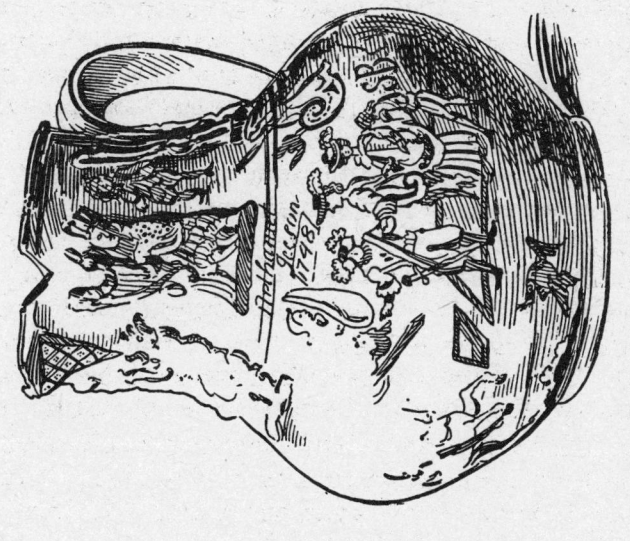

A RARE SPECIMEN, FROM CAPT. H. D. TERRY'S COLLECTION.

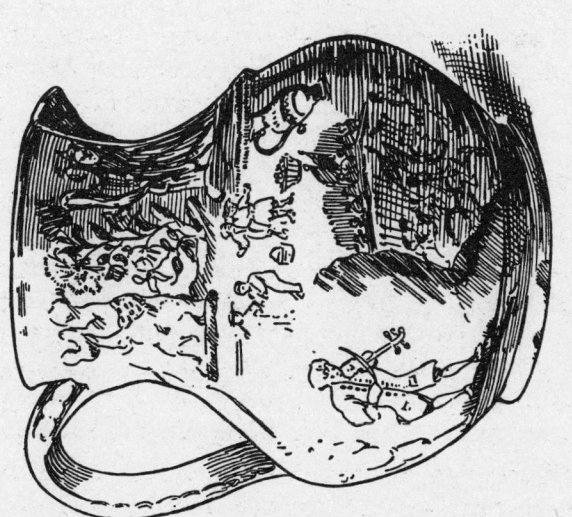

WINCANTON WARE.

tions of the rare pottery of Wincanton, Somersetshire, show to what excellence that old delft attained. Ireson, the potter, is little known, though his name is found occasionally as a mark. So is the name "Wincanton." Many bowls, jugs, dishes, and plates of this ware, probably hidden away or put back in the cabinet as being of no importance, would have better treatment if they were identified. The ware itself resembles piecrust, the glaze is good, the decoration is stencilled or painted. Oriental views, English scenes, fruit and flowers are amongst the subjects treated. If the name Clewill appears as a mark, it will be noted that he was a workman at Wincanton.

Captain H. D. Terry, to whom thanks are due for the illustrations, writing from Great Duryard, Exeter, says:—

"I have no doubt that specimens have frequently been attributed to Dutch and Bristol Delft; the body is pink, and this shows through the glaze in places. I have a pair of plates with initials S.B., dated 1746, also a bowl, richly decorated, blue, brown, and green, inscribed 'Drink fair Don't Swar 1727,' marked in blue; on the bottom 'W.' I have no doubt that transfer printing was first used on Wincanton pottery."

Other pieces are known. A plate, marked on the back "Wincanto," also a punch-bowl, inscribed inside "Wincanton, 1739." From these specimens it may be possible to identify others, as Ireson put the names of his customers on many articles ordered from him. The clay seems to be a quite unusual shade of pink. The glaze is of a bluish tinge, mostly painted in blue or in blue with yellow. Some pieces were dug up on the site of the old pottery works.

The S. B. on the jug are the initials of Samuel (Ireson) Bewesy, who was related to Ireson.

SUNDERLAND LUSTRE WARE WITH TRANSFER-PRINTED VERSES, ETC.

CHAPTER XXXIV

OLD TOBACCO PIPES

THE pipe manufactories of Broseley existed about three hundred years ago, and were even then famous. " When you ask for a Broseley pipe, see that you get it !" was not necessary as an advertisement. Was smoking prevalent in England before the advent of tobacco ? Were herbs, such as coltsfoot, yarrow, mouse-ear, and others, smoked before Sir Walter Raleigh introduced and first used tobacco ? Did he or Sir John Hawkins or Ralph Lane, Governor of Virginia, who returned to England in 1556, or somebody else, commence the widespread use of the " weed " ? The last question has not yet been solved,.

In any case, the use of tobacco in Elizabethan days must have been an expensive luxury, and the idea that early pipes must be judged by their size has much to recommend it. The *form* of the pipe cannot always be depended upon as a criterion of age. Naturally, a new taste such as smoking would be content with the form originally used, until, as tobacco became cheaper, a larger indulgence was allowed to the smoker, which resulted in a larger pipe.

The first illustration shows the shape of pipes from the time of Queen Elizabeth to the reign of William III. from the top downward. The Tudor rose, the date, the C.R., are self-explanatory. Long pipes were as English as the others, though some came from Holland. The Dutch were only copyists—that is to say, their pipes came originally from our own country. Thus we find that in 1694 only 110 gross of Dutch pipes were imported—" the very long ones and also small." The barrel-shaped bowls were types of the Commonwealth and Charles II., though they were in use at a later period. In many cases the heel of the pipe was flat—made to rest upon the table during use.

Though Broseley pipes are spoken of, it must not be concluded that the manufacture was limited to Broseley. Winchester had a famous factory in the seventeenth century. The pipes made there were noted by Ben Jonson as being the best made in his day.

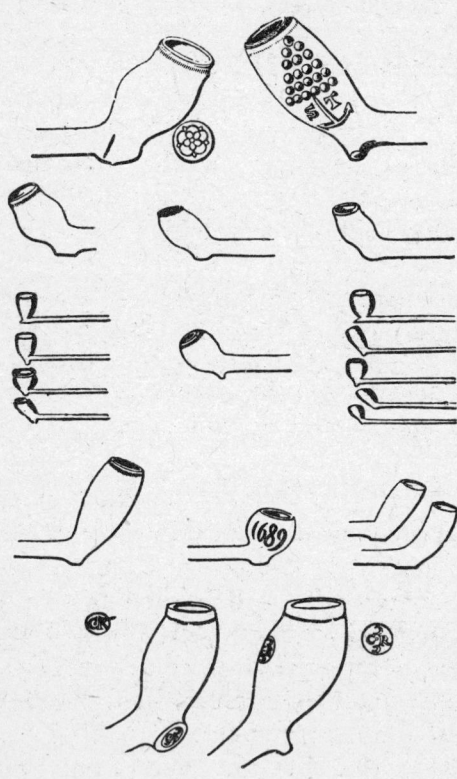

Exeter, too, at the same period, produced tobacco-pipes. A curious story of a witch committed for trial, in 1654, shows that Edward Trible, a tobacco-pipe maker, deposed that the witch — Mrs. Crosse — came to his house for fire, and for a month afterwards his pipes were either over or under burnt. A boy, too, in his employ suffered from the spell cast upon him, so that he "grew into a distracted condition, and was much consumed, and pyned away in body."

Smoking was forbidden amongst schoolmasters. In the rules of the school at Chigwell, founded in 1629, it was decreed that "the master must be of sound religion, of a grave behaviour and sober and honest conversation, no tippler or haunter of alehouses, and *no puffer of tobacco.*"

In 1621, a comedy was performed by the students of Christ Church, Oxford, before James I. at Woodstock, called

"Technogamia." In it, one of the characters, Phlegmaticus, entered exclaiming: "'Fore Jove, most meteorological tobacco! Pure Indian! not a jot sophisticated; a tobacco pipe is the chimney of perpetual hospitality." He sang a song, of which we select one verse:

> "Tobacco is a Traveller,
> Come from the Indies hither;
> It passed sea and land
> Ere it came into my hand
> And 'scaped the wind and weather.
> This makes me sing, So ho, so ho, boys,
> Ho, boys, sound I loudly,
> Earth ne'er did breed
> Such a jovial weed
> Whereof to boast so proudly."

The royal author of the "Counterblast to Tobacco" offered several times to withdraw, but was persuaded to stay "much against his will." Ben Jonson abused the "devil's own weed" in a slangy, low play, which, however, pleased the King so much that it was performed three times by royal command.

In 1619, just before the incident narrated, the pipemakers were incorporated, and their privileges were confirmed by subsequent monarchs.

At Derby, generations succeeded each other in pipemaking. Pipeclay, or *terre de pipe*, was moulded and fired in the ovens that saw the birth of the first piece of Derby china. "Bath" had a special mark—a shield with a branch of the tobacco plant. Lichfield, Newcastle-under-Lyme, and most parts of the country had their pipemakers.

From their small size the early pipes had fanciful names, such as "Fairy Pipes," "Elfin Pipes," "Old Man's Pipes," "Mab's Pipes," etc., from the rustic belief that Queen Mab carried on a fairy-pipe factory in certain favourite spots.

It is remarkable that Richard Legg, one of the old pipemakers of Broseley, had a daughter baptized in 1575, ten years before Sir Walter Raleigh brought his tobacco into England. But the Broseley pipemakers were numerous from the end of the sixteenth through the seventeenth centuries.

When were the pipes stamped on the stem? The second illustration shows the initials of the maker as a mark upon the spur. More than a hundred years ago this was largely altered by the name and address being stamped on the stem

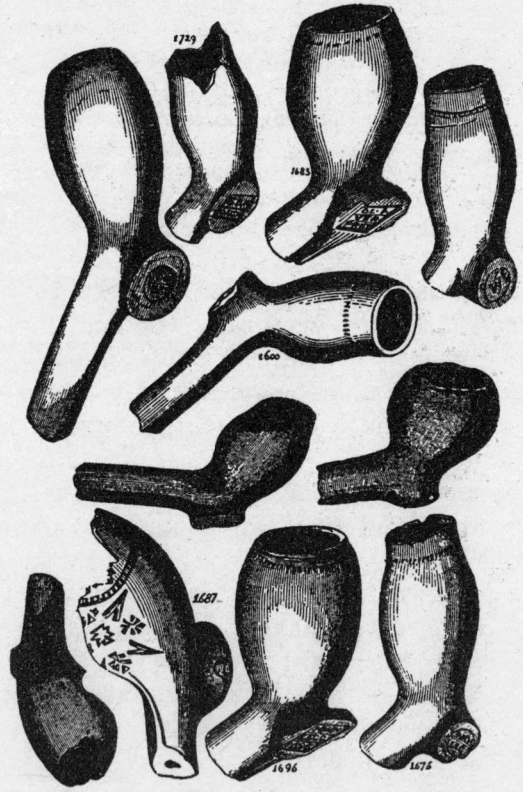

OLD PIPES FROM "JEWITT."

of the "churchwardens," which were 16 in. to 28 in. long, sometimes with a bend, or twist, at the point where the pipe could be balanced.

The chief pipemaker to the London clubs and coffee-houses was Noah Roden, who died about 1829, but his successors still produce "Real Broseleys." The Southrons, father and son, followed Roden, and manufactured enormous quantities of "churchwardens," "London straws," and many other varieties. The output has been sometimes over a million and a half in a year. The "long Broseley straws," "Lord Crewes," were 27 in. long, whilst the "long Dutch straws" added another inch. Medical testimony seems to indicate that these long clay pipes are the best. They have, however, lost much of their popularity since our childhood's days. The best pipeclay is that which is uniform in its porosity, absorbing much of the harmful nicotine. The value of individual specimens of these early pipes is but small, though a collection illustrating the various shapes and sizes is most interesting.

CHAPTER XXXV
CONCLUSION

WE have seen how from the very earliest times " pots and pans " were made from clay. From the beginnings of ornamental design rudely applied to the wet clay, we have followed the potter through many a change, due to civilisation, education, evolution, or any other force expressing the march of progress. English pottery, as contrasted with English china, has largely been a native product, free from foreign influence. It has acquired a reputation which modern manufacturers are striving to maintain, and, though the keen fight of modern competition amongst the nations for cheapness instead of quality tends to lower the artistic aim in favour of a monetary one, worthy successors are carrying on the work of Dwight, Wedgwood, and many others, whose efforts have been noted. May success attend their efforts!

There remains in the history of Old Pottery much that requires elucidation—much that further comparison and research may reveal. The vast quantity of early English ware of similar type made at the Potteries and elsewhere which never was marked will depend for its value upon its real worth, its potting, its glaze, and its decoration. Indeed, it is to the decoration that much of the added value is due. To take a type, white or drab salt-glaze ware has a certain value—not much, it is true, but a certain value; but if the glaze be coloured the price advances ten or twenty-fold.

Old Wedgwood, old Staffordshire, old Delft, old slipware, etc., all have their votaries, who delight to seek and to find. With them, indeed, putting aside profit as a consideration, the pleasure of collecting is real and abiding. Subtle, charming, inexplicable, and invigorating are the precious experiences it affords them. So ably, so dexterously, with what readiness of mind, what expedition, what confidence do they address themselves to the task of adding to the collection.

There are numberless people who possess some pottery

OLD STAFFORDSHIRE FIGURES, MAINLY LOVERS.

and like to know about it, and perhaps as many more who, for want of a guide, have never had a chance of developing tastes and capabilities which might turn the darkness of their lives into light. Busy men, men to whom a hobby would be a godsend, idle men who have practically no object in life, careful men whose knowledge may contribute something to the home purse—to them this book may be useful.

With increasing knowledge comes an earnest desire to work a field which yields so delightful a harvest, and to all those who enter upon the work of collecting with the intention of gathering in this harvest we would suggest that eager emptiness is of little worth, that knowledge " felt in the blood " and " felt along the heart " overcomes the shocks and stirs of early errors, and that with experience comes the instinctive tension of the nerves and the tingling of the pulses given to seekers when they find. To lovers of old pottery we commend the following lines from an old bowl :—

"My love is fix'd, I cannot range
I like my choice too well to change."

"Long may we live. Happy may we be
Blest with content and from misfortunes free."

320 a

BACCHUS JUG BY VOYEZ.

TOBY JUG BY ENOCH WOOD.

Lent by Mr. C. Andrade.

APPENDIX

The prices set out below are from the William Bemrose Sale, Derby, March 1909.

ELIZABETHAN STONEWARE

Brown mottled stoneware jug with handle, coat of arms incised, three heads ditto round neck, pewter lid, about 1613; h. 9 in.; and a brown jug with incised ornament and metal foot, £6 16s. 6d.

Elizabethan stoneware jug, *circa* 1581 (D), with silver-mounted neck-band; vase and scroll design, 11 gns.

An Elizabethan stoneware jug, with finely designed silver band, £25 4s.

Elizabethan stoneware jug, with silver gilt mount, repoussé lid, and acorn thumb-piece; neck-band of interlaced work; no mount at foot, £42.

DELFT WARES

White Fulham dish, and Bristol dish with Chinese subject, 10s.

Blue and white Fulham dish with garden subject; and a plate, £2 10s.

Large dish; portraits—King William III. and consort, £3 10s.

Pair of dishes with deep blue floral pattern, £2 4s.

Six Cockpit Hill plates, blue decoration, £11 0s. 6d.

Large mug and a coffee-pot similar; and a small mug, £4.

A dish with tulip design, and a large Leeds lustre dish, £5 15s. 6d.

A wall pocket with Oriental decoration; and a Delft wall vase, £1 8s.

A blue and white Delft dish, with flowers; 13 in.; and a lobed dish, £4 4s.

A large polychrome Delft dish; and a mug with pewter mounts dated 1767, £4 14s. 6d.

A dish with white decoration and view in colours, £2 2s.

APPENDIX

SALT GLAZE, WHIELDON AND OTHER POTTERY

A salt-glaze plate—embossed decoration; two leaf trays; and a fish mould, £5 15s. 6d.

Pair of white cornucopiæ—medallions representing Flora, 4 gns.

A salt-glaze basket and stand; a basket-work dish; and an embossed plate, 5 gns.

Two shaped trays—embossed ornaments; and an octagonal stand on three feet, £4 4s.

A heart-shaped flask, embossed with figures; two coffee-cups; and three other small specimens, £6 6s.

Two salt-glaze house teapots, £10 10s.

A white teapot with raised ornament; and a teapot in form of a camel, £7 17s. 6d.

A white teapot with mask spout; and a teapot with relief ornament; both slightly gilt, £12 1s. 6d.

A salt-glaze plate, with embossed and coloured flowers; and a pair of plates with prints "Queen Caroline," £1 11s. 6d.

Two coloured salt-glaze cream jugs—flower decoration, £14 14s.

A coffee mug, with banded ornaments in colours; and a saucer painted with flowers, £11 0s. 6d.

An enamelled salt-glaze punch-bowl, with figures and ships; and a smaller bowl with figures, £11 0s. 6d.

A punch-bowl, with enamelled birds and flowers; and a small bowl with flowers, £18 18s.

A bottle-shaped vase, enamelled with Kylin, birds, and flowers in the Chinese manner, £28 7s.

A coffee-pot decorated with figures (*lid missing*); and a small teapot decorated with flowers, £11 11s.

A teapot, enamelled with Chinese figures, £11 0s. 6d.

A similar teapot, £16 5s. 6d.

A small teapot, enamelled with flowers, £9 19s. 6d.

A teapot, enamelled with figures in English costumes, £7 17s. 6d.

A teapot, with groups of figures in quaint costumes, £13 13s.

A teapot with embossed and coloured vine-leaves: by Littler, £17 17s.

A similar teapot, differently coloured, £18 18s.

A similar teapot, differently coloured, £20 10s. 6d.

(*Note.—The three last mentioned are illustrated in Mr. Bemrose's Longton Hall work.*)

APPENDIX

A fine teapot, rose-coloured ground, with vine-leaves in relief, £33 12s.
A fine coffee-pot, enamelled with Chinese figures, £21.
A quart jug, richly enamelled with figures and flowers, £26 5s.
A rare farmer's jug, with long inscription and floral decoration, £21.
A fine milk jug, decorated with embossed and coloured work, small portrait of the Young Pretender in front, initialled P.C., £43 1s.
A fine basket, with coloured flowers, partly in relief, £60 18s.
A rare Whieldon teapoy, with relief portrait of Prince Charlie, £15 15s.
Two small Whieldon teapots, £7 7s. 6d.
A fine Whieldon milk jug—on feet; and a teapot, with twisted handle, £12 1s. 6d.
A large Whieldon teapot—embossed ornament; and a teapoy, with embossed borders, £13.
A brown Whieldon teapot—gilt relief ornament; a coffee-pot; and a cup and saucer to match, £24 3s. 6d.
Pair of Whieldon cornucopiæ—female masks, 7 gns.
A teapot, in form of a basket of fruit; a milk jug; and a cup, 10 gns.
Two Whieldon dishes—embossed borders; two plates; an oblong tray; and a pipe, 15 gns.
Three Astbury teapots, relief ornaments; and a saucer, £16 5s. 6d.
An Agate ware teapot; and a cream jug, 15 gns.
A slip-ware porringer " William Turnor "; and a brown glazed pigeon, £11 0s. 6d.
A teapot inscribed " Wilkes & Liberty No. 45 "; two Elers teapots; and a Dwight mug, £8 18s. 6d.
Two mask mugs; a fox head cup; a teapoy; and a small Toby jug, 10 gns.
A Lambeth ware barrel flask; a Fulham mug; and two pieces of Jackfield ware, 4 gns.

WORKS BY L. SOLON (IN PÂTE-SUR-PÂTE)

Early plaque, signed MILÈS, 69. Painted in Paris by M. Solon, just before leaving for England. Subject: " The Perplexed Maid," represented as dividing Cupid between love and money; note at back by M. Solon, £27 6s.

APPENDIX

Pair of plaques—representing "Fire" and "Water"; 4 in. square. Signed. £27 6s.

Plaque—two Cupids representing the "Battle between Fire and Water"; 7 in. by 4 in. Signed. £37 16s.

Plaque—female figure holding a bell, and a cupid tolling it by swinging on the clapper; 7 in. by 6 in. Signed. £52 10s.

Plaque—"Love's Ardour cooled," a column on which Cupid is seated in the act of delivering a douche of cold water over a female ascending a ladder reared against the column; 8 in. by 4 in. Signed. £23 2s.

Circular plaque—female figure seated, opening a box, out of which springs Cupid. (*Exhibited in the Vienna Exhibition.*) Signed. £42.

Large plaque—a nymph and her love are bound together; a group of cupids are scoffing at them, two other cupids come stealthily endeavouring to cut the binding threads and part the faithful couple; 15 in. by 8 in. Signed. One of the finest of the artist's works, £48 6s.

Plaque. Three Cupids have been attracted like butterflies by the flame burning in the candelabra—the nymph, who is an entomologist, has caught them, and is busy with hammer and nails affixing them to the stem of the candelabra. Signed. In Italian ebony frame, inlaid with ivory scrolls, animals, etc. *From the Wass Collection*, £26 5s.

Group in terra-cotta—female with child, £7 7s.

Circular plaque—three figures listening to musician, £12 1s.

CATALOGUE OF STAFFORDSHIRE WARE FORMED DURING THE PAST FORTY YEARS BY PERCY FITZGERALD, ESQ., F.S.A. SOLD AT CHRISTIE'S JANUARY 24, 1908.

Much of which was Exhibited at the Victoria and Albert Museum, and also at Dublin in 1865

STAFFORDSHIRE WARE GROUPS AND FIGURES

A pair of groups of Count Bruhl's Tailor and his Wife, riding goats, 5¼ in. high, 4 gns.

A pair of figures of a shepherd and shepherdess, with bagpipes and guitar, 6 in. high ; and two figures of gentlemen, playing the flute, 6 in. high, 4 gns.

Four figures of boys, with dogs, bird's-nest, etc., in bosquets of flowers, 6 in. high, 3 gns.

A group, emblematic of Charity, 7¼ in. high ; and a pair of figures of a gentleman, and lady with bow and arrow, 7 in. high, 3½ gns.

A pair of figures of an old man and woman, 6 in. high ; and two seated figures of men, 5¼ in. high, 5 gns.

Seven small figures of children, with flowers, 2 gns.

Nine ditto, in various attitudes, 5 gns.

Seven small figures of peasants and children, in various attitudes, 4½ gns.

A shepherdess with a lamb, 4¼ in. high ; and four other figures, 3 gns.

A pair of figures of a sportsman and lady, with gun and dog, 7 in. high ; and two figures of peasant children, 6½ in. high, 3⅓ gns.

A pair of equestrian figures, 6 in. high; and a pair of groups of a tree-trunk and figures, 3 gns.
A pair of equestrian figures of a lady and gentleman, 7¾ in. high; and a group of a lady and gentleman, 7 in. high, 4½ gns.
A pair of seated figures of a lady and gentleman, 5½ in. high; a figure of Paul Pry; and a figure of a clown, 8½ gns.
A pair of figures in Welsh costume, 6½ in. and 7 in. high, 6 gns.
Six figures of sheep and lambs, 5½ gns.
Three figures of cows; a figure of a horse; and a goat, 5 gns.
A figure of a bull; a figure of a milkmaid and cow; and two figures of lions, by Wood and Caldwell, 8½ gns.
A figure of a cock, 10 in. high; a parrot on perch, 9 in. high; and a figure of an eagle, 5 gns.
A figure of a lion, 7 in. high; an elephant, with howdah; a tiger; and an inkstand, surmounted by a lion, 6½ gns.
An inkstand, surmounted by an eagle; a figure of a peacock; three stags; and two dogs, 5½ gns.
Two figures of a shepherdess with a lamb, 5½ in. high; and a figure of a gardener with a flower-pot, 5½ in. high, 2½ gns.
Four groups of peasant children, with a lamb, flowers, etc., 5½ in., 6½ in. and 7 in. high, 3½ gns.
A pair of Whieldon figures of a peasant boy and girl, emblematic of Autumn and Winter, on octagonal plinth, 7¼ in. high; and a figure of a man, with bagpipes, 8¼ in. high, 13 gns.
A pair of groups of a peasant boy and girl, with musical instruments, 7½ in. high, 3½ gns.
A pair of figures of a peasant boy and girl, reclining in bosquets with a lamb and dog, 7 in. high; and a group of a lady and gentleman, with a basket of flowers and fruit, 6½ in. high, 7½ gns.
A pair of figures, emblematic of Truth and Justice, 9 in. high; and a figure of a wooden-legged fiddler, 8 in. high, 5½ gns.
A figure of a harlequin, 5¼ in. high; and a group of a boy and girl with bird's-nest, 4¾ in. high, 12 gns.
A pair of figures of a boy and girl crying, 8¼ in. high; and a figure of an old peasant woman, 7 in. high, 6 gns.
A group of the Tithe Pig, 7 in. high; and a group of a travelling showman with bear, 8¾ in. high, 9½ gns.
A figure of a youth; and a lady with bow and arrow, 7 in. and 7½ in. high, 5 gns.

APPENDIX

A pair of figures of Elijah and The Widow, 8½ in. high ; and a pair of candlesticks, with figures of children, 7½ in. high, 3½ gns.

A white model of a tomb, 13¾ in. high ; and four white figures, 3 gns.

A pair of white groups of children quarrelling, 7¼ in. high ; and a white group of a peasant boy and girl, 7½ in. high, 3 gns.

A figure of Charlotte at the tomb of Werther, 9¼ in. high ; and four other figures of mourning Nymphs, 6½ gns.

Napoleon, 8 in. high ; a group of lovers, 7 in. high ; and four other figures, 4½ gns.

A figure emblematic of Peace, 8¼ in. high ; Pomona, 8½ in. high ; and four other figures, 7 gns.

Romulus and Remus : a group, 8½ in. high ; and a group of a man and donkey, with panniers, 7 in. high, 7 gns.

A set of four figures, emblematic of The Elements, 8 in. high, 7 gns.

A pair of figures of haymakers, 8¼ in. high ; and a pair of figures of a boy and girl carrying packs, 8½ in. high, 9 gns.

A pair of figures of Elijah and The Widow, 9½ in. high ; and another figure of The Widow, 9¼ in. high, 5 gns.

A pair of figures of a boy and girl, with guitar and hurdy-gurdy, 9¼ in. high ; and two figures of boys, 8 in. high, 6½ gns.

A pair of figures of Iphigenia and Cymon, 9¼ in. high ; " The Lost Piece," 9¼ in. high ; and Bacchus, 9 in. high, 8½ gns.

An inkstand, with figure of Shakespeare, 5½ in. high ; and three groups of peasant children, 7 gns.

A figure of a man, in pink coat, leaning on a pedestal, 8¼ in. high ; Cupid, 7¼ in. high ; and four other figures, 7 gns.

A group, emblematic of Charity, 7½ in. high ; a reclining figure of Cupid, 6 in. high ; two vases, supported by figures ; and a pair of vases, with triple necks, supported by dolphins, 7 in. high, 5 gns.

A figure of Ceres, 10 in. high ; Neptune, 9 in. high ; and two other figures, 10½ in. high, 8 gns.

A group of lovers, seated by a tree, 7½ in. high ; and a group of a chariot, drawn by lions, 7½ in. high, 10 gns.

A Whieldon figure of King David, 12½ in. high ; and Neptune, 11½ in. high, on square pedestals, with medallions in relief, 13½ gns. (Both of these were Ralph Wood.)

APPENDIX

A group of The Crucifixion, 9 in. high ; a monk, 10 in. high, and one other figure, 3 gns.

A pair of figures of Elijah and The Widow, 9½ in. high ; and a group of Samuel anointing David, 10 in. high, 4½ gns.

Atlas supporting the Globe, 11 in. high : another figure of the same, 9¼ in. high ; a Triton, 9½ in. high ; and Hotei, 5½ in. high, 10 gns.

A group of Charity, 9 in. high ; a figure of a man with hurdy-gurdy, 9 in. high ; a pair of candlesticks supported by cupids ; and a female bust, 4 gns.

A group of Rinaldo and Armida, 10 in. high ; and three figures of reading girls, 10½ gns.

Europa, 8½ in. high ; a group, emblematic of Astronomy, 9 in. high ; and two watch-stands, 9½ gns.

A Whieldon figure of St. George and the Dragon, 11 in. high ; and a group, nearly similar, 10 gns.

A pair of military equestrian figures, 9½ in. and 10 in. high ; and a bust of an Admiral, 9½ in. high, 10 gns.

A pair of reclining figures of Antony and Cleopatra, 8 in. and 8½ in. high, 14 gns.

A small Voyez jug, modelled with a boy and girl and bird's-nest, 5 in. high ; and two small jugs, formed as a mask and figure, 6½ gns.

A bust of Prior, 9¼ in. high ; a bust of Alexander I., 10 in. high : and one other, 10 in. high, 7½ gns.

A bust of Voltaire, 8¼ in. high ; and a bust of George Washington, 8¾ in. high, 14 gns.

A bust of Shakespeare, 10¼ in. high ; a bust of a divine, 9 in. high ; and a female bust, 10¼ in. high, 11¼ gns.

A bust of Handel, 8½ in. high ; and a bust of Newton, 8½ in. high, 8 gns.

A bust of Neptune, 12 in. high ; and a bust of Miss Foote, 11 in. high, 11 gns.

Two jugs, modelled as Watchmen, 9 in. and 8 in. high ; and a small Toby-Fillpot jug and cover, modelled as a man holding a jug, 7 in. high, 7 gns.

Two Toby-Fillpot jugs, modelled as men holding jugs, 9¾ in. high ; and one, modelled as a woman, 11½ in. high, 15 gns.

Three Toby-Fillpot jugs, modelled as figures of men, seated, and holding jugs and a cup, 9½ in. high, 15½ gns.

A bowl and cover, formed as a hen and chickens, 6½ in. high ;

FAMOUS SOLON PLAQUES.
From the William Bemrose Sale, Derby, March 1909.

APPENDIX

a white figure of a bird, 10½ in. high; and a splashed figure of a cat, 6½ gns.

A bowl and cover, formed as a boar's head; and a figure of a dog, 15½ in. high, 9½ gns.

A group of a bear and dog, 10½ in. high; and a jug and cover, formed as a bear and dog, 12 in. high, 9½ gns.

A pair of figures of an elephant and camel, 8 in. high; and a reclining figure of a lion, 16 gns.

A figure of a horse, 15½ in. high; and a figure of a bull, 11 in. high, 16 gns.

A figure of a turkey-cock, dressed in costume, 10½ in. high, 13 gns.

Four figures of children, emblematic of The Seasons, 9½ in. high, 8 gns.

A group of The Assassination of Marat, 13¼ in. high; and a group of The Grecian Daughter, 8¾ in. high, 10 gns.

A group of a travelling show, 11 in. high; and a group of a girl and Cupid, 10½ in. high, 16 gns.

A figure of a sportsman, 9 in. high; a man blowing a horn, 9 in. high; and a figure of a lady, 10 in. high, 7 gns.

A figure of Sir Sidney Smith, 11½ in. high; and two figures of Britannia, by Wood and Caldwell, 10 in. high, 8 gns.

A pair of groups of The Sailor's Departure and Return, 9 in. high, 5 gns.

A pair of groups of The Toilet and the Shoeblack, 8¾ in. high, 7 gns.

A group of a shepherd and shepherdess, with a bagpipe, guitar and animals, 10 in. high; and a group of a man and woman, with performing dogs, 9 in. high, 8½ gns.

A pair of figures of Jove and Juno, 8¾ in. high, 6½ gns.

Jove, 11 in. high; Minerva, 12 in. high; and Diana, 11½ in. high, 9½ gns.

A pair of Whieldon figures of a gentleman, and a lady carrying a lamb, 9¾ in. high, 9½ gns.

A pair of Whieldon groups of lovers, with a bird-cage, lamb and dog, 10 in. and 11 in. high, 21 gns. (Ralph Wood.)

A figure of Apollo, 13 in. high; and two figures of Flora, 13 in. high, 9½ gns.

A Salopian [R. W.] group of The Vicar and Moses, 9 in. high; and a group of The Parson and Clerk, 8¾ in. high, 7½ gns.

Four figures of Pomona, Flora, and Venus, 10½ in. and 9¼ in. high, 7 gns.

APPENDIX

A group of Abraham's Sacrifice, 14¼ in. high; and two figures of Christ Preaching, 10¼ in. high, 3½ gns.

A pair of large seated figures of The Cobbler and his Wife, 12½ in. high, 12½ gns.

A pair of figures of Chaucer and Newton, with books and other attributes, 11 in. high, 15 gns.

A statuette of Shakespeare, leaning on books and pedestal, on square marbled plinth, 15 in. high, 12 gns. (*from the Collection of R. Soden Smith, Esq.*).

A group of a mother and child, 13 in. high; and a bust of Minerva, 12 in. high, 13 gns.

Three figures of St. Peter, St. Philip and St. John, on square plinths, with pateræ in relief, 13 in. and 13½ in. high, 7½ gns.

A bust of a man, 12 in. high; a silvered bust, 11½ in. high; and a bust of a man, inscribed JOHN HARRISON, 1822, 9½ in. high, 7 gns.

A bust of Shakespeare, 10 in. high; a small bust of Sterne, 7 in. high; and one other, 9 in. high, 8 gns.

A bust of Plato, 12½ in. high; and one of Homer, 12 in. high, 9 gns.

A pair of busts of Neptune and Hercules, 14 in. high, 5½ gns.

A bust of the Duke of Wellington, 13 in. high; a mug and cover, formed as head of the same; and a bust of Charlotte Corday, 11½ in. high, 7½ gns.

A figure of a sailor, seated on a chest, 10½ in. high: and a small Toby-Fillpot jug, formed as a man in green coat, 7½ in. high, 5½ gns.

Three jugs, modelled with rustic figures in relief, by Voyez, 8½ in. and 10 in. high, 21 gns.

A Toby-Fillpot jug, modelled as a man in Eastern costume, holding a cup, 10½ in. high; and one, modelled as a man holding jug and cup, 10¼ in. high, 7½ gns.

Two jugs, modelled as figures of men seated on barrels, 11½ in. high, 3½ gns.

A jug, formed as a man seated on a rock, 14 in. high; and a jug, formed as an old woman holding a cup, 12 in. high, 13 gns.

A jug, formed as a sailor seated on a chest, 11½ in. high; and one formed as boys holding a fungus, 5½ gns.

Two Toby-Fillpot jugs: one of green glaze, one of brown glaze, 2 gns.

APPENDIX

A group of The Death of Monro, 11 in. high; and a group of bull-baiting, 10 in. high, 15 gns.

A pair of figures of lions, 8½ in. high; and two other figures of a lion and tiger, 9 in. high, 9½ gns.

A bust of a man, in fur cap, 6½ in. high; and four other small busts, 6 gns.

A Whieldon vase, modelled with two figures at the side, 10 in. high; three mugs, modelled as masks; and one other piece, 8½ gns.

A flower-vase, formed as a tree-trunk, with small groups of sheep on the plinth; and a clock-case, with inscription, 2 gns.

Three flower-vases, modelled with pastoral figures and animals in high relief, 8½ in. and 10 in. high, 3½ gns.

A group of Cupid and Psyche, 20 in. high; and a figure of Cupid, 16½ in. high, 12 gns.

A group of Christ and the Woman at the Well, 16½ in. high; and a blue glaze figure of The Virgin and Child, 1½ gn.

An equestrian figure of a man in Eastern costume, 13 in. high; a figure of Jove, 16½ in. high; and a square white pedestal, with figures in relief at the corners, 9 gns.

A statuette of Franklin, on pedestal with pateræ in relief, 13 in. high; and a small figure of the same, 10 in. high, 30 gns.

A bust of Alexander the Great, 12 in. high; Napoleon as First Consul, 9½ in. high; and one of Francis II. of Austria, 10 in. high, 8½ gns.

A pair of busts, of the Rev. John Wesley and the Rev. George Whitefield, by Enoch Wood, 12½ in. and 13 in. high, 14 gns.

A group of two Cupids wrestling for a heart, 16 in. high, 9 gns.

A bust of Shakespeare, 16½ in. high; and a bust of Princess Charlotte, 19 in. high, 5½ gns.

Venus de Medici, 23½ in. high; and a white figure of an athlete, 24 in. high, 11 gns.

Cleopatra; and the Companion: a pair of statuettes, on oblong blue plinths, 19½ in. high, 15¼ gns.

Two larger figures of the same, 22½ in. high, 14¼ gns.

A pair of groups of Bacchus and Ariadne, 25 in. high; and a female figure, holding a dove, 25 in. high, 16 gns.

A pair of figures of Shakespeare and Milton, leaning on emblematic pedestals, surmounted by books, 18½ in. high, 15 gns.

A statuette of Sir Walter Raleigh, holding a roll, 21½ in. high, 18 gns.

A bust of Queen Charlotte, by J. and R. Riley, Burslem, 1819, 17 in. high; a white bust of the same; and a white bust of an admiral in uniform, 8½ gns.

A bust of the Madonna, 15 in. high; and a white bust of the same, 20 in. high, 8½ gns.

A white figure of Cupid, 13½ in. high; a figure of the Empress Josephine, 25 in. high; and a figure of the infant St. John, 21 in. high, 5½ gns.

A life-size bust of Alexander the Great, by Enoch Wood, coloured, 18 gns.

A figure of St. Paul preaching, 18½ in. high; and a figure of Hercules, 17½ in. high, 12 gns.

A figure of a lady at an altar, 28 in. high; and a figure of a girl, with dove, 29 in. high, 21 gns.

A figure of Venus after the Bath, 30 in. high; and a group of two children, 24 in. high, 6½ gns.

A bowl and cover, formed as a boar's head, 12 in. high; and a figure of a bull, of brown glaze, 15 in. high, 49 gns.

A group of St. George and the Dragon, 10½ in. high; a figure of Ganymede, 14 in. high; two busts; and two other pieces, 8½ gns.

STAFFORDSHIRE WARE

A large jug, decorated with a bird and flowers in silver lustre and white, and inscribed, " J. SIMPSON, ORIGINAL STAFFORDSHIRE WAREHOUSE, 1791," 14 gns.

A tea service, decorated with foliage in blue and copper lustre, consisting of teapot and cover, sugar-basin and cover, cream-jug, bowl, and four teacups and saucers; and three lustred goblets. No bid.

A jug, printed with a view of the Wear Bridge; four jugs, decorated in colours with figures, flowers, and grapes; a silver lustred jug; and two mugs, with figures in relief, 6 gns.

A jug, decorated with a hunting subject in relief, and with figure handle; three other jugs, with sporting and other subjects in relief; three jugs, formed as masks; and one other, 5 gns.

APPENDIX

A puzzle-jug, decorated in pale green and brown, and with a small figure in the interior; a rhyton, formed as a fox's head; a model of a hand and heart; and two pipes, modelled with a hand and figure, 8½ gns.

A pair of semicircular jardinières, with small views in lake on yellow basket-pattern ground; two candlesticks, with Cupid supports; three other candlesticks and a pair of copper lustre vases, 4½ gns.

A vase and cover, with lavender-blue ground; another, with medallions and festoons round the centre; and agate ware vase and jar; and three other pieces, 10½ gns.

A vase and cover, with laurel festoons in relief and ruins in pink on cream ground; three jardinières, with landscapes in red lustre; and a vase, with landscapes in brown, 4 gns.

A model of a column, by R. Wood; a bowl, with decorations in colours; three vases; a model of a boat; and a Wedgwood teapot, 5½ gns.

Eleven medallions, with portraits and other subjects in relief, 14 gns.

A pair of Whieldon cornucopia-shaped hanging-vases, with pastoral subjects in relief; an oval plaque, with cats in relief; a plaque, with a lion, and one with a figure of Ceres in relief, 6½ gns.

INDEX TO SUBJECTS

A

Adam and Eve dishes, 61–2
Æsop's fables, 81
Agate ware, 107–9, 151
Ale pots, 38, 42, 51–60
Amherst Japan, 291
Amphoræ, 29–31
Anchor mark, 289
Ancient British pottery, 35, 36
Anglo-Saxon pottery, 35
Animal figures, old, 40–3
Apothecaries' jars, 64, 65
Appendix—prices, 321
Arretian ware, 34
Arrow impressed, Yarmouth mark, 240
Astbury ware, 99, 110, 124, 127–8, 245

B

Barbotine ornament, 90, 96
Basaltes or Egyptian ware, 156, 166, 173
— makers of, 173
Basket work, 122
B.B " New Stone " mark, 291
Bear drinking-vessels, 242–3
Bee-hive, Ridgway's mark, 302
Bellarmines, 37, 57, 115
Bianco sopro bianco decoration, 74
Bird, Herculaneum mark, 280
Biscuit, 14
Black decoration, 17
Blue scratched ware, 90, 110, 129, 138, 141
Bowls, Roman, 31, 34
Brampton ware, 56, 269
Brislington lustre, 207
Bristol delft, 69–75; date from shape, 72

Brongniart, M., praises Roman pottery, 23
Bronze lustre, 157, 209, 215
Broseley pattern, 255
— pipes, 314–17
Burning in the kiln, 14, 104
Burslem and its slip wares, 100

C

C: Turner's mark, 255
Cadogan teapots, 261
Castleford ware, 275
Castor ware, 27–8
Cauliflower ware, 141
Chesterfield ware, 247
Cinerary urns, 35
Clays, 100
— preparation of, 101
Cock Pit Hill pottery, 68, 97, 105
Cologne ware, 31, 37, 51
Coloured delft, 62, 96
— glazes, 15, 138, 197
— salt-glaze ware, 131, 137, 138
— slip, 57, 96
Combed ware, 57, 103, 105, 109
Copper lustre, 207, 209
Costrels or pilgrims' bottles, 40, 44
Cream ware, 128, 133, 151
Crouch ware, 129, 140
Crown, Wilson's mark, 297

D

Dash decoration, 67
Death of Wolfe, 84
Delft: Bristol, 69–75
— Dutch, 87
— Lambeth, 57, 59–68
— Liverpoo , 76–88
— Wincanton, 310–12
Denby pottery, 268
Derby pipes, 315

INDEX TO SUBJECTS

Don pottery, 266
Doulton ware, 273-5
Drinking-vessels, grotesque old, 41-4
Drug pots, 64, 78
Dutch delft, 87
Dwight stoneware, 38, 52, 109, 112-19

E

Early English pottery, 35-45
Egyptian black ware, 156, 166, 173
Election plates, Bristol, 71
Elers ware, 99, 122-6
Elizabethan ware, silver mounted, 37, 38
Enamels in colours, 129, 138
— Battersea, 79
Encaustic tiles, so-called, 45-50
"England" in the mark, 275
Engobe decoration, 17
Etruria works started, 149
Etruscan ware, 17-22, 157, 195
Exeter pipes, 314

F

F: Fell's mark with anchor, 277
Fairy pipes, 315
Ferrybridge pottery, 278
Figures, not portraits, old English, 41-3
— Astbury, 128
— Leeds, 219
— Salt glaze, 137, 140
— Staffordshire, 195-200, 235, 257-61, 264, 270, 282, 292, 298-9, 303, 306-7, 319-20
— Sunderland, 208
— Wedgwood, 145-6
Flaxman's works, 20, 165, 169
Frog, the green, 173-4
Frog mugs, 250-1
Fulham ware, 112-119

G

German stoneware, 32, 36-7, 44
Gladstone on Wedgwood, 22
Glazes, enamel, 129, 197
— old soft, 201, 258
— simple, 38, 61, 75, 130, 142, 151
Glazing, process of, 15, 101, 130
Glost kiln, 15

Gold decoration, 133, 137, 156
— lustre, 206, 208
Gravestones in slip ware, 106
Greek tazzas, 18-20
— vases, 17-22
Grès de Flandres, 53
Greybeards, 51 *et seq.*
Grotesque figures as drinking-vessels, 41-43

H

Henri-Deux ware, 170
— copied, 293
Herculaneum pottery, 280
Hounslow pottery, 278

I

Imitators of Wedgwood, 186-204
Isleworth pottery, 305

J

Jackfield black ware, 230-2
Japanese ornament imitated, 124, 142
Jasper ware, 148, 162-6, 182, 190, 193, and many illustrations

K

Kilns, ancient, Castor, 15
— — New Forest, 29
— — Upchurch, 30
— seventeenth-century, 104
— various, 50

L

Lambeth delft, 57, 59-68
Lathe, turning on the, 125
Lead glaze, 61, 75, 133, 142
Leeds ware, 58, 218-25
Leopard ware, 37, 38, 54
Linthorpe pottery, 283-6
Littler's salt glaze, 137, 139
Liverpool delft, 76-88
"London," a Middlesbrough mark, 289
London strata, 26
Longton Hall pottery, 137, 139
Lowesby pottery, 288
Lustre ware, 206-17
— bronze, 209, 215
— copper, 209
— gold, 206, 208

INDEX TO SUBJECTS 337

Lustre, silver, 209, 213, 264, 266
— pink, 154, 212
— resist 210
—— makers of, 207-8, 217

M

Majolica, 61, 207, 209, 293
Mammiform bottles, 44
Marbled or clouded ware, 57, 103, 107, 109, 128, 161
Mediæval pottery, 35-45
Mermaid, 97
Metal dies for moulds, 99, 125, 131
Mexborough pottery, 300
Middlesbrough, 283, 289
Mintons', 289-95
Mortlake, 308
Moulded decoration, 96, 99, 130-1
— in the clay, 15, 130, 136
Musicians, Astbury's, 128

N

Nelson jugs, 247
New Forest kiln, 28, 29
Newcastle lustre, 217
Nottingham bears, 242-4
— wares, 55, 241-4

O

Oriental pattern plates, 71, 73
Oven, directions for firing, 177, 182

P

Painted ware, 61, 78, 138
Pancheons, 159
Parian ware, 170, 292
Parson and Clerk, 200
Pâte-sur-pâte, Solon, 294
Patents :
   Billin, 89
   Champion, 150
   Dwight, 52, 113
   Ramsey, 52
   Van Hamme, 57, 60
Pearl ware, 270
"Pelican in her piety," 95, 98
Pennington's blue, 85
Pharmacy jars, 64, 65, 78
Pilgrim bottles, 40, 44
Pine-apple ware, 142

Pink lustre, 154, 212
Pipes, old tobacco, 313
Pitchers, 38-40
Place's ware, 120-1
Portraits, 113, 116-17, 154, 156, 187-8, 194-5, 207, 300
Pots, 42, 50, 53, 64, 65, 66, 101-5
Potter's wheel, Egyptian, 14
Potting, process of, 14, 100-105
Prices, 166, 174, 249, 252, 259, and Appendix
Printed ware, 79-83, 153, 252
Printing, transfer, invention of, 79
Puzzle jugs, 55-8

Q

Queen's ware, 133, 151-2

R

Ramsey's patent, 52
Raren stoneware, 53
Redware, 22, 159
Resist lustre, 211
Rivals of Wedgwood, 186-205
Rockingham ware, 261, 270
Roman and British urns, 35-6
Roman red lustrous ware, 22
Royalty portrayed, 60, 66, 94, 113

S

S : Turner's mark, 255
Salt-glaze ware, reputed discovery of, 130
— objections to its use, 133
— makers of, 133, 135
Samian ware, 24, 305
Scratched or *graffiato* ware, 90, 110, 129, 138, 141
Sepulchral urns, 35
Silver lustre, 207-17, 266
Slip ware, 57, 89-106
Solid agate, 107-9, 161
— jasper, 148, 162
Solon's ware, 294
Staffordshire figures, 145
Stockton (Wedgewood—note "e"), 305
Sunderland lustre, 208, 217
Sun-dried pots, 13
Surface coloured jasper, 151, 193
Swansea pottery, 226-9
Swinton pottery, 261

INDEX TO SUBJECTS

T

Teapots, 131-4, 141
Tesselated pavements, 46-50
Tickenhall, 45, 105
Tiger ware, 38, 53
Tiles, old, 46-50
— Bitton and Bristol, 48
— Bristol, 71
— Chertsey, 47
— Elizabethan, 49
— Liverpool, 78, 81
— Monmouth, 49
Tin enamel, 61, 69, 75, 77
Tobacco pipes, 313-17
Toby-jugs, 256-262
— makers of, 256-7
Toft ware, 92 et seq.
— names upon, 93
Tortoiseshell ware, 109, 111, 151
Transfer printing, 79-83
Tudor jugs, 37-8, 60
Tygs, 89, 90-1

U

Upchurch ware, 29, 30

V

Van Hamme's patent, 57, 60
Variegated ware, 109, 161, 308

Vauxhall, 308
Voyez and his work, 233-6

W

W: Warburton's mark, 309
Wedgwood, 142-184
— Burslem, 143, 154
— Chelsea, 150
— Etruria, 149
— family, 158
— figures, 143-6
— finds, 180 et seq.
— marks, 177-9
— prices, 166, 174
— wares, 147 et seq.
Wedgewood, 305
Wesley, 188, 199, 272, 303,
Whieldon's ware, 107-110, 135, 161, 181, 246, 256
Whitfield, 188, 199
Willow pattern, 252-55
— — popular, 255, 269
Wilnecote pottery, 310
Wincanton delft, 310-12
Winchester pipes, 314
Wrotham ware, 92, 99, 106

Y

Yarmouth, 237-40

INDEX OF POTTERS AND DECORATORS

The latter are distinguished by the employer's name following.

A

Abbey, R., *Liverpool*, 261
Absolon, *Yarmouth*, 237–40
Adamses, The, *Staffordshire*, 189–93
Alders, *Cliff Bank*, 143
Andries & Janson, *Norwich*, 54
Ashworth, G. L., *Hanley*, 265
Astbury, J., *Shelton*, 99, 124, 127, 129
Astbury, T., *Lane Delph*, 99, 110, 124, 127, 245
Aynsley, J., *Lane End*, 208, 263

B

Baddeleys, The, *Shelton*, 263–5
Bagster & Phillips, *Hanley*, 265
Bailey & Batken, *Lane End*, 266
Baker, Bevan & Irwin, *Swansea*, 229
Barker, Sutton & Till, *Burslem*, 145–6
Barker, S., *Doncaster*, 266
Barnes, Z., *Liverpool*, 78
Baxter, T. (Dillwyn's), 227
Bell, W., *Hull*, 267
Bentley, T., *Etruria*, 149, 163
Bevington & Co., *Swansea*, 229
Billin, T., 89
Birch, E. J., *Hanley*, 267
Booth & Co., *Hanley*, 268
Booth, E., *Tunstall*, 267
Bourne, E. & J., *Denby*, 268
Bourne, S. (Minton's), 293
Bromley, W., *Brampton*, 269

Browne, *Caughley*, 269
Brown-Westhead, T. C., *Stoke*, 302
Brunton & Co., *Sunderland*, 250
Burton, S. & J., *Hanley*, 269
Butler, E., *Swinton*, 270

C

C. & H. (Cockson & Harding), 278
Cartledge, *Brackley*, 132
Chaffers, R., *Liverpool*, 83
Chetham & Woolley, *Lane End*, 270
Child, S., *Tunstall*, 271
C. J. M. (Mason), *Fenton*, 265
Clementson, I., *Shelton*, 271
Clews, J. & R., *Cobridge*, 271
Close & Co., *Stoke*, 272
Cockson & Harding, *Shelton*, 278
Copeland & Garrett, *Stoke*, 202–4

D

Dale, I., *Burslem*, 145, 272
Daniel, H., *Shelton*, 272
Daniel, R., *Cobridge*, 136, 138, 272
Daniel, T. (Wedgwood's), 151
Davenport, *Longport*, 208, 274
Dawson, *Sunderland*, 217, 274
D. D. & Co. (Dunderdale), 275
D. M. (De Morgan), *Fulham*, 206
Dillwyns, The, *Swansea*, 226–9
Dixon, Austin & Co., *Sunderland*, 146, 217, 274
Dixon & Co., *Sunderland*, 207, 274
Doulton, *Lambeth*, 274

INDEX OF POTTERS AND DECORATORS

Dunderdale, D., *Castleford*, 275
Dwight, J., *Fulham*, 38, 52, 109, 112–19

E

Eastwood (Baddeley), *Hanley*, 265
Edkins, M. (Frank's), *Bristol*, 70
E. I. B. (Birch), *Hanley*, 267
Elers, D. & J. P., *Bradwell Wood*, 99, 122–6
Evans, D. J. & Co., *Swansea*, 229

F

Fell & Co., *Newcastle*, 217, 277
Flaxman, J. (Wedgwood's), 20, 165, 169
Flower, J., *Bristol*, 70, 73
Fowke, Sir F., *Lowesby*, 286–7
Frank, R., *Bristol*, 69, 71, 207

G

Gardner, J., *Hanley*, 207
Garner, R., *Lane End*, 110, 146
Glass, J., *Hanley*, 278
Goulding, W., *Isleworth*, 278, 305
Greatbach, D., *Fenton*, 110
Green, J., *Doncaster* (Don), 266
Greens, Hartley & Co., *Leeds*, 218–25
Greens, Bingley & Co., *Swinton*, 261

H

Hackwood, W., *Shelton*, 278
Hall, R., *Tunstall*, 145
Hancock, J., *Hanley*, 207–8
Harley, T., *Lane End*, 279
Harrison & Alders, *Stoke*, 143
Harrison, T., *Linthorpe*, 283–6
Hartley, Greens, & Co., *Leeds*, 145, 218–25
Heath, J. & C., *Cock Pit Hill*, 97, 105, 279
Herculaneum Pottery, *Liverpool*, 279
Hicks & Meigh, *Shelton*, 265
Hollins, S., *Hanley*, 280–1
Hollins, T. & J., *Hanley*, 280
Horobin, *Tunstall*, 208
Humble, Green, & Co., *Leeds*, 218

I

I. or J. E. B. (Baddeley), 265
Ireson, N., *Wincanton*, 310–12
I. W. & Co., *Middlesbrough*, 289

J

J. R. (Ridgway), 301–2
J. W. R. (Ridgway), 301–2

K

Keeling, A. & E., *Tunstall*, 268
Keeling, J., *Hanley*, 281

L

Lakin & Poole, *Hanley*, 145, 208, 281, 300
Landré, Mrs. (Wedgwood's), 145, 147
Leeds Pottery Co., 224
Lessore, E. (Wedgwood's), 170
Littler, W., *Longton Hall*, 137, 139
Lockett, J., *Burslem*, 286

M

M. (Minton), also M. & Co., M. & B., 289–95
M. & N. (Mayer & Newbold), 288
Mason, M., *Fenton*, 265
Mayer & Newbold, *Lane End*, 288
Mayer, E., & Son, *Hanley*, 288
Meigh, *Shelton*, 265
Meigh, J., *Hanley*, 288
Meir, J. & T., *Cock Pit Hill*, 97–8, 105
Middlesbrough Pottery Co., 288
Miles, T., *Shelton*, 131
Mintons, The, *Stoke*, 289–95
Mitchell, *Burslem*, 136, 138
Moore & Co., *Sunderland*, 250, 295
Morley, C., *Nottingham*, 241–4
Morley & Co., *Shelton*, 265
Moseley, *Burslem*, 297
M. P. Co. (Middlesbrough), 288

N

Neale, J., *Hanley*, 195, 297
Neale & Co., *Hanley*, 145, 195, 297

INDEX OF POTTERS AND DECORATORS 341

Neale & Palmer, *Hanley*, 195-6
Neale & Wilson, *Hanley*, 195-6, 297

P

Palmer, H., *Hanley*, 193-6, 297-8
Pardoe, T. (Dillwyn's), 227
Parker, T. (Wedgwood's), 147
Pennington, S., *Liverpool*, 84-7
Phillips & Co., *Sunderland*, 298
Phillips, J., *Sunderland*, 217, 298
Pierce & Co., *Benthall*, 298
Place, W., *York*, 120-1
Plant, B., *Lane End*, 299
Pollard (Dillwyn's), 227-8
Poole, R., *Burslem*, 300

R

Ramsey, D., 52
R. B. & S. (Britton & Sons), *Leeds*, 224
Reed, J., *Mexborough*, 300
Reid, W., & Co., *Liverpool*, 84
Rhodes, *Leeds*, 138
Ridgway & Sons, *Stoke*, 302
Ridgway, J. & W., *Shelton*, 301
Ridgway, Morley, Wear & Co., *Shelton*, 265, 302
Ridgway, W., & Son, *Shelton*, 302
Ring, J., *Bristol*, 69
R., M., W. & Co. (Ridgway, etc.), 265, 302
Robinson (Pennington's), 85
Robinson, *Leeds*, 138

S

Sadler & Green, *Liverpool*, 79-83, 147, 151
Salt, R., *Hanley*, 145, 246, 303
S., B. & S. (Barker), 267
S. & G. (Shore & Goulding), 278, 305
Scott Bros., *Sunderland*, 303
Sewell & Donkin, *Sunderland*, 304
Shaw, R., *Burslem*, 109, 128, 138
Shaw, T., *Liverpool*, 76, 80, 304
Shore & Goulding, *Isleworth*, 305
Shorthose & Heath, *Hanley*, 305

Simpson, R., *Shelton*, 93, 95
Simpson, J. (Minton's), 294
Skey, G., *Wilnecote*, 310
Smith, W., *Stockton-on-Tees*, 305
Solon, L. (Minton's), 294-5
Spodes, The, *Stoke*, 156, 201-5, 208
Steele, D., *Burslem*, 305
Steele, D. (Wedgwood's), 151
Stephan, P., *Jackfield*, 232
Stevenson, R., *Cobridge*, 305
Stiff & Son, *Lambeth*, 68

T

Taylors, The, 306, 308
Thursfield, J., *Jackfield*, 230-2
Tofts, The, *Tinker's Clough*, 92
Turner, J., *Lane End*, 145, 186-8, 246
Turner, T., *Caughley*, 255
Twyford, *Shelton*, 124, 127

V

Van Hamme, *Lambeth*, 57, 60
Voyez, J., *Cobridge*, 146, 233-6

W

Wagstaffe, *Vauxhall*, 308
Wainwright & Co., *Leeds*, 224
Walton, J., *Burslem*, 145, 309
Warburton, J., *Hot Lane*, 281, 309
W. & B. (Wedgwood & Bentley), 163, 166, 179
Webber (Wedgwood's), 168-9
Wedgwood, A., *Burslem*, 158
Wedgwood & Co., *Hill Works*, 158
Wedgwood, Josiah, *Etruria*, 20, 57, 143, 145-85
Wedgwoods, The, 142, 158-9
Wedgewood (W. Smith), 305
Whieldon, T., *Fenton Low*, 107-110, 135, 161, 181, 246, 256
White, W., *Fulham*, 309
Wilson, D., & Sons, *Hanley*, 207
Wilson, R., *Hanley*, 195, 207, 297
Wood, A., *Burslem*, 110, 133-5, 196, 198
Wood, Enoch, *Burslem*, 145, 196, 198

Wood & Caldwell, *Burslem*, 145, 157, 200, 208
Wood, R. (father), *Burslem*, 140, 145, 196–7
Wood, R. (son), *Burslem*, 196–8, 246

Worthington, *Liverpool*, 280
W., R. & Co. (Ridgway), 301
W., S. & Co. (Smith), 305

Y

Young, W. W. (Dillwyn's), 227–8